HANDBOOK OF
MODEL ACCOUNTING REPORTS
AND FORMATS

HANDBOOK OF
MODEL ACCOUNTING REPORTS
AND FORMATS

Thomas M. Vickman

PRENTICE-HALL, INC.

Englewood Cliffs, N.J.

Prentice-Hall International, Inc., London
Prentice-Hall of Australia, Pty. Ltd., *Sydney*
Prentice-Hall Canada, Inc., *Toronto*
Prentice-Hall of India Private Ltd., *New Delhi*
Prentice-Hall of Japan, Inc., *Tokyo*
Prentice-Hall of Southeast Asia Pte. Ltd., *Singapore*
Whitehall Books, Ltd., Wellington, *New Zealand*
Editora Prentice-Hall do Brasil Ltda., *Rio de Janeiro*
Prentice-Hall Hispanoamericana, S.A., *Mexico*

Lotus 1-2-3 and VisiCalc are registered trademarks of
Lotus Development Corporation.

Library of Congress Cataloging-in-Publication Data

Vickman, Thomas M.
  Handbook of model accounting reports and
formats.

  Includes index.
  1. Managerial accounting—Handbooks,
manuals, etc. 2. Financial statements—
Handbooks, manuals, etc. 3. Corporation
reports-Handbooks, manuals, etc. I. Title.
HF5635.V53   1987   658.1'512   86-15068

ISBN 0-13-380338-4

Printed in the United States of America

ABOUT THE AUTHOR

Thomas M. Vickman is a Certified Public Accountant, having graduated from the University of Wisconsin with a BBA degree. He is currently Vice President of Finance of Satellite Industries, Inc. in Minneapolis. He has previously held positions with Winzen International, Inc., K-tel International, Inc., Continental Financial Corporation, and the international public accounting firm of Touche Ross and Co. Since 1970 Mr. Vickman has also advised numerous companies on reporting, financial performance strategy, and banking relationships.

Mr. Vickman is currently a member of the International Council for Small Business, the American Management Association, the American Institute of CPAs, and the Minnesota Society of CPAs. In addition to publishing one book, *Financial Officer's Manual & Guide,* he has written numerous articles on business for publications such as the *Journal of Accountancy* and the *Journal of Small Business Management.* He is an award winning author and has also spoken on financial topics before several continuing education programs.

Introduction

The *Handbook of Model Accounting Reports and Formats* is a dynamic resource to help you, the busy financial executive, communicate numbers more effectively to management, shareholders, auditors, and those who work for you.

It contains 290 detailed examples of model, ready-to-use accounting reports and graphics. Each one answers a vital management information need, and has been successfully used over and over by businesses throughout the country.

Each report will help you tackle the toughest management reporting questions instantly, with skilled, practical solutions. For example, if you want to check on a company's ability to meet its short-term obligations, Exhibit 22-2 gives you the calculations and ratios you need. If you want to compute your firm's earning power, Exhibit 13-11 will exactly show you how.

This book doesn't stop at the general purpose financial reports...it contains all the operating, internal audit, and even human resource rating reports you need to run your numbers through management and shareholders so they get an exact picture of what is happening in every phase of the business.

You'll find 13 Sales Operations Reports, including everything from daily order tallies to a sales performance report and top-10 sales account reports, sales mix and sales growth profiles. There are nine Marketing Reports...26 Manufacturing Cost Reports on material and labor...18 Purchasing Reports, and much more. Flip through the book and see how easy the hundreds of reports can make your daily information reporting requirements.

Every operation, every department within the company is covered; and not only that, many reports give you the calculations to show you how to arrange the figures and give you the tools to interpret them.

In effect, you'll not only have 90% of the reports you could ever want or need in your reporting arsenal—ready whenever you need them—but you'll have a complete and comprehensive accounting and financial reporting kit. There's even a Reportamatic Locater Index with Key Words and Phrases to guide you to the appropriate form and page. And after locating the exact report you are looking for, you will find a detailed model of the report plus a brief discussion of its key use, suggested routing, and recommended frequency of preparation.

Many of you will be able to employ these report formats as is. Others of you will find it necessary to tailor certain ones to your specific needs or the particular requirements of your data processing configuration. In any event, this book eliminates the necessity of designing reports from scratch.

For ease of use, the book has been conveniently organized into three sections.

Part I illustrates 241 reports broken down into 27 different categories. These reports emphasize all aspects of managing a company from profit planning to balance sheet control.

Part II presents an overview of the various types of graphics and charting that continues to be so popular and useful to managers. This section contains over 50 illustrations to aid you in meeting your most demanding reporting requirements. Part III centers on the techniques of reporting. Particular attention is paid to determining who gets what report, shortcuts to understandable reporting, livening up the physical appearance of reports, utilizing visual aids, and ensuring a company's reporting will help before rather than after the fact.

The *Handbook of Model Accounting Reports and Formats* with its hundreds of practical examples is a must for all of a firm's financial specialists and their staffs. This invaluable reference book should be a constant companion for anyone wishing to objectively report the results, develop a fully coherent management information system, improve the performance of his/her business, and do it all with maximum ease and efficiency.

Thomas M. Vickman

Table of Contents

Inventory Reporting (180)

Capital Expenditures and Other Financing Decisions (189)

Other Assets Reporting (208)

Liabilities and Shareholders' Investment Reports (215)

Part II

Graphics and Charting Examples

Part III

How to Design Useful and
Understandable Accounting Reports

I

Accounting
Report Examples

The 241 accounting report examples that follow include something for everyone in all sectors of business. First, it is a matter of specifically locating the report you need. Secondly, you must decide if you can use the report as is, or does it need modification to fit your exact needs. Finally, you must decide whether you want to use the report manually, program it on your desktop computer using a popular spreadsheet such as Lotus 1-2-3 or VisiCalc, or program it on your central mainframe computer if you have one. Each report will lend itself to any of these approaches.

GENERAL PURPOSE FINANCIAL STATEMENTS

The cornerstones of any financial reporting system are a firm's income statement, balance sheet, and funds flow statement. CPAs auditing a firm's books issue an opinion on them. The SEC requires these statements at a minimum annually for publicly held companies. Lenders usually want to review them monthly. Suppliers normally request updated financials once a year. Shareholders usually want to see results quarterly. Management should be reviewing these basic financials monthly to properly monitor company activities.

Generally accepted accounting principles dictate that the format of these statements pretty much must coincide with the way Exhibits 1-1 through 1-9 are presented. For a presentation at a meeting, Exhibits 1-8 and 1-9 generally have a very strong impact. At a glance the percentages can be reviewed on an item-by-item basis to detect differences between accounting periods.

Exhibit 1-1

INCOME STATEMENT

	CURRENT MONTH			YEAR TO DATE		
	ACTUAL	BUDGET	VARIANCE +(-)	ACTUAL	BUDGET	VARIANCE +(-)
Gross sales	$ 635,000	$ 675,000	$ (40,000)	$5,890,000	$5,500,000	$ 390,000
Sales returns and allowances	4,500	2,500	(2,000)	41,300	37,000	(4,300)
Net sales	630,500	672,500	(42,000)	5,848,700	5,463,000	385,700
Cost of Sales:						
Direct labor	87,000	90,000	3,000	801,325	810,000	8,675
Material	168,500	175,000	6,500	1,463,000	1,500,000	37,000
Overhead (attached schedule)	110,000	116,000	6,000	979,000	1,025,000	46,000
Change in inventories	(30,000)	(40,000)	(10,000)	10,500	25,000	14,500
Total cost of sales	335,500	341,000	5,500	3,253,825	3,360,000	106,175
Gross profit	295,000	331,500	(36,500)	2,594,875	2,103,000	491,875
Selling expense (attached schedule)	42,000	45,000	3,000	397,000	375,000	(22,000)
General and administrative expense (attached schedule	67,500	70,000	2,500	615,000	640,000	25,000
Operating income	185,500	216,500	(31,000)	1,582,875	1,088,000	494,875
Non-operating income:						
Interest	1,500	--	1,500	5,900	7,500	(1,600)
Dividends	--	--		--	10,000	(10,000)
Total non-operating income	1,500	--	1,500	5,900	17,500	(11,600)
Non-operating expenses:						
Interest	18,000	18,500	500	182,500	150,000	(32,500)
Other	2,000	2,200	200	14,500	10,000	(4,500)
Total non-operating expense	20,000	20,700	700	197,000	160,000	(37,000)
Income (loss) before income taxes	167,000	195,800	(28,800)	1,391,775	945,500	446,275
Income taxes:						
Federal and state	67,000	79,000	12,000	575,000	370,000	(205,000)
Deferred	8,000	9,000	1,000	29,000	25,000	(4,000)
Total income taxes	75,000	88,000	13,000	604,000	395,000	(209,000)
Net income (loss)	$ 92,000	$ 107,800	$ (15,800)	$ 787,775	$ 550,500	$ 237,275

Profit and loss statement in conformity with generally accepted accounting principles. Included is a semi-detailed cost of sales breakdown and examples of non-operating income and expenses.

MODEL REPORT #1-1

Key Use of Report:

Itemizes revenues and expenses for a period culminating with profit or loss from operations. It explains the financial progress of a firm and accounts for all changes in net assets.

Suggested Routing:

Board of Directors, Top Management, Major Creditors, Shareholders.

Frequency of Preparation:

Monthly.

Alternative Reports:

Model Report #1-3, #1-9, #2-1, #2-2, #13-1, #13-2, #23-2.

Exhibit 1-2

SUPPLEMENTARY INCOME STATEMENT DATA

| | CURRENT MONTH | | | YEAR TO DATE | | |
	ACTUAL	BUDGET	VARIANCE +(-)	ACTUAL	BUDGET	VARIANCE +(-)
Overhead:						
Indirect labor	$ 59,300	$ 61,000	$ 1,700	$ 495,000	$ 515,000	$ 20,000
Maintenance & repairs	2,500	3,000	500	25,300	20,000	(5,300)
Property taxes	2,200	2,500	300	20,000	25,000	5,000
Heat, light & power	22,000	25,000	3,000	220,000	245,000	25,000
Supplies	5,500	5,000	(500)	50,100	55,000	4,900
Insurance	3,800	4,000	200	33,700	35,000	1,300
Depreciation	10,500	10,500	--	95,000	95,000	--
Miscellaneous	4,200	5,000	800	39,900	35,000	4,900
Total overhead	$ 110,000	$ 116,000	$ 6,000	$ 979,000	$1,025,000	$ 46,000
Selling expenses:						
Sales salaries and commissions	$ 27,000	$ 27,500	$ 500	$ 245,000	$240,000	$ (5,000)
Advertising	12,000	14,000	2,000	117,000	112,000	(5,000)
Misc. selling exp.	3,000	3,500	500	35,000	23,000	(12,000)
	$ 42,000	$ 45,000	$ 3,000	$ 397,000	$ 375,000	$ (22,000)
General & administrative expenses:						
Officers' salaries	$ 18,000	$ 18,000	$ --	$ 166,000	$ 175,000	$ 9,000
Office salaries	34,550	35,000	450	325,000	330,000	5,000
Office supplies	1,800	2,300	500	15,000	17,500	2,500
Insurance	3,500	3,500	--	30,000	32,000	2,000
Repairs and Maint.	750	1,000	250	7,000	8,000	1,000
Depreciation	4,500	4,500	--	42,000	42,000	--
Property taxes	1,200	1,500	300	15,000	16,500	1,500
Miscellaneous	3,200	4,200	1,000	15,000	19,000	4,000
	$ 67,500	$ 70,000	$ 2,500	$ 615,000	$ 640,000	$ 25,000

Sales backlog	$ 360,000
Next month's sales projections	$ 685,000
Number of employees:	
Direct	89
Indirect	27
Average hourly wage:	
Direct - this month	$9.04
- last month	$8.90
% of direct labor utilization:	
This month	63%
Last month	69%
Weighted average short-term interest rate	12.8%

Detailed breakdown of overhead, selling, and general and administrative expenses. Additionally, various other key operating data are presented for management use—sales backlog, projections, number of employees, etc.

MODEL REPORT #1-2

Key Use of Report:

Provides a detailed analysis of important income statement expense categories. Furnishes several important statistics to help management evaluate operations.

Suggested Routing:

Board of Directors, Top Management, Major Creditors, Shareholders.

Frequency of Preparation:

Monthly.

Exhibit 1-3

PROFIT AND LOSS SUMMARY

| | (Dollar amounts in Thousands) | | | | | |
| | CURRENT MONTH | | | YEAR TO DATE | | |
	ACTUAL	BUDGET	VARIANCE +(-)	ACTUAL	BUDGET	VARIANCE +(-)
Sales	$ 630,500	$ 672,500	$ (42,000)	$5,848,700	$5,463,000	$ 385,700
Gross profit	295,000	331,500	(36,500)	2,594,875	2,103,000	491,875
(% of sales)	47%	49%		44.3%	39%	
Expenses:						
Selling	42,000	45,000	3,000	397,000	375,000	(22,000)
General & Administrative	67,500	70,000	2,500	615,000	640,000	25,000
Interest	18,000	18,500	500	182,500	150,000	(32,500)
Other expenses (income)	500	2,200	1,700	8,600	(7,500)	(16,100)
Income before tax	167,000	195,800	(28,800)	1,391,775	945,500	446,275
Income tax	75,000	88,000	13,000	604,000	395,000	(209,000)
Net income (loss)	$ 92,000	$ 107,800	$ (15,800)	$ 787,775	$ 550,500	$ 237,275

Profit and loss statement in conformity with generally accepted accounting principles in capsule form. This summary displays the major income and expense categories for management use.

MODEL REPORT #1-3

Key Use of Report:

Allows management to examine operating results without becoming absorbed in all the details.

Suggested Routing:

Board of Directors, Top Management.

Frequency of Preparation:

Monthly.

Alternative Reports:

Model Reports #1-1, #2-1, #2-2, #13-1, #13-2, #23-2.

Exhibit 1-4

BALANCE SHEET

		YEAR END	
	ACTUAL	BUDGET	VARIANCE +(-)
Assets			
Current assets:			
Cash and short-term investments	$ 210,000	$ 170,000	$ 40,000
Accounts and notes receivable, net of allowance for doubtful accounts of $75,000	473,000	425,000	48,000
Inventories	881,000	839,000	42,000
Prepaid expenses	67,000	82,000	(15,000)
Total current assets	1,631,000	1,516,000	115,000
Property, plant and equipment, at cost:			
Building	825,000	825,000	
Furniture and fixtures	137,000	125,000	12,000
Machinery and equipment	1,253,875	1,174,800	79,075
	2,215,875	2,124,800	91,075
Less accumulated depreciation	(389,000)	(374,800)	(14,200)
Total property, plant and equipment	1,826,875	1,750,000	76,875
Other assets	116,000	114,000	2,000
Total assets	$3,573,875	$3,380,000	$ 193,875
Liabilities and Shareholders' Equity			
Current liabilities:			
Current portion of long-term debt	$ 60,000	$ 58,000	$ 2,000
Accounts payable	410,000	390,000	20,000
Accrued expenses	75,000	50,000	25,000
Income taxes	100,500	75,000	25,500
Other	57,375	8,000	49,375
Total current liabilities	702,875	581,000	121,875
Long-term debt	420,000	420,000	
Deferred income taxes	118,000	105,000	13,000
Shareholders' equity:			
Common stock, $.50 par value, authorized 400,000 shares, issued and outstanding 215,000 shares	107,500	107,500	
Additional paid-in capital	320,000	320,000	
Retained earnings	1,935,000	1,876,000	59,000
	2,362,500	2,303,500	59,000
Less treasury stock, at cost	(29,500)	29,500	
Total shareholders' equity	2,333,000	2,274,000	59,000
Total liabilities and shareholders' equity	$3,573,875	$3,380,000	$ 193,875

Balance sheet complete with major asset, liability, and shareholder equity categories that are most common in commercial enterprises.

MODEL REPORT #1-4

Key Use of Report:

This statement of financial position shows the cumulative results of all asset, liability, and capital transactions of the business from its inception.

Suggested Routing:

Board of Directors, Top Management, Major Creditors, Shareholders.

Frequency of Preparation:

Monthly.

Alternative Reports:

Model Report #1-5, #1-8, #13-1, #23-1.

Exhibit 1-5

BALANCE SHEET AND RELATED STATISTICS

	YEAR END		
	ACTUAL	BUDGET	VARIANCE +(−)
Assets			
Current assets:			
Cash	$ 210,000	$ 170,000	$ 40,000
Receivables	473,000	425,000	48,000
Inventories	881,000	839,000	42,000
Prepaid expenses	67,000	82,000	(15,000)
Total current assets	1,631,000	1,516,000	115,000
Property, plant and equipment:			
Building	825,000	825,000	
Furniture and Fixtures	137,000	125,000	12,000
Machinery and equipment	1,253,875	1,174,800	79,075
	2,215,875	2,124,800	91,075
Less accumulated depreciation	(389,000)	(374,800)	(14,200)
Total property and equipment	1,826,875	1,750,000	76,875
Other assets	116,000	114,000	2,000
Total assets	$3,573,875	$3,380,000	$ 193,875
Liabilities and Shareholders' Equity			
Current liabilities:			
Current portion of long-term debt	$ 60,000	$ 58,000	$ 2,000
Accounts payable	410,000	390,000	20,000
Accrued expenses and other	232,875	133,000	99,875
Total current liabilities	702,875	581,000	121,875
Long-term debt	420,000	420,000	
Deferred income taxes	118,000	105,000	13,000
Shareholders' equity:			
Common stock	107,500	107,500	
Additional paid-in capital	320,000	320,000	
Retained earnings	1,935,000	1,876,000	59,000
	2,362,500	2,303,500	59,000
Less Treasury stock, at cost	(29,500)	(29,500)	
Total shareholders' equity	2,333,000	2,274,000	59,000
Total liabilities and shareholders' equity	$3,573,875	$3,380,000	$ 193,875
Balance Sheet Statistics			
Cash dividends	$ 10,750	$ 10,750	
Cash dividends per share	.05	.05	
Capital expenditures	127,500	89,500	
Return on average shareholders' equity	40.5%	27.5%	
Debt-to-equity ratio	20.6%	21.0%	
Net working capital	928,125	935,000	
Current ratio	2.32	2.60	
Book value per share	10.85	10.46	
Average common shares outstanding	215,000	217,200	

A second example of a balance sheet with less detailed captions. Related statistics include important financial ratios and measurements of special significance to management, creditors, and shareholders.

MODEL REPORT #1-5

Key Use of Report:

This report not only summarizes the current financial positon of a company but also presents nine vital balance sheet ratios and measurements to be used in analyzing and interpreting the data.

Suggested Routing:

Board of Directors, Top Management, Major Creditors, Shareholders.

Frequency of Preparation:

Monthly.

Alternative Reports:

Model Report #1-4, #1-8, #13-1.

Exhibit 1-6

STATEMENT OF CHANGES IN FINANCIAL POSITION— VERSION I

	Year Ended December 31, 1986 ACTUAL	1987 PLAN
Working capital provided from (used for):		
Operations:		
Net earnings	$ 787,775	$ 320,000
Add (deduct) items not affecting working capital:		
Depreciation and amortization	103,000	130,000
Deferred income taxes	19,000	12,000
Loss (gain) on sale of equipment	7,000	(11,000)
Total from operations	916,775	451,000
Increase in long-term financing	5,000	20,000
Proceeds from sale of property, plant and equipment	1,700	22,000
Total working capital provided	923,475	493,000
Working capital used to:		
Pay dividends	10,750	48,000
Acquire property plant and equipment	235,000	264,125
Reduce long-term debt	60,000	60,000
Increase (decrease) other investments	115,000	(36,000)
Total working capital used	420,750	336,125
Increase (decrease) in working capital	$ 502,725	$ 156,875
Increase (decrease) in working capital resulted from:		
Increase (decrease) in current assets:		
Cash	$ 136,900	$ 90,000
Receivables	128,000	52,000
Inventories	240,000	119,000
Other	0	(17,000)
Total	504,900	244,000
Increase (decrease) in current liabilities:		
Payables and accruals	2,175	87,125
Notes payable	0	0
Total	2,175	87,125
Increase (decrease) in working capital	$ 502,725	$ 156,875

A detailed funds flow statement delineating the various sources and uses of working capital.

MODEL REPORT #1-6

Key Use of Report:

Describes the activities responsible for changes in a company's financial resources during a period of time. It is useful for controlling working capital and how it is employed.

Suggested Routing:

Board of Directors, Top Management, Major Creditors, Shareholders.

Frequency of Preparation:

Monthly.

Alternative Reports:

Model Report #1-7.

Exhibit 1-7

STATEMENT OF CHANGES IN FINANCIAL POSITION— VERSION II

	Year Ended December 31,	
	1986 ACTUAL	1987 PLAN
Internally generated funds:		
Net earnings	$ 787,775	$ 320,000
Expenses not requiring the use of cash:		
Depreciation and amortization	103,000	130,000
Deferred income taxes	19,000	12,000
Loss (gain) on sale of equipment	7,000	(11,000)
	916,775	451,000
Decrease (increase) in receivables	(128,000)	(52,000)
Decrease (increase) in inventories	(240,000)	(119,000)
Decrease (increase) in other assets	0	17,000
Increase (decrease) in payables	2,175	87,125
Funds provided from (used in) operations	550,950	384,125
Funds used to pay dividends	(10,750)	(48,000)
Net internally generated funds (used) available for investment	540,200	336,125
Capital investment activities:		
Acquisition of property, plant and equipment	(235,000)	(264,125)
Other investments (increase) decrease	(115,000)	(36,000)
Sale or retirements of property, plant and equipment	1,700	22,000
Net funds (used by) available for investment activities	(191,900)	(130,000)
Financing activities:		
Financing acquired: Long-term debt	5,000	20,000
Financing discharged -- long-term debt	(60,000)	(60,000)
Net funds provided by (used in) financing activities	55,000	40,000
Increase (decrease) in cash	$ 136,900	$ 90,000

The "new look" funds flow that reconciles a firm's sources and uses of cash. The three broad sources and uses of cash include internally generated cash, capital investment activities, and financing activities.

MODEL REPORT #1-7

Key Use of Report:

This cash-flow statement shows the movement of cash in and out of a business by listing all sources and uses. It is an important starting point for analyzing future cash needs and where it will come from.

Suggested Routing:

Board of Directors, Top Management, Major Creditors, Shareholders.

Frequency of Preparation:

Monthly.

Alternative Reports:

Model Report #1-6, #14-5.

Exhibit 1-8

COMMON-SIZE BALANCE SHEET

Description	Amounts, December 31 (in thousands)			Common-Size Percentages, December 31		
	198 ACTUAL	198 PLAN	198 PLAN	198 ACTUAL	198 PLAN	198 PLAN
Assets						
Current assets:						
Cash	$ 210,000	$ 300,000	$ 375,000	6%	8%	9%
Receivables	473,000	525,000	550,000	13	13	13
Inventories	881,000	1,000,000	1,100,000	25	26	26
Other	67,000	50,000	50,000	2	1	2
Total current assets	1,631,000	1,875,000	2,075,000	46	48	50
Property, plant and equipment, net	1,826,875	1,950,000	2,000,000	51	50	48
Other noncurrent assets:	116,000	80,000	100,000	3	2	2
Total assets	$3,573,875	$3,905,000	$4,175,000	100%	100%	100%
Liabilities & Shareholders' Equity						
Current liabilities:						
Current portion of long-term debt	$ 60,000	$ 60,000	$ 60,000	2%	1%	1%
Accounts payable	410,000	455,000	525,000	12	12	13
Accrued expenses and other	232,875	275,000	290,000	7	7	7
Total current liabilities	702,875	790,000	875,000	21	20	21
Long term debt	420,000	380,000	360,000	12	10	9
Deferred taxes:	118,000	130,000	138,000	2	3	2
Total liabilities	1,240,875	1,300,000	1,373,000	35	33	32
Shareholders' equity:						
Common stock	107,500	107,500	107,500	3	3	3
Paid-in capital	320,000	320,000	320,000	9	8	8
Retained earnings	750,000	802,250	681,000	54	57	58
	2,362,500	2,634,500	2,831,500	66	68	69
Less treasury stock	(29,500)	(29,500)	(29,500)	(1)	(1)	(1)
Total shareholders' equity	2,333,000	2,605,000	2,802,000	65	67	68
Total liabilities and equity	$3,573,875	$3,905,000	$4,175,000	100%	100%	100%

A comparative balance sheet that displays vertical percentages for all balance sheet categories without showing dollar values. All items are shown as a percentage of total assets or total liabilities/shareholders' equity.

MODEL REPORT #1-8

Key Use of Report:

Shows the percent of total assets invested in each type of asset and the percent of the total liabilities and equity obtained from each source. It is valuable in determining whether a firm has over-invested in a specific asset category or obtained too much debt or equity from one source.

Suggested Routing:

Top Management, Controller, Financial Analyst.

Frequency of Preparation:

Monthly.

Alternative Reports:

Model Report #1-4, #1-5, #23-1.

Exhibit 1-9

COMMON-SIZE INCOME STATEMENT

Description	Amounts, December 31 (in thousands)			Common-Size Percentages, December 31		
	198_ ACTUAL	198_ PLAN	198_ PLAN	198_ ACTUAL	198_ PLAN	198_ PLAN
Net sales	$5,848,700	$5,432,000	$5,954,000	100%	100%	100%
Cost of sales	3,253,825	3,204,000	3,573,000	56	59	60
Gross profit	2,594,875	2,228,000	2,381,000	44	41	40
Selling expense	397,000	510,000	635,000	7	9	11
General and administrative	615,000	725,000	775,000	11	13	13
Operating income	1,582,875	993,000	971,000	26	19	16
Interest expense	182,500	273,000	315,000	3	5	5
Other expenses (income)	8,600	115,000	146,000	-	2	2
Income (loss) before taxes	1,391,775	605,000	510,000	23	12	9
Income taxes	604,000	285,000	235,000	10	6	4
Net income (loss)	$ 787,775)	$ 320,000	$ 275,000	13%	6%	5%

A comparative income statement that displays vertical percentages of income statement categories without showing dollar values. This statement starts with sales as 100%, and all items are shown as percentage of sales.

MODEL REPORT #1-9

Key Use of Report:

Simplifies studying revenue, cost, and expense relationships by the use of percentages.

Suggested Routing:

Top Management, Controller, Financial Analyst.

Alternative Reports:

Model Report #1-1, #23-2.

RESPONSIBILITY REPORTING

Responsibility Reporting establishes a basis for segregating costs in centers of responsibility for each manager. It is a scorecard for evaluating how well department heads are doing in controlling the costs associated with the activities they manage. Exhibit 2-1 breaks down responsibility by division and presents a detailed analysis of costs for high level monthly operating meetings. Exhibit 2-2 summarizes divisional results for the Board of Directors. Exhibits 2-3 through 2-6 analyze operating results for profit center managers and are exceptionally useful in monitoring individual products, departments, divisions, and product groups. The key information to be highlighted in these reports is the breakdown of costs by type.

Exhibit 2-1

RESPONSIBILITY OPERATING REPORT

	TOTAL		DIVISION A		DIVISION B	
	ACTUAL	PLAN	ACTUAL	PLAN	ACTUAL	PLAN
Net sales actual	$4,230,000	$4,000,000	$2,980,000	$3,000,000	$1,250,000	$1,000,000
Variable cost of sales at standard	1,650,000	1,500,000	1,200,000	1,200,000	450,000	300,000
Marginal profit at standard	2,580,000	2,500,000	1,780,000	1,800,000	800,000	700,000
Fixed cost of sales at standard	510,000	500,000	300,000	325,000	210,000	290,000
Gross profit at standard	2,070,000	2,000,000	1,480,000	1,475,000	590,000	525,000
% standard gross profit	49%	50%	50%	49%	49%	53%
Variances on variable cost of sales: (unfavorable)						
Materials - prices	(12,000)		(1,000)		(11,000)	
usage	(15,000)		5,000		(20,000)	
yield	7,500		2,100		5,400	
Labor - payroll	(2,900)		(4,300)		1,400	
pay rates	(3,500)		(4,900)		1,400	
Overhead						
- productivity	8,000		5,000		3,000	
- spending	(3,000)		(9,000)		6,000	
Total	(20,900)	--	(7,100)	--	(13,800)	
Variances on fixed cost of sales: (unfavorable)						
Overhead - spending	(4,900)		(2,000)		(2,900)	
volume	(10,200)		(8,000)		(2,200)	
Total	(15,100)		(10,000)		(5,100)	
Total variances	(36,000)		(17,100)		(18,900)	
Gross profit at actual	2,034,000	2,000,000	1,462,900	1,475,000	571,100	525,000
% actual gross profit	48%	50%	49%	49%	46%	53%
Other expenses:						
General and administrative	575,000	550,000	350,000	390,000	225,000	160,000
Selling	342,000	325,000	210,000	220,000	132,000	105,000
Interest	175,000	200,000	100,000	130,000	75,000	70,000
Total	1,092,000	1,075,000	660,000	740,000	432,000	335,000
Pretax profit	$ 942,000	$ 925,000	$ 802,900	$ 735,000	$ 139,100	4 190,000
% net profit	22%	23%	27%	25%	11%	19%

A divisional profit and loss statement which discloses operating
variances from plan and the specific reasons for them.

MODEL REPORT #2-1

Key Use of Report:

Itemizes operational detail by division including cost variances by type for analysis and planning purposes.

Suggested Routing:

Top Management, Divisional Heads.

Frequency of Preparation:

Monthly.

Alternative Reports:

Model Report #1-1, #1-2.

Exhibit 2-2

SUMMARY OF DIVISIONAL PERFORMANCE FOR THE BOARD
OF DIRECTORS

	CURRENT YEAR		
	ACTUAL	BUDGET	% OF BUDGET
Net sales:			
Midwest division			
Month	$ 325,000	$ 315,000	103%
Year-to-date	2,250,000	2,300,000	98
Products			
Month	175,000	150,000	117%
Year-to-date	1,200,000	1,300,000	92
Shelter group			
Month	97,000	110,000	88%
year-to-date	560,000	600,000	93
Export			
Month	210,000	200,000	105%
Year-to-date	1,340,000	1,300,000	103
Consolidated			
Month	807,000	775,000	104%
Year-to-date	$5,350,000	$5,500,000	97%
Pretax income (loss):			
Midwest division			
Month	$ 30,500	$ 29,200	105%
Year-to-date	199,000	204,000	98
Products			
Month	15,600	13,000	120%
Year-to-date	109,000	118,500	92
Shelter group			
Month	14,050	15,550	90%
Year-to-date	63,800	66,000	97
Export			
Month	16,700	15,850	105%
Year-to-date	114,000	119,000	96
Consolidated			
Month	76,850	73,600	104%
Year-to-date	$ 485,800	$ 507,500	96%

Summary of net sales and pretax income (loss) by major product classification.

MODEL REPORT #2-2

Key Use of Report:

Presents a look at sales and income totals by division for review purposes.

Suggested Routing:

Board of Directors.

Frequency of Preparation:

Monthly.

Alternative Reports:

Model Report #1-1, #1-2, #2-1, #13-1.

Exhibit 2-3

PRODUCT CONTRIBUTION REPORT

	PER UNIT	$ TOTAL	%
Budgeted sales units	66,250		
Net sales	$ 40.00	$2,650,000	100%
Variable cost of sales:			
Raw material	13.58	900,000	34
Direct labor	6.04	400,000	15
Direct product expenses:			
Delivery	1.13	75,000	3
Freight - in and warehousing	.91	60,000	2
Spoilage	.26	17,000	1
Sales commissions	2.00	133,000	5
Energy	1.03	68,000	3
Royalties	.15	10,000	-
Total variable cost of sales	25.10	1,663,000	63
Variable product contribution	14.90	987,000	37
Fixed direct product expenses:			
Product advertising		200,000	8
Product administration		100,000	4
Promotion		60,000	2
Research and development		42,000	1
Market research		33,000	1
Total fixed direct product expenses		435,000	16%
Direct product contribution		552,000	21
(project manager's responsibility)			
Fixed corporate period expenses:			
General and administrative		145,000	5
Sales		85,000	3
Public relations		21,000	1
Manufacturing period expenses		93,000	4
Interest expense		65,000	2
Total fixed corporate period expenses		409,000	15
Net profit (loss)		$ 143,000	5

A product profit and loss statement that first discloses by how much sales exceeds variable costs (variable product contribution) and is then available to cover fixed expenses and provide a firm's profit.

MODEL REPORT #2-3

Key Use of Report:

Analyzes the significant components of a product sales dollar: (1) variable cost of sales, (2) fixed direct product expenses, (3) fixed corporate expenses, and (4) net income.

Suggested Routing:

Divisional Heads, Product Group Managers, Product Managers.

Frequency of Preparation:

Monthly.

Alternative Reports:

Model Report #2-4, #2-5, #2-6, #5-1, #5-2, #5-4, #13-14.

Exhibit 2-4

INTERIM CONTRIBUTION REPORT

Net sales			$1,200,000
Variable direct product expenses			
Raw material		325,000	
Direct labor		160,000	
Delivery		42,000	
Sales commissions		30,000	
Energy		46,000	603,000
Variable product contribution	(1)		597,000
Fixed direct product expenses (budget for year)			
Product advertising		410,000	
Product administration		212,000	
Product development		65,000	687,000
Fixed corporate period expenses (budget for year)			
General and administrative		342,000	
Sales		69,000	
Manufacturing		110,000	
Interest expense		62,000	583,000
Total fixed expenses for year	(2)		1,270,000
Budgeted fixed expenses yet to be recovered	(1)-(2)		(673,000)
Actual fixed costs first quarter (30%)	(4)		381,000
Net profit, first quarter 198__	(1)-(4)		$ 216,000

Note: Under responsibility reporting profits do not occur until all fixed costs for the year have been paid for. In the above example, the company recovered 30% of the fixed costs in the first quarter and thus reports $216,000 in profits, but in reality they will not show a true profit until all of the $673,000 in fixed costs have been recovered.

An interim profit and loss statement that uses the variable product contribution concept and a dual view of fixed expenses—actual fixed costs incurred and budgeted fixed costs yet to be recovered.

MODEL REPORT #2-4

Key Use of Report:

Analyzes on a quarterly basis the significant components of a product sales dollar: (1) variable cost of sales, (2) fixed direct product expenses, (3) fixed corporate expenses, and (4) net income.

Suggested Routing:

Divisional Heads, Product Group Managers, Product Managers.

Frequency of Preparation:

Monthly.

Alternative Reports:

Model Report #2-3, #2-5, #2-6, #5-1, #5-2.

Exhibit 2-5

EARNINGS REPORT FOR PRODUCT MANAGERS

		$	
	ACTUAL	BUDGETED	ACTUAL OVER(UNDER) BUDGET
Net sales	$3,400,000	$3,750,000	$ (350,000)
Variable expenses:			
Variable cost of sales	1,900,000	2,130,000	(230,000)
Freight	176,000	197,000	(21,000)
Sales commissions	75,000	83,000	(8,000)
Total variable expenses	2,151,000	2,410,000	(259,000)
Marginal income	1,249,000	1,340,000	(91,000)
Direct product expenses			
Advertising	165,000	170,000	(5,000)
Administration	89,000	93,000	(4,000)
Total direct product expenses	254,000	263,000	(9,000)
Product income (1)	995,000	1,077,000	(82,000)
Product group expenses:			
Fixed group overhead	130,000	122,000	8,000
Product group income (2)	865,000	955,000	(90,000)
Division expenses:			
Administration	95,000	107,000	(12,000)
Marketing	110,000	102,000	8,000
Interest	67,000	79,000	(12,000)
Total division expenses	272,000	288,000	(16,000)
Division income	593,000	667,000	(74,000)
Corporate overhead	189,000	201,000	(12,000)
Net profit	$ 404,000	$ 466,000	$ (62,000)

(1) Product manager responsibility level
(2) Group product manager responsibility level

An operating earnings report (using the marginal contribution concept) that breaks down the profits and losses by responsibility level; in this example, a product manager and product group manager.

MODEL REPORT #2-5

Key Use of Report:

Itemizes profits by level of responsibility: (1) product manager, (2) group product manager, (3) divisional general managers, and (4) corporate management.

Suggested Routing:

Same management as is listed under "Key Use of Report."

Frequency of Preparation:

Monthly.

Alternative Reports:

Model Report #2-3, #2-4, #2-6, #5-1, #5-2, #13-14.

Exhibit 2-6

PRODUCT GROUP RESULTS

	ACTUAL SALES $			BUDGET SALES $			VARIANCE FROM BUDGET OVER (UNDER)
	TOTAL	PER UNIT	% OF SALES	TOTAL	PER UNIT	% OF SALES	
Units sold	15,200			14,400			
Net sales	$1,216,000	$80.00	100%	$1,152,000	$80.00	100%	(64,000)
Variable expenses:							
Variable cost of sales	625,000	41.12	51	610,000	42.36	53	(15,000)
Sales commissions	73,000	4.80	6	59,000	4.10	5	(14,000)
Total variable expenses	698,000	45.92	57	669,000	46.46	58	(29,000)
Marginal income	518,000	34.08	43	483,000	33.54	42	(35,000)
Direct product expenses:							
Advertising	165,000	10.86	14	160,000	11.11	14	(5,000)
Administration	130,000	8.55	11	130,000	9.03	11	--
Total direct product expenses	295,000	19.41	25	290,000	20.14	25	(5,000)
Product income	223,000	14.67	18	193,000	13.40	17	(30,000)
Fixed group overhead	111,000	7.30	9	105,000	7.29	9	(6,000)
Product group income	$ 112,000	$ 7.37	9%	$ 88,000	$ 6.11	8%	$ (24,000)

A summary P&L that shows marginal income, product income, and product group income variance from budget for the period.

MODEL REPORT #2-6

Key Use of Report:

Summarizes income by product and product group for review purposes.

Suggested Routing:

Product Group Managers.

Frequency of Preparation:

Monthly.

Alternative Reports:

Model Report #2-3, #2-4, #2-5, #5-1, #5-2, #13-14.

SALES OPERATIONS REPORTS

This series of 14 reports will help management analyze the productivity and efficiency of the sales department. They concentrate on examining individual salesperson performance, sales statistics, department performance ratios, customer profiles and activity, manpower requirements, and departmental expense analysis. This vital information is critical to effectively managing day-to-day sales department activities. Overall these reports highlight how the sales department is getting the job done.

Exhibit 3-1
DAILY BILLING REPORT

| | MONTH'S BUDGET | ACTUAL BILLINGS | | % MONTH'S BUDGET TO DATE |
		TODAY	MONTH TO DATE	
Beck sheeting	$ 85,000	$ 1,300	$ 52,700	*62%
Deli wrap	42,000	2,700	25,200	*60%
Embossed scale sheets	30,000	5,200	14,400	**48%
Colored tissue	38,000	3,950	20,140	**53%
Flex-o-wrap	93,000	7,900	63,240	*68%
	$ 288,000	$ 21,050	$ 175,680	*61%

Budget to date: 18 days
 out of 30 days = 60%

   60% x $288,000 = $ 172,800   60%

      * ahead of budget

      ** behind budget

Daily report giving actual billings for the day and comparing month to date billings against budget.

MODEL REPORT #3-1

Key Use of Report:

   Computes the percentage of the monthly sales budget achieved to date.

Suggested Routing:

   Top Management, Sales Manager.

Frequency of Preparation:

   Daily.

Exhibit 3-2

CUSTOMER CALL ANALYSIS

CUSTOMER ANNUAL PURCHASES	CUSTOMERS		CALLS		SALES	
	NUMBER	% OF TOTAL	NUMBER	% OF TOTAL	AMOUNT	% OF TOTAL
$600,000 and over	5	3%	22	6%	$ 4,120,000	18%
$500,000 to $599,000	7	5%	27	7%	4,900,000	21%
$400,000 to $499,000	12	8%	39	11%	5,275,000	23%
$300,000 to $399,000	6	4%	21	6%	2,125,000	9%
$200,000 to $299,000	16	10%	28	8%	3,423,000	15%
$100,000 to $199,000	12	8%	32	9%	1,656,000	7%
$ 50,000 to $ 99,000	9	6%	27	7%	571,500	3%
Less than $50,000	87	56%	168	46%	957,000	4%
	154	100%	364	100%	$23,027,500	100%

The number of sales calls and the dollar amount of sales made to customers of different sizes.

MODEL REPORT #3-2

Key Use of Report:

Highlights statistical information on the customer base for sales planning purposes.

Suggested Routing:

Sales Manager.

Frequency of Preparation:

Quarterly.

Exhibit 3-3

WEEKLY REPORT OF SALESMAN PERFORMANCE

	TOTAL SALES	GROSS PROFIT(a) AMOUNT	%	DIRECT EXPENSES AMOUNT	%	NET MARGIN	# OF CALLS MADE	NEW CUSTOMERS
Abbott	$ 11,560	$ 4,046	35%	$ 750	6.5%	$ 3,296	15	0
Blakely	7,200	2,808	39%	425	5.9%	2,383	12	0
Connors	5,930	2,491	42%	460	7.8%	2,031	9	2
DeVoe	9,560	3,442	36%	590	6.2%	2,852	17	3
Earling	14,530	4,940	34%	610	4.2%	4,330	18	1
TOTAL	$ 48,780	$ 17,727	36%	$2,835	5.8%	$14,892	71	6

(a) Cumulative actual gross profit percent through the end of the previous month.

A weekly report by salesman showing total dollar sales, gross profit accruing to the firm on those sales, direct salesman expenses, the number of sales calls made, and the number of new customers opened.

MODEL REPORT #3-3

Key Use of Report:

Monitors sales performance of each salesperson including an estimate of their profit contribution.

Suggested Routing:

Sales Manager.

Frequency of Preparation:

Weekly.

Alternative Reports:

Model Report #3-6, #3-11, #3-12.

Exhibit 3-4
SALES ORDER ANALYSIS—VERSION I

ELECTRONIC PROFILE MEASURING DEVICE

MARKET SEGMENT

	OEM		INDUSTRIAL/COMMERCIAL		GOVERNMENT		EXPORT		TOTAL	
	MONTH	YTD	MONTH	YTD	MONTH	YTD	MONTH	YTD	MONTH	YTD
TOTAL CONTROL										
Budget	$87,000	$400,000	$170,000	$860,000	$35,000	$140,000	$8,000	$40,000	$300,000	$1,440,000
Actual	79,200	378,000	162,580	913,500	28,410	129,430	--	32,480	270,190	1,453,410
ON-LINE Q.C.										
Budget	50,000	265,000	10,000	53,000	30,000	140,000	13,000	68,000	103,000	526,000
Actual	37,500	319,000	20,580	72,480	39,870	167,000	13,500	51,620	111,450	610,100
LAB Q.C.										
Budget	35,000	209,000	10,000	40,000	5,000	30,000	5,000	31,000	55,000	310,000
Actual	30,550	213,000	13,770	36,200	7,620	24,820	4,975	44,620	56,915	318,640
REPLACEMENT ACCESSORY										
Budget	9,500	50,000	1,000	5,000	2,500	13,500	1,000	5,000	14,000	73,500
Actual	6,231	42,500	2,950	6,782	8,960	5,897	1,925	3,250	20,066	58,429
TOTALS										
Budget	$181,500	$924,000	$191,000	$958,000	$72,500	$323,500	$27,000	$144,000	$472,000	$2,349,500
Actual	153,481	952,500	199,880	1,028,962	84,860	327,147	20,400	131,970	458,621	2,440,579

Report showing product sales by different market segments—OEM, Industrial/Commercial, Government, and Export.

MODEL REPORT #3-4

Key Use of Report:

Subdivides sales orders by product and market segment for sales and marketing planning.

Suggested Routing:

Sales Manager.

Frequency of Preparation:

Monthly.

Alternative Reports:

Model Report #3-5.

Exhibit 3-5

SALES ORDER ANALYSIS—VERSION II

	ELECTRONIC PROFILE MEASURING DEVICE			
	TOTAL CONTROL	ON-LINE QC	LAB QC	REPLACEMENT ACCESSORY
Orders:				
Current month $ - this year	$ 160,000	$ 87,000	$ 113,000	$ 48,000
Current month $ - last year	238,000	89,000	70,500	55,000
Amount increase (decrease)	(78,000)	(2,000)	42,500	(7,000)
% increase (decrease)	(33%)	(2%)	60%	(13%)
Year to date $ - this year	675,000	410,500	539,000	246,000
Year to date $ - last year	660,000	438,200	560,000	239,200
Amount increase (decrease)	15,000	(27,700)	(21,000)	6,800
% increase (decrease)	2%	(6%)	(4%)	3%
Sales:				
Current month $ - this year	300,000	103,000	55,000	14,000
Current month $ - last year	275,000	118,400	62,300	5,240
Amount increase (decrease)	25,000	(15,400)	(7,300)	8,760
% increase (decrease)	9%	(13%)	(12%)	167%
Year to date $ - this year	1,440,000	526,000	310,000	73,500
Year to date $ - last year	1,258,500	482,376	329,000	85,050
Amount increase (decrease)	181,500	43,624	(19,000)	(11,550)
% increase (decrease)	14%	9%	(6%)	(14%)
Cancelled Orders:				
Current month $	--	5,640	2,540	250
Year to date $	$ 18,550	$ 23,840	$ 2,540	$ 690

Report showing assorted order and sales statistics broken down by product type.

MODEL REPORT #3-5

Key Use of Report:

Monitors sales orders and dollars by product line for planning and control purposes.

Suggested Routing:

Sales Manager.

Frequency of Preparation:

Monthly.

Alternative Reports:

Model Report #3-4.

Exhibit 3-6

SALES PERFORMANCE MEASUREMENT REPORT

	ACTUAL	BUDGET
Net sales	$395,000	$440,000
Variable expenses:		
Variable cost of sales	210,000	224,000
Sales commissions	24,000	26,400
Total	234,000	250,400
Marginal income:	$161,000	$189,600
Salesmen's calls:		
Total	110	125
Total on new accounts only	15	20
Number of orders:		
Total	73	70
New accounts	5	7
New products	8	4
Number of accounts:		
Total	60	65
Number sold during year	48	65
New accounts opened and sold during the year	5	7

NOTE: Companies should prepare one of these reports for each of their salesmen.

Report by salesman showing marginal income, number of sales calls, number of orders, and number of accounts.

MODEL REPORT #3-6

Key Use of Report:

Informs sales management about salesperson activity levels compared with plan.

Suggested Routing:

Sales Manager.

Frequency of Preparation:

Monthly.

Alternative Reports:

Model Report #3-3, #3-11, #3-12.

Exhibit 3-7

SALES PERFORMANCE RATIO REPORT

1.	Net sales $ divided by total # of orders	$ 3,800
2.	Selling expenses as percentage of sales	4%
3.	Total quotations divided by total calls	62%
4.	New account quotations divided by new account calls	42%
5.	New account sales divided by:	
	o Net sales	11%
	o New account calls	31%
6.	New product sales divided by:	
	o Net sales	7%
	o Total calls	$140
	o New product quotes	70%
7.	Total orders divided by total quotations	75%
8.	Total orders divided by 100 calls	10.5
9.	Number of accounts sold divided by number of accounts	90%
10.	Sales expenses divided by total calls	$ 80
11.	Net sales divided by number of man days	$961

NOTE: Companies use this report not only for the sales function
        in total but also by individual salesman.

Sales report depicting the calculation of 11 key sales performance ratios.

MODEL REPORT #3-7

Key Use of Report:

Analyzes sales performance using a series of special ratios and measurements.

Suggested Routing:

Top Management, Sales Manager.

Frequency of Preparation:

Quarterly.

Exhibit 3-8
PREFERRED CUSTOMER SALES ANALYSIS

CUSTOMER (1)	SALESMAN	JANUARY	FEBRUARY	MARCH	APRIL	MAY	JUNE	AVERAGE MONTHLY	# OF ORDERS YTD
George Stein & Co.	DB	$101,990	$ 67,829	$ 92,140	$363,520	$129,820	$260,000	$169,217	97
NSBF	CR	79,620	22,390	58,620	238,620	--	163,420	93,778	123
Maryland Packaging	CR	38,637	16,829	106,938	43,243	159,820	108,000	78,910	79
Packing Systems	AR	13,876	29,543	68,375	31,105	53,486	79,600	45,998	147
Advanced Sheeting	DB	37,690	51,421	66,352	27,862	4,248	84,350	45,320	101
Meyers Meats	CR	18,680	48,295	18,650	48,295	27,685	50,825	35,405	162
National Deli. Assoc.	AC	4,827	31,321	37,625	31,350	49,531	52,300	34,492	107
Charman	DB	16,950	41,862	30,540	39,285	29,085	37,620	32,543	125
TOTAL SALES		$312,260	$309,490	$479,240	$823,280	$453,595	$836,115	$535,663	941

(1) Preferred customers can be defined any way a company wishes but it is usually based on dollar volume of sales.

Actual monthly sales, average monthly sales, and the number of orders year to date by key customers.

MODEL REPORT #3-8

Key Use of Report:

Tracks sales activity of large, repeat customers for sales planning purposes.

Suggested Routing:

Sales Manager.

Frequency of Preparation:

Monthly.

Alternative Reports:

Model Report #4-5.

Exhibit 3-9
SAFETY FACTOR SALES VOLUME REPORT

	(1) SALES VOLUME	(2) $ BREAKEVEN POINT	(3) SAFETY FACTOR (1)-(2)	(4) SAFETY FACTOR % (3)÷(2)
Product A:				
Budget	$ 835,000	$ 702,000	$ 133,000	18.9%
Actual	750,000	702,000	48,000	6.8%
Product B:				
Budget	455,000	400,000	55,000	13.8%
Actual	495,000	400,000	95,000	23.8%
Product C:				
Budget	690,000	610,000	80,000	13.1%
Actual	640,000	610,000	30,000	5.0%
TOTAL SALES:				
Budget	$1,980,000	$1,712,000	$ 268,000	15.7%
Actual	$1,885,000	$1,712,000	$ 173,000	10.1%

Report showing a firm's sales safety factor (sales volume minus breakeven sales) by product.

MODEL REPORT #3-9

Key Use of Report:

A control report that alerts management to what extent a product's sales volume exceeds its breakeven sales level; i.e., what a product's safety factor is.

Suggested Routing:

Top Management, Sales Manager.

Frequency of Preparation:

Monthly.

Alternative Reports:

Model Report #13-13, #14-9.

Exhibit 3-10

SALES PER EMPLOYEE REPORT

		SALES PER EMPLOYEE			
MONTH	ACTUAL EMPLOYEES	ACTUAL	BUDGET	VARIANCE +(-)	% VARIANCE
Jan	205	$2,439	$2,350	$ 89	4%
Feb	207	3,140	3,400	(260)	(8%)
Mar	210	2,976	3,400	(424)	(13%)
Apr	227	3,744	4,000	(256)	(6%)
May	226	4,097	4,000	97	2%
June	230	3,850	4,000	(150)	(4%)
July					
Aug					
Sept					
Oct					
Nov					
Dec					

Monthly report comparing actual and budgeted sales dollars by employee.

MODEL REPORT #3-10

Key Use of Report:

A measure of employee productivity.

Suggested Routing:

Top Management.

Frequency of Preparation:

Monthly.

Exhibit 3-11

ANALYSIS OF SALES CALLS

| | SALES CALLS | | | # OF ORDERS | TOTAL $ |
	PHONED	PERSONAL VISIT	TOTAL		
Existing accounts	16	8	24	8	$114,320
Targeted accounts	7	4	11	2	89,780
Prospective accounts	13	3	16	3	13,540
New accounts	1	4	5	1	8,250
	37	19	56	14	$225,890

1st time calls
(included above)

	Comments
Warte Brothers	$3500 order placed with us
Juston Company	Small user with little potential
Bryan Corp.	Loyal Bloomquist customer - probably will remain so
Tillman Co.	Owner on vacation
Andrews Co.	May be interested next spring
Wheaton Co.	With persistence we may see a bag order by Oct.

Number of sales calls and number and dollar value of orders by account type (existing, targeted, prospective, new), including written comments on first-time calls.

MODEL REPORT #3-11

Key Use of Report:

Monitors a salesperson's activity and sales production.

Suggested Routing:

Sales Manager.

Frequency of Preparation:

Monthly.

Alternative Reports:

Model Report #3-3, #3-6, #3-12.

Exhibit 3-12
SALES QUOTA REPORT

	MONTH				YEAR TO DATE			
	QUOTA	ACTUAL	OVER (UNDER)	% OF QUOTA ATTAINED	QUOTA	ACTUAL	OVER (UNDER)	% OF QUOTA ATTAINED
New parts:								
Salesman A	$ 67,000	$ 76,000	$ 9,000	113%	$320,000	$347,000	$ 27,000	108%
Salesmen B	50,000	53,000	3,000	106	300,000	287,000	(13,000)	96
Salesman C	60,000	49,000	(11,000)	82	310,000	301,500	(8,500)	97
Salesman D	62,000	59,000	(3,000)	95	310,000	297,000	(13,000)	96
Manufacturing reps.	189,000	175,000	(14,000)	93	865,000	942,000	77,000	109
Replacement parts	13,800	15,000	1,200	109	80,000	67,000	(13,000)	84
	$441,800	$427,000	$(14,800)	97%	$2,185,000	$2,241,500	$ 56,500	103%

Actual sales dollars compared to sales dollar quotas by salesman.

MODEL REPORT #3-12

Key Use of Report:

Measures actual sales activity compared to quota for control purposes.

Suggested Routing:

Sales Manager.

Frequency of Preparation:

Monthly.

Alternative Reports:

Model Report #3-3, #3-6, #3-11.

Exhibit 3-13
LONG-RANGE MANLOADING

DIVISION		198__	198__	198__	198__
Sales:					
Electronics	Budget	$1,300,000	$1,750,000	$1,900,000	$2,300,000
	Backlog	360,000	--	--	--
Plastic Packaging	Budget	1,250,000	1,500,000	2,000,000	2,300,000
	Backlog	110,000	--	--	--
Engineering	Budget	980,000	1,100,000	1,400,000	1,600,000
	Backlog	240,000	--	--	--
Total budget sales		$4,240,000	$4,350,000	$5,300,000	$6,200,000
Manloading:					
Direct labor (22% of budget sales) (1)		$ 932,800	$ 957,000	$1,166,000	$1,364,000
Average wage rate (2)		$8	$8	$8.70	$9.10
Hours needed (1) -- (2) (3)		116,600	119,625	134,023	149,891
Hours per man year (4)		2080	2080	2080	2080
Direct employees needed (3) -- (4) (5)		56	58	64	72
Indirect employees (50% of direct) (5)x.50		28	29	32	36
Total manloading		84	87	96	108

Number of direct and indirect employees needed to reach the budgeted sales dollar number.

MODEL REPORT #3-13

Key Use of Report:

Establishes the number of employees needed to reach the budgeted sales level.

Suggested Routing:

Top Management.

Frequency of Preparation:

As often as sales are budgeted or rebudgeted.

Alternative Reports:

Once the headcount is established, it can best be monitored using Model Report #21-1 and #21-2.

Exhibit 3-14
SELLING EXPENSES

	CURRENT MONTH			YEAR TO DATE		
	ACTUAL	BUDGET	VARIANCE +(-)	ACTUAL	BUDGET	VARIANCE +(-)
Salesmen						
- salaries	$ 8,000	$ 8,000	--	$ 40,000	$ 40,000	--
- commissions	3,200	2,500	$ (700)	14,350	13,800	$ (550)
Travel	2,150	2,000	(150)	10,600	11,000	400
Advertising						
- media space	7,825	6,000	(1,825)	36,700	35,000	(1,700)
- dealer display	3,150	3,500	350	13,950	15,000	1,050
- salaries	2,650	2,600	(50)	12,350	12,000	(350)
Payroll taxes	1,260	1,200	(60)	5,825	6,000	175
Group insurance	875	850	(25)	4,200	4,300	100
Sales office occupancy						
- rent	1,100	1,100	--	5,500	5,500	--
- utilities	770	850	80	5,450	5,000	(450)
depreciation	510	500	(10)	2,500	2,500	--
Telephone	2,740	2,350	(390)	12,830	12,000	(830)
Car expenses	480	400	(80)	2,750	2,500	(250)
Bad debts	--	250	250	--	1,250	1,250
Miscellaneous	200	100	(100)	675	500	(175)
	$ 34,910	$ 32,200	$ (2,710)	$ 167,680	$ 166,350	$ (1,330)

An actual versus budget comparison of detailed selling expenses.

MODEL REPORT #3-14

Key Use of Report:

Compares actual versus budgeted selling expenses for control purposes.

Suggested Routing:

Top Management, Sales Manager.

Frequency of Preparation:

Monthly.

SALES ACTIVITY REPORTS

This group of reports tracks the sales effort; i.e., orders, shipments, backlogs, quotations, number of accounts, and so on. The data is most effectively presented when compared to budget or prior period's actual. Top management refers to this information continually in assessing company performance. One highly effective method to detail sales activity is to present it by product type such as Exhibits 4-1, 4-3, 4-4, 4-7 through 4-9, and 4-12 do. Another common breakdown of key sales data is by geographic territory as shown in Exhibit 4-11. The remaining Exhibits in this section highlight other special sales information that is important in the overall management of the sales function.

Exhibit 4-1

SUMMARY OF ORDERS BOOKED

PRODUCT	DAY			WEEK		
	# OF ORDERS	TOTAL DOLLARS	AVERAGE ORDER SIZE	# OF ORDERS	TOTAL DOLLARS	AVERAGE ORDER SIZE
Big number clock	38	$ 1,875	$ 49	125	$ 5,006	$ 40
Travel alarm	16	1,410	88	80	5,440	68
Alpha quartz	8	390	49	62	2,790	45
Denim watch	111	5,895	53	410	24,190	59
Dannish watch	23	1,110	48	132	5,280	40
SOS alarm	46	3,480	76	218	14,170	65
Digital dashboard	65	2,785	43	305	14,030	46
	307	$16,945	$ 55	1,332	$70,906	$ 53

Daily report of orders booked, total dollars, and average order size by product.

MODEL REPORT #4-1

Key Use of Report:

Itemizes order activity for informational purposes.

Suggested Routing:

Sales Manager.

Frequency of Preparation:

Daily.

Alternative Reports:

Model Report #4-3, #4-4.

Exhibit 4-2

NUMBER OF ACCOUNTS REPORT

	ACTUAL	BUDGET
Number of accounts sold during year	140	153
Existing accounts not sold during year	13	5
Total number of existing accounts	153	158
New accounts opened and sold during year	16	12
Existing top priority accounts (sales greater than $50,000)	14	11

Summary analysis of customer account activity compared to last year.

MODEL REPORT #4-2

Key Use of Report:

Summarizes the number of accounts for informational and planning purposes.

Suggested Routing:

Sales Manager.

Frequency of Preparation:

Annually.

Exhibit 4-3

DAILY REPORT OF ORDERS AND SHIPMENTS

MARKET SEGMENT		TODAY	THIS WEEK	THIS MONTH	THIS MONTH LAST YEAR	THIS MONTH BUDGET
Commercial:						
Orders	- number	2	7	31	29	33
	dollars	$ 13,500	$ 62,400	$293,500	$228,000	$305,000
Shipments	- number	4	6	35	40	45
	dollars	62,400	128,200	398,400	360,000	407,000
Industrial:						
Orders	- number	--	--	5	9	9
	- dollars	--	--	85,921	168,520	142,300
Shipments	- number	1	1	4	6	8
	- dollars	8,270	8,270	68,530	97,250	103,000
Residential:						
Orders	- number	3	4	7	7	10
	- dollars	38,200	46,550	124,300	96,000	210,000
Shipments	- number	1	1	5	7	9
	- dollars	10,500	10,500	84,710	114,580	163,520
TOTAL						
Orders	- number	5	11	43	45	52
	- dollars	$ 51,700	$108,950	$503,721	$492,520	$657,300
Shipments	- number	6	8	44	53	62
	- dollars	81,170	146,970	551,640	571,830	673,520

Daily, weekly, and monthly totals of orders and shipments by market segment compared to budget and the previous year.

MODEL REPORT #4-3

Key Use of Report:

Documents orders and shipments by market segment for informational purposes.

Suggested Routing:

Sales Manager.

Frequency of Preparation:

Daily.

Alternative Reports:

Model Report #4-1, #4-4.

Exhibit 4-4

REPORT OF ORDERS AND SHIPMENTS

PRODUCT	EXTRUDERS		BLOW MOLDING		LABORATORY		TOTAL	
	ACTUAL	BUDGET	ACTUAL	BUDGET	ACTUAL	BUDGET	ACTUAL	BUDGET
Model 10 thickness gauge								
Orders	$ 42,000	$ 50,000	--	$ 22,000	$ 74,500	$ 82,000	$116,500	$154,000
Shipments	20,000	35,000	--	22,000	31,850	30,000	51,850	87,000
Model 40A on-line gauge								
Orders	--	17,000	31,700	16,000	--	--	31,700	33,000
Shipments	37,420	29,500	17,200	19,800	--	--	54,620	49,300
Model 40B on-line gauge								
Orders	48,300	50,000	89,420	70,000	--	--	137,720	120,000
Shipments	19,750	25,000	65,800	50,000	--	--	85,550	75,000
TOTALS								
Orders	$ 90,300	$117,000	$121,120	$108,000	$ 74,500	$ 82,000	$285,920	$307,000
Shipments	77,170	89,500	83,000	91,800	31,850	30,000	192,020	211,300

BUYER TYPE

Reports of orders and shipments by product and by type of buyer.

MODEL REPORT #4-4

Key Use of Report:
Documents orders and shipments by product for planning and informational purposes.

Suggested Routing:
Sales Manager.

Frequency of Preparation:
Monthly.

Alternative Reports:
Model Report #4-1, #4-3.

Exhibit 4-5
TOP TEN SALES ACCOUNT REPORT

	CUSTOMERS	NUMBER OF ORDERS		DOLLARS		AVERAGE ORDER SIZE	
		CURRENT YEAR	PRIOR YEAR	CURRENT YEAR	PRIOR YEAR	CURRENT YEAR	PRIOR YEAR
1.	Babcock Co.	717	759	$ 342,580	$ 311,220	$478	$410
2.	Anderson	665	472	297,650	273,548	448	579
3.	Swanson Co.	430	316	214,395	197,300	499	624
4.	Menhart	304	448	212,410	228,560	698	510
5.	Sell & Jones	180	164	107,650	99,890	598	609
6.	Aaron Co.	177	207	93,200	109,920	527	531
7.	Sherman	107	185	90,582	83,250	847	450
8.	Ring Specialties	140	--	79,980	--	571	--
9.	Evert	152	146	77,540	89,270	510	611
10.	Dun & Brown	101	109	63,211	51,325	625	471
	Total Top 10	2,973	2,806	$1,579,198	$1,444,283	$531	$514
	Total company	7,760	7,422	$3,872,548	$3,629,506	$499	$489
	Top 10 % of total	38%	38%	41%	40%		

Top ten customers ranked by sales dollar. Also included in the report are the number of orders and average order size.

MODEL REPORT #4-5

Key Use of Report:

Ranks largest customers by sales volume for sales analysis and planning.

Suggested Routing:

Sales Manager.

Frequency of Preparation:

Monthly.

Alternative Reports:

Model Report #3-8.

Exhibit 4-6

SALES QUOTATION REPORT

	NUMBER OF QUOTES	
	MONTH	YTD
New accounts and products:		
Prospective new accounts	3	11
New products:		
Shrink Pac	5	8
Glass Flex	8	26
Total new products	13	31
Existing accounts and products:		
Accounts over 1 year old	39	142
Accounts less than 1 year old	16	61
Existing products:		
Electro Tape	25	63
Shrink Film	14	83
Shrink Belt	93	160
Total existing products	132	306
Cumulative total - new and existing accounts	58	214
- new and existing products	145	337

Analysis of sales quotations for new and existing accounts and new and existing products.

MODEL REPORT #4-6

Key Use of Report:

Monitors where sales emphasis is being placed.

Suggested Routing:

Sales Manager.

Frequency of Preparation:

Monthly.

Exhibit 4-7

SALES MIX AND ADJUSTMENTS REPORT

DESCRIPTION	SALES $	SALES OVER(UNDER) BUDGET	GROSS PROFIT %	GROSS PROFIT $	GROSS PROFIT OVER(UNDER) BUDGET
Valves:					
1/4"	$ 175,000	$ 15,000	31%	$ 54,250	$ 4,650
1/2"	238,000	32,000	28	66,640	8,960
3/4"	343,000	(19,000)	27	92,610	(5,130)
1-1/4"	197,000	27,000	36	70,920	9,720
TOTAL	953,000	55,000	30%	284,420	18,200
Gauges:					
Insulation gauge	376,000	62,000	39%	146,640	24,180
Cover gauge	438,000	(48,000)	37	162,060	(17,760)
Assembly gauge	210,000	5,600	42	88,200	2,352
Casting gauge	218,000	(18,000)	33%	71,940	(5,940)
TOTAL	1,242,000	1,600	38%	468,840	2,832
Replacement parts	67,500	8,250	96%	64,800	7,920
TOTAL	2,262,500	64,850	36%	818,060	28,952
Sales adjustments - discounts, rebate, freight	(183,200)	(3,950)		(183,200)	(3,950)
TOTAL	$2,079,300	$ 60,900	31%	$ 634,860	$ 25,002

Sales and gross profit dollars by product compared to budget. Also includes sales adjustments (discounts, rebates, freight) versus budget.

MODEL REPORT #4-7

Key Use of Report:

Monitors sales and gross profits by product compared to budget for control purposes.

Suggested Routing:

Top Management, Sales Manager.

Frequency of Preparation:

Monthly.

Alternative Reports:

Model Report #13-12.

Exhibit 4-8

LOST SALES REPORT

	$ Amount of Lost Sale	PRICING	DELIVERY TERMS	PROMOTIONAL ALLOWANCE	CREDIT TERMS	FREIGHT	NEW PRODUCTS	OTHER
				REASONS FOR LOST SALE				
1 Mil Packing Wrap:								
Carls Co.	$ 4,500	X		X				
Moore Co.	3,900				X	X		
Diamond Co.	13,200	X						
Hall Co.	1,100				X			
	22,700							
.7 Mil Shrink Wrap:								
Rollie Co.	3,900						X	
Pizza House	17,800	X						
Deli Supply	2,950	X						
Deli Express	8,235	X			X			
	32,885							
TOTAL	$ 55,585							

Listing of each lost sale and the reasons for it.

MODEL REPORT #4-8

Key Use of Report:

For planning purposes, it tracks the specific reasons expected orders were lost to the competition.

Suggested Routing:

Sales Manager.

Frequency of Preparation:

Monthly.

Exhibit 4-9

PROFILE OF SALES GROWTH

PRODUCT GROUP	1st YEAR		2nd YEAR		3rd YEAR		AVERAGE 3 YEAR	
	SALES $	% GAIN OVER PREVIOUS YEAR	SALES $	% GAIN OVER PREVIOUS YEAR	SALES $	% GAIN OVER PREVIOUS YEAR	$ INCREASE	% GAIN
Commercial furnishings	$ 973,000	6%	$ 925,000	(5%)	$1,010,000	9%	$ 31,800	3.4%
Home furnishings	1,380,000	4%	1,465,000	6%	1,610,500	10%	95,200	6.7%
Leisure products	675,000	9%	710,000	5%	760,000	7%	48,600	7.4%
Industrial rental	1,825,650	11%	2,060,000	13%	2,132,000	4%	169,000	9.5%
Commercial apparel	1,123,550	6%	1,250,000	11%	1,305,000	4%	82,900	7.4%
	$5,977,200	7%	$6,410,000	7%	$6,817,500	6%	$ 427,500	7.0%

Sales dollars and percent of sales dollar gain over the previous year by product line.

MODEL REPORT #4-9

Key Use of Report:

Identifies sales trends over a three-year period for budgeting and planning purposes.

Suggested Routing:

Top Management, Sales Manager.

Frequency of Preparation:

Annually.

Exhibit 4-10

SALES—ACTUAL VS. BUDGETED BACKLOG

MONTH	E.O.M. BACKLOG		ACTUAL OVER(UNDER)BUDGET	
	ACTUAL	BUDGET	$	%
Jan	$ 350,420	$ 400,000	$(69,580)	(17)%
Feb	313,870	375,000	(61,130)	(16)
Mar	462,380	500,000	(37,620)	(8)
Apr	270,600	410,000	(139,400)	(34)
May	597,300	500,000	97,300	20
June	782,362	725,000	57,362	8
July	920,380	1,000,000	(79,620)	(8)
Aug		1,250,000		
Sept		600,000		
Oct		425,000		
Nov		375,000		
Dec		300,000		

Actual end-of-month backlog compared to budget by month.

MODEL REPORT #4-10

Key Use of Report:

Monitors the status of sales backlog for both sales and production planning purposes.

Suggested Routing:

Sales Manager, Production Planning.

Frequency of Preparation:

Monthly.

Exhibit 4-11

SALES BY GEOGRAPHIC TERRITORY

| | CURRENT MONTH | | | YEAR TO DATE | | | # OF ACCOUNTS WITH ACTIVITY | | AVG. SALES FOR MONTH | |
	ACTUAL	BUDGET	VARIANCE +(-)	ACTUAL	BUDGET	VARIANCE +(-)	CURRENT YEAR	PRIOR YEAR	CURRENT YTD ACTUAL	PRIOR YTD ACTUAL
Northeast	$ 483,000	$ 500,000	$ (17,000)	$1,365,000	$1,427,000	$ (62,000)	260	253	$ 455,000	$ 431,500
Southeast	362,100	375,000	(12,900)	1,050,380	878,900	171,480	159	148	350,127	340,182
Midwest	597,000	450,000	147,000	1,760,500	1,665,000	95,500	328	313	586,833	496,523
Rocky Mountain	162,000	175,000	(13,000)	397,950	348,000	49,950	120	113	132,650	147,625
Northwest	158,000	150,000	8,000	582,625	550,000	32,625	162	148	194,208	206,829
Southwest	261,500	185,000	76,500	509,500	445,000	64,500	143	149	169,833	139,888
TOTAL	$2,023,600	$1,835,000	$ 188,600	$5,665,955	$5,313,900	$ 352,055	1,172	1,124	$1,888,651	$1,762,547

Current month and year-to-date sales, numbers of accounts with activity, and average sales for the month broken down by region of the country.

MODEL REPORT #4-11

Key Use of Report:

Summarizes sales activity by territory for analysis purposes.

Suggested Routing:

Sales Manager.

Frequency of Preparation:

Monthly.

Exhibit 4-12

SALES BY PRODUCT GROUP BY MONTH

	MONTH				YTD	
	BUDGET	ACTUAL	VARIANCE +(-)	% VARIANCE	LAST YEAR'S ACTUAL	CURRENT YEAR	LAST YEAR
Commercial furnishings	$ 210,000	$ 267,540	$ 57,540	27%	$ 232,380	$ 768,150	$ 827,360
Home furnishings	175,000	238,345	63,345	36	227,410	529,438	582,618
Leisure products	327,000	162,500	(164,500)	(50)	289,470	408,620	387,100
Industrial rental	211,000	76,900	(134,100)	(64)	138,200	697,280	505,420
Commercial apparel	295,000	382,420	87,420	30	338,520	976,240	723,248
TOTAL	$1,218,000	$1,127,705	$ (90,295)	(7)%	$1,225,980	$3,379,728	$3,025,746

Monthly and year-to-date budgeted versus actual sales by product group.

MODEL REPORT #4-12

Key Use of Report:

Breaks down sales by product line compared with the plan to monitor which products are performing the best.

Suggested Routing:

Sales Manager.

Frequency of Preparation:

Monthly.

Exhibit 4-13

FORECAST OF SALES BY SALESMAN

PRODUCT GROUP	1st QUARTER				QUARTERS			TOTALS	
	JAN	FEB	MAR	TOTAL	2nd	3rd	4th	CURRENT YEAR	PRIOR YEAR
On-line:									
Multi-line	$ 38,600	$ 21,500	$ 18,250	$ 78,350	$ 84,000	$ 90,000	$ 103,000	$ 355,350	$ 310,000
Single line	9,750	27,620	23,580	60,950	65,000	70,000	70,000	265,950	225,000
Specialty	15,400	15,000	21,550	51,950	55,000	60,000	66,500	233,450	225,000
Subtotal	63,750	64,120	63,380	191,250	204,000	220,000	239,500	854,750	760,000
Lab:									
Multi-location	27,820	16,540	22,500	66,860	60,000	65,000	70,000	261,860	250,000
Single facility	32,870	18,010	23,800	74,680	80,000	80,000	80,000	314,680	280,000
Subtotal	60,690	34,550	46,300	141,540	140,000	145,000	150,000	576,540	530,000
Replacement parts	4,000	4,000	4,000	12,000	12,000	12,000	12,000	48,000	48,000
	$128,440	$ 102,670	$ 113,680	$ 344,790	$ 356,000	$ 377,000	$ 401,500	$1,479,290	$1,338,000

Budgeted sales by salesman and by product group.

MODEL REPORT #4-13

Key Use of Report:

Lays out a salesman's goals by quarter and by product for the upcoming year.

Suggested Routing:

Sales Manager.

Frequency of Preparation:

Monthly.

MARKETING REPORTS

Marketing encompasses activities designed to plan, price, promote, sell, and distribute products and services to customers. The reports contained in this section are especially helpful in monitoring overall marketing performance. Exhibits 5-1 through 5-5 concentrate on how products are contributing to a firm's bottom line. Exhibit 5-6 displays a marketing plan in units that is extremely valuable for marketing managers, and also for production planning and cash flow forecasting. Exhibits 5-7 through 5-9 depict various marketing ratios and cost status reports that are essential for controlling departmental operations.

Exhibit 5-1

MARKETING PERFORMANCE REPORT

	BUDGET	ADJUSTED BUDGET(a)	ACTUAL	VARIANCE VOLUME/ MIX	VARIANCE PRICE/ COST
Net sales	$ 847,250	$ 689,000	$687,000	$ (158,250)	$ (2,000)
Variable costs:					
Material	351,000	285,000	291,000	66,000	(5,000)
Direct labor	37,850	32,550	33,400	5,300	(850)
Marketing commissions	41,200	33,975	33,450	7,225	525
Marketing freight	35,070	28,100	27,620	6,970	480
Total	465,120	379,625	385,470	85,495	(5,845)
Marginal income	382,130	309,375	301,530	(72,755)	(7,845)
Marginal income percentage	45.10%	44.90%	43.89%		
Direct fixed costs:					
Production	59,450	56,000	55,502	3,450	498
Marketing	83,600	81,400	81,535	2,200	(135)
Total	143,050	137,400	137,037	5,650	363
Product contribution	239,080	171,975	164,493	(67,105)	(7,482)
Territory direct fixed costs:					
Administration	62,500	58,700	59,580	3,800	(880)
Advertising	45,000	43,000	43,509	2,000	(509)
	107,500	101,700	103,089	5,800	(1,389)
Territory contribution	$ 131,580	$ 70,275	$ 61,404	$ (61,305)	$ (8,871)

(a) Actual sales x budgeted selling prices and costs.

NOTE: The information contained in Exhibits 5-2 through 5-4 is based on the contents of Exhibit 5-1.

Analysis of differences in budget, adjusted budget, and actual results. This report focuses on marginal income, product contribution, and territory contribution.

MODEL REPORT #5-1

Key Use of Report:

Analyzes product and territory profitability and the specific reasons for variances from budget.

Suggested Routing:

Top Management, Marketing Manager.

Frequency of Preparation:

Monthly.

Alternative Reports:

Model Report #2-3, #2-4, #2-5, #2-6, #5-2, #5-3, #5-4, #5-5.

Exhibit 5-2

MARKETING REPORT—CONTRIBUTION BY PRODUCT

		PRODUCTS		
	RECORDS	SPECIAL PRODUCTS	MAIL ORDER	TOTAL
Net sales	$ 295,000	$ 207,000	$ 185,000	$ 687,000
Variable costs:				
Material	89,000	102,500	99,500	291,000
Direct labor	14,500	18,900	--	33,400
Marketing commissions	20,600	12,850	--	33,450
Marketing freight	8,420	5,230	13,970	27,620
	132,520	139,480	113,470	385,470
Marginal income	162,480	67,520	71,530	301,530
Direct fixed costs:				
Production	28,050	21,555	5,897	55,502
Marketing	21,675	23,620	36,240	81,535
	49,725	45,175	42,137	137,037
Product contribution	112,755	22,345	29,393	164,493
Territory direct fixed costs:				
Administration				59,580
Advertising				43,509
				103,089
Territory contribution				$ 61,404

Profit and loss statement by product that shows marginal income, product contribution, and territory contribution totals.

MODEL REPORT #5-2

Key Use of Report:

Measures individual product and consolidated territory profitability.

Suggested Routing:

Top Management, Marketing Manager.

Frequency of Preparation:

Monthly.

Alternative Reports:

Model Report #2-3, #2-4, #2-5, #2-6, #5-1, #5-3, #5-4, #5-5, #13-14.

Exhibit 5-3

MARKETING VARIANCE REPORT—ONE TERRITORY

```
Budgeted territory contribution for period            $  131,580

    Volume variance ($158,250 x .4510)                   (71,375)
    Mix variance ( .4510 - .4490 x $689,000)              (1,380)
    Cost variance ($143,050 + $107,500 - $137,400 - $101,700)  11,450

Standard marginal income at actual sales volume           70,275

    Price variances:
        Change in selling price                           (2,000)
        Change in variable costs                          (5,845)
                                                          (7,845)

    Cost variances:
        Direct fixed costs                                   363
        Territory direct fixed costs                      (1,389)

                                                          (1,026)
Actual territory contribution for the period          $   61,404
```

Refer to Exhibit 5-2

A reconciliation of budgeted territory and actual territory profit contribution for the period.

MODEL REPORT #5-3

Key Use of Report:

Itemizes the specific reasons for the variance between budgeted and actual territory profit contribution.

Suggested Routing:

Marketing Manager, Territory Manager.

Frequency of Preparation:

Monthly.

Alternative Reports:

Model Report #5-1, #5-2, #5-4, #5-5.

Exhibit 5-4

PRODUCT VARIANCE REPORT—ONE TERRITORY

		PRODUCTS		
	RECORDS	SPECIAL PRODUCTS	MAIL ORDER	TOTAL
Budgeted product contribution	$158,550	$ 41,600	$ 38,930	$239,080
Volume variance	(48,445)	(14,735)	(8,195)	(71,375)
Mix variance	2,820	(3,760)	(440)	(1,380)
Price variance	(4,130)	(2,010)	(1,705)	(7,845)
Cost variance (a)	3,960	1,250	803	6,013
Actual product contribution	$112,755	$ 22,345	$ 29,393	$164,493

(a) See direct fixed costs, Exhibit 5-1

$143,050 - $137,037 = $6,013

A reconciliation of budgeted product and actual product profit contribution for each product in one marketing territory.

MODEL REPORT #5-4

Key Use of Report:

Itemizes the specific reasons for the variance between budgeted and actual product profit contribution.

Suggested Routing:

Marketing Manager, Territory Manager, Product Manager.

Frequency of Preparation:

Monthly.

Alternative Reports:

Model Report #5-1, #5-2, #5-3, #5-5.

Exhibit 5-5

MARKETING VARIANCE REPORT—ALL TERRITORIES

	VOLUME	MIX	VARIANCES +(-) PRICE	COST	TOTAL
One	$ (71,375)	$(1,380)	$(7,845)	$ 6,013	$ (74,587)
Two	(36,250)	4,260	(1,520)	(2,825)	(36,335)
Three	5,820	(1,910)	3,760	(4,620)	3,050
Four	(27,820)	(2,475)	2,223	1,340	(26,732)
Corporate office	--	--	--	4,820	4,820
	$(129,625)	$(1,505)	$(3,382)	$ 4,728	$(129,784)
Total Planned Contribution					460,000
Total Actual Contribution					$330,216

A reconciliation of actual and planned profit contributions using marketing variances (volume, mix, price, and cost) by territory.

MODEL REPORT #5-5

Key Use of Report:

Summarizes specific variances from plan for all territories.

Suggested Routing:

Marketing Manager, Territory Manager.

Frequency of Preparation:

Monthly.

Alternative Reports:

Model Report #5-1, #5-2, #5-3, #5-4.

Exhibit 5-6

MARKETING PLAN SUMMARY

Customer Classification	UNIT BUDGET BY QUARTERS					PREVIOUS THREE YEARS		
	1st	2nd	3rd	4th	TOTAL	1st	2nd	3rd
Chemical Companies	870	950	900	900	3,620	3,200	2,809	2,950
Plastic Processors:								
Blow Molders	560	400	425	450	1,835	1,700	1,610	1,580
Extruders	1,325	1,250	1,300	1,350	5,225	5,060	4,950	4,500
OEMs	410	500	500	525	1,935	1,810	1,730	1,650
Exports	618	600	610	625	2,453	1,850	--	--
	3,783	3,700	3,735	3,850	15,068	13,620	11,099	10,680
Increase (decrease) from prior year					1,448	2,521	419	1,083
% Increase (decrease) from prior year					10.6%	22.7%	3.9%	11.3%

Unit sales budget by quarter for each major customer classification.
Additionally, the prior three years unit sales totals are included.

MODEL REPORT #5-6

Key Use of Report:

Shows the sales budget (in units) by quarter compared to the previous three years to measure how the company has progressed.

Suggested Routing:

Top Management, Marketing Manager.

Frequency of Preparation:

Annually.

Exhibit 5-7

MARKETING MANAGEMENT MEASUREMENT REPORT

		CURRENT YEAR	PRIOR YEAR
1.	Sales this year divided by prior year	111.1%	103.2%
2.	Sales or % of estimated industry sales (market penetration)	2.1%	2.0%
3.	Marketing costs divided by sales	6.9%	7.0%
4.	Discounts divided by sales	.8%	.7%
5.	Bad debts divided by sales	1.2%	1.3%
6.	Finished inventory divided by sales	12.5%	15.3%
7.	Accounts receivable as % of average daily sales	41 days	50 days
8.	Sales divided by number of orders	$1,333	$1,241
9.	Marketing costs divided by number of orders	$ 86	$ 86
10.	Orders outstanding divided by average daily sales	9.1 days	16.7 days

Ten key marketing/sales ratios for use by marketing management to measure performance.

MODEL REPORT #5-7

Key Use of Report:

Analyzes the effectiveness of marketing management.

Suggested Routing:

Top Management, Marketing Manager.

Frequency of Preparation:

Quarterly.

Exhibit 5-8

MARKETING COST REPORT

		$	ACTUAL OVER(UNDER) BUDGET
	ACTUAL	BUDGETED	
Marketing costs:			
Call costs	$ 54,000	$ 65,000	$ (11,000)
Service costs	16,000	12,000	4,000
Delivery costs	38,000	35,000	3,000
Marketing administration	95,000	90,000	5,000
Marketing research costs	11,000	10,000	1,000
Advertising and promotion	129,000	118,000	11,000
	$ 343,000	$ 330,000	$ 13,000
Marketing costs as a % of:			
Net sales	7.6%	7.4%	
# of active accounts (160 accounts)	$ 2,143	$ 2,062	
# of personnel	$57,100	$55,000	

Analysis comparing major categories of actual marketing costs against budgeted costs.

MODEL REPORT #5-8

Key Use of Report:

Analyzes marketing costs by category for control purposes.

Suggested Routing:

Marketing Manager.

Frequency of Preparation:

Monthly.

Exhibit 5-9
PRODUCT PROMOTION EXPENSE STATUS REPORT

PRODUCT/ PROGRAM	EXPECTED COMPLETION DATE	ORIGINAL BUDGET	(1) ACTUAL EXPENDI- TURES TO DATE	(2) APPROVED EXPENDI- TURES	(3) FUTURE ESTIMATED EXPENDI- TURES	(1)+(2)+(3) TOTAL	TOTAL OVER(UNDER) COMMITTED
Reflective tape	9/1	$ 25,000	$ 1,800	$ 13,200	$100,000	$ 25,000	--
Deli sheets	6/30	148,000	27,500	42,000	78,500	148,000	--
Sandwich wrap	6/30	20,000	16,000	3,000	3,800	22,800	(2,800)
Pick-up tissue	7/30	12,000	--	4,800	6,500	11,300	700
Scale sheet	8/10	10,000	5,500	600	3,000	9,100	900
Total product/program		$215,000	$ 50,800	$ 63,600	$101,800	$216,200	$ (1,200)

Analysis of budgeted and actual promotion expenditures for major products and marketing programs.

MODEL REPORT #5-9

Key Use of Report:

Monitors the promotional expense budget by specific program.

Suggested Routing:

Marketing Manager, Promotion and/or Advertising Manager.

Frequency of Preparation:

Monthly.

Alternative Reports:

Model Report #27-6.

MANUFACTURING COST REPORTS—MATERIAL

Material often comprises the biggest dollar item in cost of sales and cash flow. The material cost reports included in this section will help management understand the makeup of the material dollars and their movement through the plant. Specifically they are detailed reports used most often by plant management to keep material losses to a minimum, appraise management of any trouble spots needing attention, and help increase production efficiencies.

Exhibit 6-1

DAILY MATERIALS USAGE REPORT

| | DAY | | | | MONTH | | | |
| | USAGE IN POUNDS | | | | USAGE IN POUNDS | | | |
DATE	ACTUAL	STANDARD	VARIANCE +(-)	VARIANCE % +(-)	ACTUAL	STANDARD	VARIANCE +(-)	VARIANCE % +(-)
1	4,800	5,000	200	4	4,800	5,000	200	4
2	2,950	2,775	(175)	(6)	7,750	7,775	25	--
3	13,275	12,450	(825)	(7)	21,025	20,225	(800)	(4)
4	9,843	9,650	(193)	(2)	30,868	29,875	(993)	(3)
5	8,240	8,425	185	2	39,108	38,300	(808)	(2)
6	7,605	7,525	(80)	(1)	46,713	45,825	(888)	(2)
7	9,200	9,420	220	2	55,913	55,245	(668)	(1)
8	8,420	8,305	(115)	(1)	64,333	63,550	(783)	(1)
9	9,500	9,150	(350)	(4)	73,833	72,700	(1,133)	(2)
10	9,825	9,610	(215)	(2)	83,658	82,310	(1,348)	(2)
11	7,205	7,400	195	3	90,863	89,710	(1,153)	(1)

Daily and month-to-date material usage in units (pounds, feet, number) compared against standard usage.

MODEL REPORT #6-1

Key Use of Report:

Measures how efficiently materials are being used in the plant.

Suggested Routing:

Production Manager.

Frequency of Preparation:

Daily.

Alternative Reports:

Model Report #6-2.

Exhibit 6-2

DAILY YIELD REPORT

	GOOD UNITS OF PRODUCTION	MATERIALS USED			
		ACTUAL	PLANNED	USAGE +(-)	% DEVIATION
Assembly line #1	9,250	10,430	10,920	490	4.5%
#2	14,320	15,700	16,300	600	3.7%
#3	10,150	12,430	11,180	(1,250)	(11.2)%
#4	2,938	3,250	3,000	(250)	(8.3)%
#5	7,650	8,950	8,800	(150)	(1.7)%

Actual amount of material used compared against plan for each assembly line.

MODEL REPORT #6-2

Key Use of Report:

Measures how efficiently materials are being used in the plant.

Suggested Routing:

Production Manager.

Frequency of Preparation:

Daily.

Alternative Reports:

Model Report #6-1.

Exhibit 6-3

STOCKROOM REPORT

PART #	DESCRIPTION	UNIT OF MEASURE	LOCATION	LAST ISSUE DATE	ON-HAND STOCK	ON-ORDER STOCK	RE-ORDER POINT LEVEL	SAFETY STOCK LEVEL	NEXT PHYSICAL INVENTORY DATE
37215	A/C Coupler	#	BIN 62	5/1	1,197	500	1,400	800	7/15
62854	B/R Coupler	#	BIN 67	5/13	870	--	500	250	7/15
66630	Hex-connector	#	BIN 48	4/10	629	150	750	450	7/15
70442	Arc-connector	#	BIN 42	5/08	420	600	750	400	8/15
82841	Feed hose .09"	ft	SPOOL X6	4/27	1,860	--	1,000	800	9/15
62845	M/F Jack Stand	#	DRA 26A	5/8	240	--	100	75	9/15

Analysis of parts inventory status—location, on-hand quantity, on-order quantity, reorder point, and safety stock level.

MODEL REPORT #6-3

Key Use of Report:

Itemizes the location and extent of parts inventory on hand. It is the critical report for controlling raw material levels in the plant.

Suggested Routing:

Production Manager, Materials Manager, Stockroom Supervisor, Inventory Supervisor.

Frequency of Preparation:

Daily.

Alternative Reports:

Model Report #16-1.

Exhibit 6-4

MATERIALS LEDGER REPORT

Part # 30B-C

Bin 13, Row 13

	RECEIVED				ISSUED			BALANCE		
DATE	QUANTITY	UNIT PRICE	AMOUNT	DATE	REG #	QUANTITY	AMOUNT	QUANTITY	AMOUNT	UNIT PRICE
3/1	425	1.00	425.00					425	425.00	1.00
3/3	560	1.00	560.00					985	985.00	1.00
				3/9	C302	275	275.00	710	710.00	1.00
				3/18	C309	350	350.00	360	360.00	1.00
3/24	500	1.10	510.00					860	870.00	1.01
3/26	800	1.11	888.00					1,660	1,758.00	1.06
				4/5	C428	610	646.60	1,050	1,111.40	1.06
				4/17	C483	350	371.00	700	740.40	1.06
5/8	500	1.12	560.00					1,200	1,300.40	1.08

Details of material received into stock, issued from stock, and the running net balance on hand.

MODEL REPORT #6-4

Key Use of Report:

Establishes a perpetual inventory record for each type of material used. It tells from an accounting standpoint how much inventory is on hand by tracking all receipts and issuances.

Suggested Routing:

Inventory Supervisor.

Frequency of Preparation:

Continuously kept up to date.

Alternative Reports:

Model Report #6-6.

Exhibit 6-5

MATERIALS UTILIZATION REPORT

	EXTRUDER	HOURS RUNNING TIME AVAILABLE	TOTAL PRODUCTION UNITS		EFFICIENCY % (1)	RESIN CONSUMPTION(2)		UTILIZATION % (3)
			ACTUAL	STANDARD		ACTUAL LBS USED	BUDGETED LBS USED	
#1	3-1/2"	8,000	740,000	880,000	84%	310,000	291,500	94%
#2	3-1/2"	8,000	810,000	920,000	88%	438,000	410,000	94%
#3	2-1/2"	6,500	610,000	650,000	94%	192,158	182,000	95%
#4	4-1/2"	7,200	873,000	1,260,000	69%	297,000	267,000	90%
#5	4-1/2"	8,000	675,000	960,000	70%	210,000	191,000	91%

NOTE: In a highly automated environment machine hours becomes the key index rather than direct labor hours.

(1)   Actual -- Standard production units

(2)   Key material ingredient in production process

(3)   Budgeted lbs. -- actual lbs.

Analysis shows plant efficiency (actual versus standard production units) and key raw material utilization (actual units versus budgeted units used in production).

MODEL REPORT #6-5

Key Use of Report:

Measures how efficiently each production line is functioning for control purposes.

Suggested Routing:

Plant Manager, Production Managers.

Frequency of Preparation:

Monthly.

Exhibit 6-6

WEEKLY MATERIALS UTILIZATION REPORT

PART DESCRIPTION	PART NO.	(1) BEGINNING INVENTORY	(2) ISSUES TO FLOOR	(3) RETURNS FROM FLOOR	(4) ENDING INVENTORY	(5) MATERIAL USAGE (1)+(2)-(3)-(4)	(6) GOOD PRODUCTION	(7) UTILIZATION (%)
Inflation tube (feet)	031	347,200	85,700	1,250	179,500	252,150	234,500	93%
Bag liners (lbs)	925	58,200	12,600	1,900	25,000	43,900	38,195	87%
HS-stock (lbs)	145	83,950	45,382	2,820	53,200	73,312	70,380	96%
RAR sheeting (lbs)	163	110,200	13,500	1,000	84,500	38,200	35,908	94%
Phillips (lbs)	R3	10,650	8,420	--	11,500	7,570	6,889	91%
Antiblock (lbs)	R7	6,550	540	--	5,730	1,360	1,265	93%

Detailed breakdown by inventory part number showing raw material usage for the week—issues to the plant, return from the floor, ending inventory.

MODEL REPORT #6-6

Key Use of Report:

Establishes a perpetual inventory record for each part on hand. Whereas Model Report 6-4 is the accounting inventory control report, this report is strictly used in the plant.

Suggested Routing:

Production Manager, Materials Manager.

Frequency of Preparation:

Weekly.

Alternative Reports:

Model Report #6-4.

Exhibit 6-7

WEEKLY REPORT OF MATERIALS USAGE VARIANCES

RAW MATERIAL	$ QUANTITY USED STANDARD	ACTUAL	VARIANCE +(−)	REASON FOR VARIANCE BAD MATERIAL	OVER(UNDER) RUN	SCRAP	OTHER (EXPLAIN)
Dowlex	$ 8,325	$ 8,107	$ 218				$ 218 (1)
U.C. high density	3,890	3,358	532			$ 532	
Gulf poly	4,762	5,142	(380)	$ (200)	$ (180)		
Eastman 082	11,582	12,375	(793)		(300)	(250)	(243) (2)
TOTAL	$28,559	$28,982	$ (423)	$ (200)	$ (480)	$ 282	$ (25)

(1) Changed product specification. Standard quantity should be reduced.

(2) Unexplained

Analyses of reasons for material variances by raw material category.

MODEL REPORT #6-7

Key Use of Report:

Explains the reasons for variances in material usage.

Suggested Routing:

Plant Manager, Production Manager, Materials Manager.

Frequency of Preparation:

Weekly.

Alternative Reports:

Model Report #6-8.

Exhibit 6-8
MATERIAL VARIANCES REPORT

INVEN-TORY # / MATERIAL	PURCHASES		PURCHASE VARIANCES			USAGE		USAGE VARIANCES		
	STANDARD	ACTUAL	VARIANCE ACTUAL+(-)	BUDGETED	OVER(UNDER) BUDGET	STANDARD	ACTUAL	VARIANCE ACTUAL+(-)	BUDGETED	OVER(UNDER) BUDGET
R-102 Gulf Resin	$28,250	$27,590	$ (660)	--	$ 660	$ 8,620	$ 8,560	$ (60)	--	$ 60
R-183 Union Carbide Resin	39,100	38,625	(475)	--	475	10,020	9,940	(80)	--	80
R-202 Eastman Chemical Resin	85,250	87,410	2,160	1,000	(1,160)	10,100	10,375	275	150	(125)
R-209 Dow Chemical Resin	8,000	8,110	110	--	(110)	8,750	8,975	225	150	(75)
R-214 Dupont Resin	4,000	3,950	(50)	100	150	2,950	2,930	(20)	--	20
R-223 American Chemical Resin	9,475	9,750	275	200	(75)	7,400	7,620	220	--	(220)
	$174,075	$175,435	$1,360	$1,300	$ (60)	$47,840	$48,400	$ 560	$ 300	$ (260)

Detailed analysis of materials purchase and usage variances by raw material category.

MODEL REPORT #6-8

Key Use of Report:

Monitors the dollar impact of the two material variances (price and usage).

Suggested Routing:

Production Manager, Materials Manager.

Frequency of Preparation:

Monthly.

Alternative Reports:

Model Report #6-7.

Exhibit 6-9

REPORT OF SCRAP MATERIAL AND REWORK—VERSION I

MACHINE	SCRAP			REWORK		RETURNED TO STOCK	BUDGETED SCRAP	OVER (UNDER) BUDGET
	TOTAL	RECOVERY	NET	LABOR	OVERHEAD			
Extruder #1	$1,375	$ 475	$ 900	$ 129	$ 271	$ 875	$ 500	$ 400
Extruder #2	2,850	1,942	908	242	508	2,692	500	408
Extruder #3	1,250	520	730	110	231	861	500	230
Extruder #4	627	580	47	118'	248	946	400	(353)
Beck Sheeter #1	1,295	873	422	138	207	1,218	500	(89)
Beck Sheeter #2	993	629	364	97	146	872	350	14
TOTAL	$8,390	$5,019	$3,371	$ 834	$1,611	$7,464	$2,750	$ 621

Analysis of scrap and rework dollars by machine.

MODEL REPORT #6-9

Key Use of Report:

Monitors material scrap dollars to help spot and eliminate excessive waste.

Suggested Routing:

Production Manager.

Alternative Reports:

Model Report #6-10, #6-11.

Exhibit 6-10

REPORT OF SCRAP MATERIAL AND REWORK—VERSION II

| PRODUCT | SCRAP RATE | | | | REWORK | | |
	GOOD UNITS	REJECTS	% OF REJECTS	BUDGET % OF REJECTS	STANDARD LABOR ON REJECTED MATERIAL	REWORK LABOR	% OF STD. LABOR
Hex nut 1/8"	5,975	180	3%	2%	.02 hr	.022 hr	110%
Hex nut 1/4"	8,250	165	2%	2%	.02 hr	.02 hr	100%
Hex nut 1/2"	7,700	231	3%	2%	.02 hr	.023 hr	115%
Hex nut 5/8"	7,550	302	4%	2%	.025 hr	.028 hr	112%
Kotter pin 1-1/2"	8,920	268	3%	2%	.02 hr	.022 hr	110%
Kotter pin 2-1/2"	7,150	215	3%	2%	.022 hr	.026 hr	118%

Analysis of scrapped units and rework labor hours for each appropriate inventory category.

MODEL REPORT #6-10

Key Use of Report:

Monitors scrapped production units to help eliminate excessive waste.

Suggested Routing:

Production Manager.

Frequency of Preparation:

Monthly.

Alternative Reports:

Model Report #6-9, #6-11.

Exhibit 6-11

REPORT OF SCRAP MATERIAL VARIANCES

| | POUNDS OF MATERIAL | | | | |
| | SCRAP MATERIAL | | | | |
	ACTUAL	BUDGET	ACTUAL VARIANCE +(-)	BUDGETED VARIANCE	OVER(UNDER) BUDGET
Extruder #1	620	500	(120)	(150)	(30)
Extruder #2	480	500	20	(100)	(120)
Extruder #3	562	500	(62)	(100)	(38)
Extruder #4	897	1,000	103	(100)	(203)
Beck Sheeter #1	1,420	1,250	(170)	(100)	70
Beck Sheeter #2	942	1,000	58	(50)	(108)
TOTAL	4,921	4,750	(171)	(600)	(429)

Analysis of units of scrap material compared to budget by machine.

MODEL REPORT #6-11

Key Use of Report:

Monitors scrapped production material to help eliminate excessive waste.

Suggested Routing:

Production Manager.

Frequency of Preparation:

Monthly.

Alternative Reports:

Model Report #6-9, #6-10.

Exhibit 6-12

MATERIAL REQUIREMENTS REPORT

REQUIRED MATERIALS	DEPARTMENT	TOTAL REQUIREMENT (IN UNITS)	1st QUARTER APRIL	MAY	JUNE	QUARTERS 1st	2nd	3rd	4th
Transform measure -- Units to be produced									
Digital meter	Electronics	1,780	135	150	125	410	390	450	530
Motor servo	Electronics	3,560	270	300	250	820	780	900	1,060
Relay 4 PDT	Electronics	8,900	675	750	625	2,050	1,950	2,250	2,650
Cable Coax	Machine Shop	3,560	270	300	250	820	780	900	1,060
Servo Zero Board	Electronics	1,780	135	150	125	410	410	450	530
On-line Timer	Electronics	5,340	405	450	375	1,230	1,170	1,350	1,590
Signal Module	Electronics	7,120	540	600	500	1,640	1,560	1,800	2,120
Gear, Drive	Machine Shop	1,780	135	150	125	410	410	450	530
Transformer	Electronics	3,560	270	300	250	820	780	900	1,060
Transport	Machine Shop	1,780	135	150	125	410	410	450	530
Shipping Carton	Shipping	1,780	135	150	125	410	410	450	530

Summary of raw material requirements in units by quarter for each part included in a bill of materials.

MODEL REPORT #6-12

Key Use of Report:

A production planning tool that lays out the timing of material needs for the year for each bill of material item.

Suggested Routing:

Production Manager, Purchasing Agent.

Frequency of Preparation:

Annually but updated monthly.

Exhibit 6-13
BILL OF MATERIALS UPDATE REPORT

PART DESCRIPTION	PART #	STANDARD COST 1/1/85	CHANGES INCREASE	CHANGES DECREASE	STANDARD COST 6/30/85	COMMENTS
Blow vent	1382	$ 13.95			$ 13.95	
Copper tubing	1597	16.50			16.50	
Oscillator	2076	185.25	$ 5.85		191.10	Vendor price increase
Discriminator	1377	16.95		$ (5.10)	11.85	Substitute part from alternate supplier
Double Wrung	0976	8.40			8.40	
Washers	0182	1.10			1.10	
Rollers	3012	62.50	4.50		67.00	Slightly enhanced part - thicker rubber by 1/8"
Front plate	1613	29.50			29.50	
Cabinet	2110	137.50			137.50	
3Ac Plug	0039	1.89			1.89	
Clamps	0993	1.50			1.50	
		$475.04	$10.35	$ (5.10)	$480.29	

Analysis of standard cost changes and the reasons for them for each bill of materials part.

MODEL REPORT #6-13

Key Use of Report:

Documents any changes in the bill of materials and the reasons for them.

Suggested Routing:

Production Manager, Purchasing Agent, Materials Manager.

Frequency of Preparation:

Whenever a price change takes place.

MANUFACTURING COST REPORTS—LABOR

In recent years labor has been a rapidly escalating cost for most businesses. The reports in this section are valuable aids for management to measure, analyze, and control this volatile cost. They will specifically help in monitoring labor dollars and hours by employee, job, and department; eliminating all unnecessary hours; scheduling current and future manpower requirements; increasing productivity; and contributing to lowering the cost of production. Although plant level personnel will get the most benefit from these reports due to their detailed nature, corporate management will find value in periodically reviewing Exhibits 7-9 and 7-10.

Exhibit 7-1

DAILY DIRECT LABOR REPORT

EMPLOYEE	PROJECT #	(1) QUANTITY PRODUCED	(2) BUDGETED HOURS PER UNIT	(3) BUDGETED HOURS EARNED (1)x(2)	(4) ACTUAL HOURS	(5) % EFFICIENCY (3)--(4)
1410	92100	210	.036	7.56	7.40	102%
1415	92350	56	.13	7.28	8.00	91%
1421	92100	84	.08	6.72	8.00	84%
1428	92400	111	.056	6.22	6.50	96%
1430	92150	29	.07	2.03	2.30	
	93160	84	.04	3.36	3.80	
	93900	40	.035	1.40	1.90	
				6.79	8.00	85%
TOTAL				34.78	37.90	92%

Actual hours incurred versus budgeted hours for each employee by project number.

MODEL REPORT #7-1

Key Use of Report:

Monitors labor efficiency by employee.

Suggested Routing:

Production Manager.

Frequency of Preparation:

Daily.

Alternative Reports:

Model Report #7-11.

Exhibit 7-2

DAILY IDLE TIME REPORT

DEPARTMENT	TOTAL AVAILABLE HOURS	DIRECT CHARGEABLE HOURS		LACK OF ORDERS		LACK OF MATERIAL		MACHINE DOWNTIME		OTHER	
		AMOUNT	%	AMOUNT	%	AMOUNT	%	AMOUNT	%	AMOUNT	%
Extrusion	420	375	89	35	9	5	1	5	1		
Sheeting	160	82	51	56	35	8	5	6	4	8	5
Conversion	160	153	96					7	4		
Machine Shop	245	210	86	25	10			5	2	5	2
Electronics	380	328	86	30	8	11	3	1	1	10	2

Analysis by department giving specific reasons for idle time.

MODEL REPORT #7-2

Key Use of Report:

   Monitors the causes of idle time within each department in the plant.

Suggested Routing:

   Production Manager.

Frequency of Preparation:

   Daily.

Exhibit 7-3

WEEKLY LABOR COST DISTRIBUTION SUMMARY REPORT

LABOR CLASSIFICATION	JOB NUMBER				
	37498	42379	42384	45784	TOTAL
Direct labor:					
Direct charges	$ 2,975	$ 862	$4,384	$ 510	$8,731
Overtime	185	174	260	--	619
Shift differential	--	--	182	--	182
Vacation		587	67		654
Other	82				82
Subtotal	3,242	1,623	4,893	510	10,268
Indirect labor:					
Direct charges	284	170	663	--	1,117
Overtime		10	87		97
Shift differential					
Vacation				142	142
Other			66		66
Subtotal	284	180	816	142	1,422
TOTAL	$ 3,526	$ 1,803	$ 5,709	$ 652	$11,690

Dollars of direct and indirect labor broken down and totaled by job numbers.

MODEL REPORT #7-3

Key Use of Report:

Allocates both direct and indirect labor to specific jobs.

Suggested Routing:

Production Manager, Inventory Supervisor.

Frequency of Preparation:

Weekly.

Exhibit 7-4
WEEKLY OVERTIME REPORT

DEPARTMENT	CURRENT YEAR OVERTIME		PRIOR YEAR OVERTIME	
	HOURS	DOLLARS	HOURS	DOLLARS
Extruding	121	$ 1,125	25	$ 225
Sheeting	19	149	9	67
Packaging	21	126	15	104
Machine Shop	--	--	42	412
Warehousing	16	96	8	47
Week's Total	177	1,496	99	855
Month's Total - Ac.	462	3,467	310	2,263
- Bu.	340	2,605	280	2,030
Year to Date - Ac.	769	5,897	648	4,834
- Bu.	508	3,759	600	4,505

Hours and dollars of overtime by department compared with the prior year. In addition to the weekly total, there are running totals for the month and year.

MODEL REPORT #7-4

Key Use of Report:

Summarizes the amount of overtime by department for control purposes.

Suggested Routing:

Production Manager.

Frequency of Preparation:

Weekly.

Exhibit 7-5

WEEKLY REPORT OF DIRECT LABOR ON INDIRECT WORK

INDIRECT WORK	WEEK			CURRENT MONTH		
	ACTUAL	BUDGET	VARIANCE (+/-)	ACTUAL	BUDGET	VARIANCE (+/-)
Quality control	$ 78	$ 50	$ (28)	$ 205	$ 160	$ (45)
Inspection	36	100	64	137	300	163
R & D	88	125	37	291	275	(16)
Maintenance	39	50	11	162	150	(12)
Repairs	41	75	34	131	200	69
Total indirect labor	$ 282	$ 400	$ 118	$ 926	$1,085	$ 159
Total direct labor	$2,385	$2,200		$7,350	$7,625	
% indirect/direct labor	11.9%	18.2%		12.6%	14.2%	

Weekly and month-to-date totals of direct labor employees putting in hours on indirect work.

MODEL REPORT #7-5

Key Use of Report:

Analyzes how much direct labor was incurred on indirect jobs and thus becomes part of overhead. Unless closely watched as this report allows, significant burden rate swings can occur.

Suggested Routing:

Production Manager.

Frequency of Preparation:

Weekly.

Exhibit 7-6

WEEKLY REPORT OF DIRECT HOURLY VARIANCES

PART DESCRIPTION	QUANTITY PRODUCED	STANDARD HOURS	% ACTUAL HOURS OVER (UNDER) STD	COMMENTS
Electronics:				
Crystal watching	65	65	23	Excessive bad crystals
Back Panels	110	48	4	
Side Panels	65	29	7	
Cabinet Assembly	22	11	(9)	
Painting	22	22	14	Various interruptions
Board Assembly	162	40	(5)	
Regulator Assembly	58	10	--	
Polishing	31	39	10	New trainee

Analysis of actual labor hours compared to standard hours for each production part.

MODEL REPORT #7-6

Key Use of Report:

Measures inefficiencies in direct labor and the specific reasons for them.

Suggested Routing:

Production Manager.

Frequency of Preparation:

Weekly.

Alternative Reports:

Model Report #7-7, #7-10.

Exhibit 7-7

WEEKLY REPORT OF DIRECT LABOR COST VARIANCE

DEPARTMENT	ACTUAL HOURS	ACTUAL COST	STANDARD HOURS	STANDARD COST	VARIANCES PERFORMANCE	VARIANCES RATE	TOTAL
Machine Shop:							
Milling #1	35	$ 359	40	$ 400	$ 50	$ (9)	$ 41
Milling #2	33	340	40	410	72	(2)	70
Lathe #1	40	440	40	440	--	--	--
Lathe #2	43	473	20	220	(253)	--	(253)
Punch Press	40	360	50	450	90	--	90
Band Saw	31	244	25	195	(47)	(2)	(49)
Subtotal	222	2,316	215	2,115	(88)	(13)	(101)
Electronics:							
Assembly	167	1,336	160	1,280	(56)	--	(56)
Wiring	48	360	40	300	(60)	--	(60)
Testing	28	231	40	350	105	14	119
Repair	20	170	30	258	86	2	88
Subtotal	263	2,097	270	2,188	75	16	91
TOTAL	485	$4,413	485	$4,303	$ (13)	$ 3	$ (10)

Analysis of direct labor variances (performance and pay) for each manufacturing department.

MODEL REPORT #7-7

Key Use of Report:

Pinpoints the specific reasons for labor cost variances for cost control purposes.

Suggested Routing:

Production Manager.

Frequency of Preparation:

Weekly.

Alternative Reports:

Model Report #7-6, #7-10.

Exhibit 7-8

LABOR VARIANCE BY REPORTING AREA

DESCRIPTION	ACTUAL $	ACTUAL % OF SALES	BUDGET $	BUDGET % OF SALES	VARIANCE $
Net sales	$4,302,500		$4,050,000		$252,500
Labor:					
Direct	565,000	13%	535,000	13%	(30,000)
Indirect	348,000	8%	340,000	8%	(8,000)
Selling	75,000	2%	72,500	2%	(2,500)
General and Administrative	297,000	7%	310,000	8%	13,000
Total company labor	$1,285,000	30%	$1,257,500	31%	$(27,500)

Comparison of actual versus budgeted labor dollars for each major labor category in the income statement (direct, indirect, selling, general, and administrative).

MODEL REPORT #7-8

Key Use of Report:

Compares actual with budgeted labor dollars by major labor category for control purposes.

Suggested Routing:

Top Management.

Frequency of Preparation:

Monthly.

Alternative Reports:

Model Report #7-9.

Exhibit 7-9
LABOR HOURS CONTRIBUTION REPORT

	ACTUAL	BUDGETED	VARIANCE +(−)
Net sales	$7,830,460	$7,995,000	$(164,540)
Manpower hours:			
Direct labor	162,000	159,500	(2,500)
Indirect labor	75,000	76,000	1,000
Selling	15,000	14,500	(500)
General and Administrative	60,000	58,500	(1,500)
Total hours	312,000	308,500	(3,500)
Sales/manpower hour ratio: (a)			
Direct labor	$ 48.34	$ 50.13	$ 1.79
Indirect labor	104.40	105.20	.80
Selling	522.03	551.38	29.35
General and Administrative	130.50	136.67	35.52
Total labor ratio	$ 25.09	$ 25.91	$ .82
% gain (loss) to plan			3.165%

(a) Manpower hours ÷ net sales

Analysis of sales dollars for each labor hour. Labor hours are grouped by major income statement labor accounts (direct, indirect, selling, general, and administrative).

MODEL REPORT #7-9

Key Use of Report:

Measures the productivity of labor hours by major profit and loss labor category.

Suggested Routing:

Top Management.

Frequency of Preparation:

Monthly.

Alternative Reports:

Model Report #7-8.

Exhibit 7-10
DIRECT LABOR VARIANCE REPORT

DEPARTMENT	MONTH					YEAR TO DATE				
	TOTAL LABOR DOLLARS		VARIANCE		ACTUAL VARIANCE OVER(UNDER) BUDGET	TOTAL LABOR DOLLARS		VARIANCE		ACTUAL VARIANCE OVER(UNDER) BUDGET
	ACTUAL	BUDGET	ACTUAL	BUDGET	VARIANCE	ACTUAL	BUDGET	ACTUAL	BUDGET	VARIANCE
Machine shop:										
Milling #1	$ 1,558	$ 1,775	$ (217)	$ (100)	$ (117)	$ 4,720	$ 5,400	$ (680)	$ (400)	$ (230)
Milling #2	1,477	1,785	(308)	(250)	(58)	4,409	5,550	(1,141)	(500)	(641)
Lathe #1	1,862	1,905	(43)	(50)	7	5,920	5,850	70	(100)	170
Lathe #2	2,120	1,000	1,120	250	870	6,420	4,750	1,670	400	1,270
Punch Press	1,566	1,950	(384)	(50)	(334)	5,125	5,500	(375)	(100)	(275)
Band Saw	1,089	875	214	250	(36)	2,620	2,350	270	100	170
	9,672	9,290	382	50	332	29,214	29,400	(186)	(600)	414
Electronics:										
Assembly	5,827	5,542	285	200	85	17,420	18,000	(580)	300	(880)
Wiring	1,630	1,300	330	200	130	5,120	4,700	420	100	320
Testing	1,001	1,516	(515)	(150)	(365)	3,162	3,000	162	(100)	262
Repairing	815	1,120	(305)	--	(305)	2,060	2,250	(190)	--	(190)
	9,273	9,478	(205)	250	(455)	27,762	27,950	(188)	300	(488)
	$18,945	$18,768	$ 177	$ 300	$ (123)	$56,976	$57,350	$ (374)	$ (300)	$ (74)

NOTE: This report combines both rate and performance variances. Many firms set up a separate report for each of the variances.

Total labor dollars variance by task within each department. Monthly and year-to-date totals are included.

MODEL REPORT #7-10

Key Use of Report:

Measures labor variances by department for control purposes.

Suggested Routing:

Plant Manager, Production Manager.

Frequency of Preparation:

Monthly.

Alternative Reports:

Model Report #7-6, #7-7.

Exhibit 7-11

EMPLOYEE EFFICIENCY REPORT

CLOCK #	EMPLOYEE	ACCT#	JOB DESCRIPTION	LABOR HOURS			DIRECT LABOR % EFFICIENCY	INDIRECT AS % OF TOTAL ACTUAL HOURS
				INDIRECT	DIRECT	STANDARD DIRECT		
1610	Art Baker	6021	Quality Control	10				
		6078	Machine Cleanup	9				
		6091	Maintenance	13				
		9821	13.7 MCF Balloon		48	45	94%	
		9826	21.0 MCF Balloon		97	99	102%	18%
1635	James Hildebrand	6091	Maintenance	6				
		9821	13.7 MCF Balloon		107	105	98%	
		9826	21.0 MCF Balloon		48	50	104%	
		9829	Sounding System		6	10	167%	
		9831	Gibson Project		16	15	94%	3%

Direct labor hours as a percent of standard hours and indirect hours as a percent of total hours for each job each employee worked on.

MODEL REPORT #7-11

Key Use of Report:

Measures the efficiency of direct labor hours by employee.

Suggested Routing:

Production Manager.

Frequency of Preparation:

Monthly.

Alternative Reports:

Model Report #7-1.

Exhibit 7-12

DIRECT LABOR BUDGET

	AVERAGE LABOR RATE	TOTAL HOURS	TOTAL LABOR COST	ESTIMATED PRODUCTION UNITS	TOTAL LABOR HOURS PER UNIT	DIRECT LABOR HOURS	DIRECT LABOR COSTS	UNASSIGNED TIME(1) HOURS	%
January				15,000					
Machining	10.50	694	$ 7,287		.046	640	$ 6,720	54	8%
Electronics	8.70	346	3,010		.023	339	2,949	7	2%
Assembly	7.95	519	4,126		.035	502	3,991	17	3%
		1,559	14,423		.104	1,481	13,660	78	5%
February:				12,500					
Machining	10.50	708	7,434		.057	643	6,752	65	9%
Electronics	8.70	358	3,115		.029	332	2,888	26	7%
Assembly	7.95	540	4,293		.043	509	4,047	31	6%
		1,606	14,842		.129	1,484	13,687	122	8%
March				16,110					
Machining	10.50	690	7,245		.043	631	6,626	59	9%
Electronics	8.70	320	2,784		.020	308	2,680	12	4%
Assembly	7.95	495	3,935		.030	463	3,681	32	7%
		1,505	$13,964		.093	1,402	$12,987	103	7%

(1) Some companies call these hours unassigned and some call them indirect labor.

Direct labor hours and dollars budgeted by department by month.

MODEL REPORT #7-12

Key Use of Report:

Itemizes budgeted direct labor hours and dollars by department for planning purposes.

Suggested Routing:

Plant Manager, Production Manager.

Frequency of Preparation:

Quarterly.

Alternative Reports:

Model Report #12-4.

Exhibit 7-13
MANPOWER BY ASSIGNMENT

Project: G.E.B 103

FUNCTION	CURRENT MONTH			PROJECT TO DATE			ESTIMATE AT COMPLETION		
	PLAN	ACTUAL	VARIANCE +(-)	PLAN	ACTUAL	VARIANCE +(-)	PLAN	ESTIMATED ACTUAL	ESTIMATED VARIANCE
Machine Shop	540 hrs	513 hrs	27 hrs	700 hrs	677 hrs	23 hrs	950 hrs	970 hrs	(20)hrs
Electronic Technician	692	670	22	700	708	(8)	925	925	--
Assembly	1,384	1,390	(6)	1,500	1,438	62	1,750	1,750	--
Fabrication	460	435	25	580	575	5	625	640	(15)
Quality Control	495	473	22	525	497	28	675	635	40
Testing	560	582	(22)	570	567	3	600	585	15
TOTAL	4,131 hrs	4,063 hrs	68 hrs	4,575 hrs	4,462 hrs	113 hrs	5,525 hrs	5,505 hrs	20 hrs

Analysis of labor hours on a specific project by function broken down as follows—current month, project-to-date, and estimate at completion.

MODEL REPORT #7-13

Key Use of Report:

Schedules project hours by department for planning purposes.

Suggested Routing:

Project Manager, Department Supervisors.

Frequency of Preparation:

Monthly.

Exhibit 7-14

MANPOWER VS. WORKLOAD REPORT

| MONTH | DIRECT HOURS | | |
	ANTICIPATED AVAILABLE	ESTIMATED REQUIRED	ACTUAL USED
January	7,250	6,750	6,840
February	7,430	6,430	6,550
March	7,600	7,220	6,920
April	7,800	7,550	7,460
May	7,620	7,150	6,580
June	7,500	7,200	7,410
July			
August			
September			
October			
November			
December			

Total direct labor hours by month segregated as follows—anticipated available, estimated required, and actual used.

MODEL REPORT #7-14

Key Use of Report:

Monitors direct labor hours in total.

Suggested Routing:

Plant Manager.

Frequency of Preparation:

Monthly.

MANUFACTURING COST REPORTS—OVERHEAD

Overhead represents all production costs other than direct labor and material. Unlike direct labor and material, overhead does not easily trace into a finished product. Whereas you can examine time cards showing hours charged to a job or requisitions showing material in a job, overhead is applied through periodic accounting entries. The most convenient way to keep control of overhead expenses is to first charge them to the originating department (Exhibits 8-4, 8-5, and 8-7) and then set up a predetermined overhead rate to equitably charge overhead to products produced (Exhibits 8-2 and 8-3). As production volumes change, cost patterns also change. Exhibits 8-6 through 8-8 detail how to budget with this fact in mind.

Exhibit 8-1

MANUFACTURING EXPENSE VARIANCE REPORT

DEPT./WORK STATION	POUNDS PRODUCED (1)	RATE PER POUND VARIABLE (2)	FIXED (3)	PLANNED TOTAL APPLIED VARIABLE (4)	FIXED (5)	ACTUAL EXPENSE VARIABLE (6)	FIXED (7)	VARIANCE +(−) CURRENT MONTH VARIABLE (4-6)	FIXED (5-7)	YEAR TO DATE VARIABLE	FIXED
Interlever bag .008	2,975	.60	.39	$ 1,785	$ 1,160						
Center fold bags .006	10,870	.60	.39	6,522	4,239	$20,100	$ 9,500	$(1,866)	$ 2,352	$(6,952)	$ 1,620
Center fold bags .009	16,545	.60	.39	9,927	6,453						
HS slip wrap	8,960	.75	.39	6,720	3,494	14,970	6,420	(784)	956	2,890	582
LD clear wrap	9,954	.75	.39	7,466	3,882						
Grip perforated .005	13,650	.69	.39	9,419	5,323	9,294	4,430	125	893	1,360	190
	62,954			$41,839	$24,551	$44,364	$20,350	$(2,525)	$ 4,201	$(2,702)	$ 2,392

Analyses of variable and fixed manufacturing expense variances by department/work station.

MODEL REPORT #8-1

Key Use of Report:

Computes variable and fixed overhead manufacturing variances by department for control purposes.

Suggested Routing:

Plant Manager, Production Manager.

Frequency of Preparation:

Monthly.

Exhibit 8-2

COMPUTATION OF PREDETERMINED OVERHEAD RATE REPORT—VERSION I

EXPENSES	TOTAL	PRODUCTION DEPARTMENTS			SUPPORT FUNCTIONS				
		EXTRUSION	BALLOONS	SHEETING	QUALITY CONTROL	WAREHOUSING	UTILITIES	OCCUPANCY	DEPRECIATION
Plant supervision	$110,000	$ 35,000	$ 27,000	$ 20,000	$ 14,000	$ 14,000			
Indirect labor	185,000	79,000	47,500	41,500	9,000	8,000			
Downtime/unassigned	31,000	10,000	11,000	10,000					
Receiving/shipping	22,500					22,500			
Fringe costs	71,000	25,000	17,000	14,000	6,000	9,000			
Repairs to equipment	27,500	8,000	2,000	8,000	1,000	3,500		$ 5,000	
Misc. supplies	15,500	3,800	3,000	3,000	2,000	3,700			
Material samples	18,200	7,100	0	11,100	0	0			
General hauling	19,000	5,000	2,500	4,000		7,500			
Real estate taxes	45,000							45,000	
Insurance-property	18,450							18,450	
Utilities	143,000						$143,000		
Depreciation-buildings	79,000								79,000
Depreciation-equipment	10,000								10,000
Other	25,000	5,000	5,000	5,000		5,000	2,500	2,500	
TOTAL	$820,150	$177,900	$115,000	$116,600	$ 32,000	$ 73,200	$145,500	$ 70,950	$ 89,000
Transfer of:									
Quality control		15,000	10,000	5,000	(32,000)	2,000			
Warehousing		35,000	10,500	29,700		(75,200)			
Utilities		95,000	17,000	33,500			(145,500)		
Occupancy		26,950	34,000	10,000				(70,950)	
Depreciation		56,000	13,000	20,000					(89,000)
Total estimated expenses	$820,150	$405,850	$199,500	$214,800	--	--	--	--	--
Rate calculation:									
Direct labor dollars		$231,900	$ 81,400	$143,200					
Overhead rate		$ 1.75	$ 2.45	$ 1.50					

Detailed analysis showing overhead rate calculations for each production department.

MODEL REPORT #8-2

Key Use of Report:

Calculates departmental burden rates.

Suggested Routing:

Plant Manager, Production Manager.

Frequency of Preparation:

Annually.

Alternative Reports:

Model Report #8-3.

Exhibit 8-3

COMPUTATION OF PREDETERMINED OVERHEAD RATE REPORT—VERSION II

EXPENSE	BASIS OF DISTRIBUTION	SERVICE DEPARTMENTS		PRODUCTION DEPARTMENTS			TOTAL
		QUALITY CONTROL	MATERIAL HANDLING	EXTRUSION	BALLOONS	SHEETING	
Plant supervision	Actual salaries per department	$18,500	$43,000	$75,000	$42,000	$38,000	$216,500
Indirect labor	Actual salaries per department	11,000	35,000	110,000	67,000	14,000	237,000
Fringes	Total payroll per department	6,000	16,000	37,000	22,000	10,000	91,000
Property taxes-building	Square feet per department	1,500	4,800	10,900	21,500	4,200	42,900
Insurance-building	Square feet per department	700	2,300	5,100	10,000	1,900	20,000
Depreciation-building	Square feet per department	1,800	5,900	13,200	26,000	5,100	52,000
Depreciation-equipment	Actual equipment per department	1,250	5,200	28,500	2,900	4,150	42,000
Insurance-equipment	Book value of equipment	450	1,000	4,300	1,150	2,000	8,900
Supplies	Actual per department	3,000	12,700	19,200	14,300	12,500	61,700
Utilities	Engineering survey	6,000	11,400	78,000	8,500	6,100	110,000
Other	Actual per department	2,500	8,200	13,000	5,000	4,000	32,700
TOTAL		$ 52,700	$145,500	$394,200	$220,350	$101,950	$914,700
Transfer of:							
Quality Control		(52,700)		17,000	19,000	16,700	--
Material Handling			(145,500)	78,500	43,200	23,800	--
Total estimated expenses		--	--	$489,700	$282,550	$142,450	$914,700
Rate calculation:							
Direct labor dollars				$222,600	$ 91,150	$101,750	
Overhead rate				$ 2.20	$ 3.10	$ 1.40	

Same as Exhibit 8-2 but more detail is shown for expense category distribution.

MODEL REPORT #8-3

Key Use of Report:

Calculates departmental burden rates.

Suggested Routing:

Plant Manager, Production Manager.

Frequency of Preparation:

Annually.

Alternative Reports:

Model Report #8-2.

Exhibit 8-4

DEPARTMENTAL FACTORY OVERHEAD REPORT

EXPENSE ITEM	WEEK ENDED			MONTH			YEAR TO DATE		
	ACTUAL	PLAN	SAVINGS (OVERAGE)	ACTUAL	PLAN	SAVINGS (OVERAGE)	ACTUAL	PLAN	SAVINGS (OVERAGE)
Indirect labor	$ 1,909	$ 1,900	$ (9)	$ 8,250	$ 8,200	$ (50)	$ 24,750	$ 25,000	$ 250
Payroll taxes	212	200	(12)	875	800	(75)	2,540	2,600	60
Group benefits	430	410	(20)	1,238	1,250	12	3,796	3,850	54
Repairs and maintenance	275	100	(175)	1,240	1,500	260	6,240	4,100	(2,140)
Travel	--	250	250	950	1,000	50	2,210	3,000	790
Supplies	370	275	(95)	1,346	1,250	(96)	4,710	4,250	(460)
Rental of equipment	125	125	--	529	550	21	1,610	1,675	65
Utilities	600	450	(150)	2,420	2,700	280	7,990	7,500	(490)
Other	242	100	(142)	1,620	1,400	(220)	3,210	2,500	(710)
TOTAL	$ 4,163	$ 3,810	$ (353)	$ 18,468	$ 18,650	$ 182	$ 57,056	$ 54,475	$ (2,581)

Actual weekly, monthly, and year-to-date factory expenses compared to budget.

MODEL REPORT #8-4

Key Use of Report:
Lists Actual Manufacturing Expenses compared to budget for measurement and control purposes.

Suggested Routing:
Department Manager.

Frequency of Preparation:
Weekly.

Alternative Reports:
Model Report #13-7.

Exhibit 8-5

STATEMENT OF MANUFACTURING OVERHEAD EXPENSE

EXPENSE ITEM	VARIABLE 100%	VARIABLE 75%(1)	FIXED	TOTAL SPENDING ALLOWANCE	ACTUAL	SPENDING VARIANCE (UNFAVORABLE)
Variable - controllable:						
Salaries and indirect labor:						
Supervisory salaries	$ 98,000	$ 73,500	$ 20,000	$ 93,500	$ 90,200	$ 3,300
Office salaries	110,000	82,500	18,500	101,000	98,500	2,500
Quality control	21,000	15,750	6,500	22,250	22,000	250
TOTAL	229,000	171,750	45,000	216,750	210,700	6,050
Fringe benefits:						
Payroll taxes	23,500	17,625	4,600	22,225	22,100	125
Group insurance	17,800	13,350	3,500	16,850	17,300	(450)
Vacation pay	9,400	7,050	1,850	8,900	8,610	290
Profit sharing	12,900	9,675	2,550	12,225	10,500	1,725
TOTAL	63,600	47,700	12,500	60,200	58,510	1,690
General expenses:						
Repair and maintenance	5,800	4,350	1,000	5,350	8,950	(3,600)
Travel	8,200	6,150	750	6,900	8,420	(1,520)
Truck expense	6,900	5,175	1,000	6,175	7,410	(1,235)
Supplies	8,200	6,150	1,200	7,350	9,580	(2,230)
Rental of equipment	6,750	5,063	3,000	8,063	7,425	638
Insurance - general	5,800	4,350	1,800	6,150	6,000	150
Telephone	10,100	7,575	3,000	10,575	11,250	(675)
Utilities	21,340	16,005	4,500	20,505	21,850	(1,345)
TOTAL	73,090	54,818	16,250	71,068	80,885	(9,817)
Total variable controllable	365,690	274,268	73,750	348,018	350,095	(2,077)
Fixed expenses-noncontrollable:						
Building rent	60,000		60,000	60,000	60,000	--
Real estate taxes	28,000		28,000	28,000	28,500	(500)
Depreciation	37,000		37,000	37,000	37,000	--
Total fixed-noncontrollable	125,000		125,000	125,000	125,500	(500)
Total expenses	$490,690	$274,268	$198,750	$473,018	$475,595	$ (2,577)

(1) Normal plant activity level.

Detailed breakdown of both fixed and variable manufacturing expenses.

MODEL REPORT #8-5

Key Use of Report:

Measures budget variances for each factory expense account for control purposes.

Suggested Routing:

Top Management, Plant Manager.

Frequency of Preparation:

Monthly.

Exhibit 8-6

STEP BUDGET

	ANNUAL BUDGET	MONTHLY BUDGET RANGES			
Planned level of hours:	135,000	12,000 – 15,000	9,000 – 11,999	6,000 – 8,999	3,000 5,999
Expense item					
Supervision	$ 65,000	$ 5,500	$ 5,500	$ 5,500	$ 4,300
Indirect labor	138,000	12,000	10,500	9,500	7,700
Overtime premium	7,500	1,000	750	200	--
Repairs and maintenance	13,500	1,150	1,000	900	900
Utilities	89,000	7,500	6,500	5,500	4,500
Fringe benefits	33,000	2,900	2,600	2,300	1,850
Insurance	20,000	1,700	1,400	1,300	1,100
Real estate taxes	25,000	2,083	2,083	2,083	2,083
Depreciation	36,000	3,000	3,000	3,000	3,000
	$427,000	$ 36,833	$ 33,333	$ 30,283	$ 25,433

Detailed manufacturing expense breakdown for several levels of plant direct labor hours.

MODEL REPORT #8-6

Key Use of Report:

Exhibits budgeted expenses at various levels of monthly production hours for planning purposes.

Suggested Routing:

Plant Manager, Production Manager.

Frequency of Preparation:

Quarterly.

Alternative Reports:

Model Report #8-7, #8-8, #8-9.

Exhibit 8-7

VARIABLE BUDGET

EXPENSE ITEM	ANNUAL BUDGET TOTAL	FIXED	VARIABLE	VARIABLE RATE PER HOUR(1)	FIXED EXPENSES PER MONTH
Supervision	$ 65,000	$ 40,000	$ 25,000	$ .185	$ 3,333
Indirect labor	138,000	39,000	99,000	.733	3,250
Overtime premium	7,500	1,000	6,500	.048	83
Repairs and maintenance	13,500	3,000	10,500	.078	250
Utilities	89,000	7,500	81,500	.604	625
Fringe benefits	33,000	13,000	20,000	.148	1,083
Insurance	20,000	10,000	10,000	.074	833
Real estate taxes	25,000	25,000	--		2,083
Depreciation	36,000	36,000	--		3,000
	$427,000	$174,500	$252,500	$ 1.870	$ 14,540

(1) Based on a 135,000 planned level of hours.

Detailed manufacturing expense breakdown showing fixed costs, variable costs, and the variable rate per hour based on the planned level of labor hours.

MODEL REPORT #8-7

Key Use of Report:

Assists in evaluating expense levels based on varying activity (planned hours) levels.

Suggested Routing:

Plant Manager, Production Manager.

Frequency of Preparation:

Annually.

Alternative Reports:

Model Report #8-6, #8-8, #8-9.

Exhibit 8-8
NORMAL LEVEL BUDGET

EXPENSES	MACHINE SHOP FIXED	VARIABLE RATE PER UNIT	ELECTRONIC ASS'YS FIXED	VARIABLE RATE PER UNIT	ELECTRONIC TESTING FIXED	VARIABLE RATE PER UNIT	QUALITY CONTROL FIXED	VARIABLE RATE PER UNIT	PURCHASING FIXED	VARIABLE DOLLARS
Indirect labor	$23,000	.80	$19,750	.95	$14,750	.52	$16,350	.35	$26,380	--
Fringe benefits	2,450	.09	2,010	.10	1,500	.05	1,680	.04	2,675	--
Supplies	1,960	.29	1,500	.90	1,500	.20	1,000	.15	500	650
Small tools	1,500	.48	1,000	1.10	1,000	.19	1,000	.04	600	--
Utilities	10,000	.79	7,000	.62	7,000	.20	5,000	.18	3,500	3,000
Repairs and maintenance	1,000	.19	1,000	.17	1,000	.19	500	.09	200	500
Depreciation	9,400	--	4,000	--	4,500	--	1,500	--	850	--
Insurance	2,100	.07	1,700	.03	1,700	.02	800	.02	500	650
Property taxes	4,200	--	3,600	--	3,600	--	2,000	--	1,400	--
Other overhead	3,000	.14	3,800	.12	3,700	.09	2,300	.07	2,000	1,000
	$58,610	$2.85	$45,360	$3.99	$40,250	$1.46	$32,130	$ .94	$38,605	$ 5,800

NOTE: Variable rate per unit is calculated by dividing variable expenses for the period by the planned number of plant hours.

Detailed manufacturing expense breakdown by department showing fixed costs and the variable rate per hour based on the planned level of labor hours.

MODEL REPORT #8-8

Key Use of Report:

Establishes a plant's normal activity level which is the basis for establishing sales prices and calculating a product's standard cost.

Suggested Routing:

Plant Manager, Production Manager.

Frequency of Preparation:

Annually.

Alternative Reports:

Model Report #8-6, #8-7, #8-9.

Exhibit 8-9
OVERALL MANUFACTURING EXPENSE BUDGET

EXPENSE ITEM	JANUARY	FEBRUARY	MARCH	1st QUARTER	2nd QUARTER	3rd QUARTER	4th QUARTER	YEAR'S TOTAL
Supervisory salaries	$ 17,340	$ 17,620	$ 17,620	$ 52,580	$ 53,000	$ 53,000	$ 55,800	$214,380
Office salaries	13,350	13,420	13,420	40,190	40,250	40,250	42,900	163,590
Quality control	4,250	4,400	4,400	13,050	13,200	13,200	14,300	53,750
Payroll taxes	3,400	3,450	3,450	10,300	10,500	10,500	11,750	43,050
Group insurance	2,275	2,300	2,300	6,875	7,000	7,000	7,000	27,875
Vacation pay	1,320	890	1,250	3,460	2,500	4,250	4,580	14,790
Profit sharing	1,500	1,500	1,500	4,500	4,500	4,500	4,500	18,000
Repairs & maintenance	780	2,950	3,840	7,570	5,000	4,000	4,000	20,570
Travel	1,250	1,000	1,000	3,250	3,000	3,000	3,000	12,250
Truck expense	375	600	500	1,475	1,300	1,500	1,500	5,775
Supplies	1,320	1,500	1,500	4,320	4,500	4,500	4,500	17,820
Rental of equipment	580	580	675	1,835	1,900	1,900	1,900	7,535
Insurance - general	610	610	610	1,830	1,850	1,850	1,850	7,380
Telephone	1,790	2,200	2,100	6,090	6,500	6,500	6,500	25,590
Utilities	3,285	3,800	4,620	11,705	8,500	13,000	15,000	48,205
Building rent	5,520	5,520	5,520	16,560	16,560	16,560	16,560	66,240
Real estate taxes	3,000	3,000	6,000	12,000	12,000	12,000	12,000	48,000
Depreciation	4,620	4,620	5,300	14,540	15,900	15,900	15,900	62,240
TOTAL	$ 66,565	$ 69,960	$ 75,605	$212,130	$207,960	$213,410	$223,540	$857,040

Detailed manufacturing expense breakdown by quarter.

MODEL REPORT #8-9

Key Use of Report:

Schedules budgeted dollar amounts for each overhead expense item for planning purposes.

Suggested Routing:

Top Management, Plant Manager.

Frequency of Preparation:

Annually.

Alternative Reports:

Model Report #8-6, #8-7, #8-8.

MANUFACTURING COST REPORTS—SUMMARY

The three exhibits in this section are overview reports that Plant Managers and Operational VPs would find valuable. Exhibits 9-1 and 9-3 highlight material, labor, and overhead variances to plan, while Exhibit 9-2 monitors product cost increases and their effect on annual projected profits.

Exhibit 9-1
VOLUME AND SPENDING VARIANCE REPORT

DEPARTMENT	ACTUAL OVERHEAD	BUDGETED OVERHEAD		ACTUAL VARIANCE		BUDGETED VARIANCE		ACTUAL OVER (UNDER) BUDGETED VARIANCE	
		ACTUAL VOLUME	STANDARD VOLUME	(a)SPENDING	(b)VOLUME	SPENDING	VOLUME	SPENDING	VOLUME
Extrusion:									
Materials handling	$ 58,500	$ 59,400	$ 51,000	$ (900)	$ 8,400	$ 400	$ 4,000	$ (1,300)	$ 4,400
Production control	63,200	60,150	57,350	3,050	2,800	1,500	2,000	1,550	800
Extruder operations	123,500	119,420	107,500	4,080	11,920	1,500	6,000	2,580	5,920
Cleanup	18,250	19,750	16,200	(1,500)	3,550	500	1,000	(2,000)	2,550
Purchasing	42,350	44,620	37,500	(2,270)	7,120	500	2,000	(2,770)	5,120
Warehousing	39,870	41,900	38,500	(2,030)	3,400	500	2,000	(2,530)	1,400
Traffic	23,500	23,200	20,000	300	3,200	250	1,000	50	2,200
TOTAL	$369,170	$368,440	$328,050	$ 730	$ 40,390	$ 5,150	$ 18,000	$ (4,420)	$ 22,390

(a) Actual overhead minus actual volume
(b) Actual volume minus standard volume

Budgeted overhead at actual and standard volumes compared with actual overhead by department.

MODEL REPORT #9-1

Key Use of Report:

Identifies the specific reasons for departmental overhead variances and the dollar amount of such variances.

Suggested Routing:

Plant Manager, Production Manager.

Frequency of Preparation:

Monthly.

Exhibit 9-2

FLASH COST CHANGE REPORT

```
┌─────────────────────────────────────────────────────────────────────────┐
│                                                                           │
│  PRODUCT:        Thickness Measurer      CURRENT DATE:            10/1     │
│                                                                           │
│  PRODUCT CODE:        438-C              EFFECTIVE DATE OF CHANGE:  10/15   │
│                                                                           │
│  ANNUAL PRODUCTION QUANTITY:    738      DISTRIBUTION: Pro.Ma, SM, VP/Mkt., CEO, Pur. │
│                                                                           │
│                                                                           │
│  1.   Present cost                                    $  4,395            │
│                                                                           │
│  2.   New cost                           **           $  4,720            │
│                                                                           │
│  3.   $ change                           (2)-(1)      $    325            │
│                                                                           │
│  4.   % change                           (2)÷(1)      $    7.4%           │
│                                                                           │
│  5.   Present sales price                             $  6,800            │
│                                                                           │
│  6.   Mark-up above present cost         (5)-(1)      $  2,405            │
│                                                                           │
│  7.   Mark-up above new cost             (5)-(2)      $  2,080            │
│                                                                           │
│  8.   Annual projected unit sales                          700           │
│                                                                           │
│  9.   Annual projected profit decrease   (8)x(3)      $227,500           │
│                                                                           │
│                                                                           │
│       **  Cost increase due to (explain below):                          │
│                                                                           │
│              Purchased material            X                              │
│              Wage increases            _____                            │
│              Fringe benefits increase  _____                            │
│              Overhead increases        _____                            │
│                                                                           │
│  Specific reasons for increase:  Two purchased parts increased a total of $325.  Chart │
│                                                                           │
│       recorder $210 and master drive $115.                                │
│                                                                           │
│                                                                           │
│                                                                           │
│                                                                           │
│       A summary of the reasons for a product cost change, and the impact on │
│       the product markup and profits.                                     │
│                                                                           │
└─────────────────────────────────────────────────────────────────────────┘
```

MODEL REPORT #9-2

Key Use of Report:

Immediately notifies management of a production cost change.

Suggested Routing:

Top Management, Sales Manager, Purchasing Agent, Production Manager.

Frequency of Preparation:

Whenever a cost increase occurs above a certain minimum dollar level as defined by the company.

Exhibit 9-3
COMPLETED JOBS VARIANCE REPORT—MATERIAL AND LABOR

CUSTOMER	JOB #	MATERIAL			LABOR			JOB VARIANCE	
		ACTUAL	PLANNED	VARIANCE +(-)	ACTUAL	PLANNED	VARIANCE +(-)	$	% (1)
Allison Co.	1653	$ 29,387	$ 28,200	$ (1,187)	$ 18,250	$ 16,350	$ (1,900)	$ (3,087)	(7)%
Bartlet Co.	1951	75,842	73,500	(2,342)	31,510	32,600	1,090	(1,252)	(1)
Homby Co.	983	16,300	17,900	1,600	4,628	5,200	572	2,172	9
Matson Co.	1720	85,148	84,100	(1,048)	38,410	39,000	590	(458)	--
Pearl Co.	3821	29,360	26,950	(2,410)	16,830	15,100	(1,780)	(4,190)	(10)
TOTAL		$236,037	$230,650	$ (5,387)	$109,678	$108,250	$ (1,428)	$ (6,815)	(2)%

(1) Job variance $ -- planned material + labor.

- Material, labor, and completed job variance analysis by customer and job number.

MODEL REPORT #9-3

Key Use of Report:

Identifies the reasons for cost variances on completed jobs.

Suggested Routing:

Top Management, Plant Manager.

Frequency of Preparation:

Monthly.

PURCHASING REPORTS

Materials are often the largest component of cost of sales. By intensely monitoring the purchasing function, it is likely you can significantly cut costs and streamline operations. The reports in this section allow management to do just this. Instead of simply leaving the purchasing function to roll on as long as goods arrive on time, in usable condition and at the agreed upon price, management must be alert to locate profitable changes. These reports help not only in analyzing required purchases (Exhibit 10-5) and commitments (Exhibit 10-2), but also in spotting purchasing variances (Exhibit 10-1), efficiency (Exhibit 10-3), and individual vendor activity (Exhibit 10-4), and backorders (Exhibit 10-6).

Exhibit 10-1
DAILY REPORT OF PURCHASE VARIANCES

PART DESCRIPTION	TOTAL PURCHASE $			REASON FOR VARIANCE	
	STANDARD	ACTUAL	VARIANCE +(-)	PRICE	QUANTITY
Coupling	$ 4,932	$ 5,120	$ (188)	$ (188)	
Cabinet	8,762	8,540	222	222	
Copper leads	185	140	45	32	$23
Servo motor	397	438	(41)	(41)	
1/8" wiring	428	475	(47)	(56)	9
Panel meter	760	582	178	178	
Regulator	385	350	35		35
	$15,849	$15,645	$ 204	$ 147	$67

Analysis of price and quantity purchase variances by inventory part.

MODEL REPORT #10-1

Key Use of Report:

Measures a purchasing department's efficiency.

Suggested Routing:

Vice President Manufacturing, Purchasing Manager.

Frequency of Preparation:

Daily.

Exhibit 10-2

PURCHASE COMMITMENT BALANCES REPORT

	BALANCE PRIOR PERIOD	CURRENT PERIOD POs	INVOICES PAID	BALANCE CURRENT PERIOD
Production Material:				
Product A	$ 53,000	$ 27,000	$(18,500)	$ 61,500
Product B	17,000	8,000	(15,000)	10,000
Product C	111,000	--	(42,300)	68,700
Supplies:				
Factory	22,000	--	(5,000)	17,000
Office	3,800	850	(1,700)	2,950
Other	1,100	--	(800)	300
TOTALS	$207,900	$ 35,850	$(83,300)	$160,450
Planned commitment per budget				143,200
Over (under) plan				$17,250

Reconciliation of purchasing activity for the period.

MODEL REPORT #10-2

Key Use of Report:

Details purchasing activity by product. It is commonly used by the purchasing department to track the level of outstanding POs.

Suggested Routing:

Purchasing Manager.

Frequency of Preparation:

Weekly.

Exhibit 10-3

PURCHASING MANAGEMENT MEASUREMENT REPORT

		CURRENT YEAR	PRIOR YEAR
1.	Dollars of purchases divided by gross sales	37.5%	35%
2.	Purchasing department costs divided by dollars of purchase	2.5%	2.8%
3.	Purchasing department costs divided by number of purchases	$25	$ 29
4.	Purchases divided by purchasing hours (productivity)	$605	$508
5.	Dollars of purchases divided by number of purchases	$1,001	$1,054
6.	% of purchases rejected	4%	2.8%
7.	% of orders overdue	7%	5%
8.	% of rejected invoices	1%	1.1%
9.	Purchases from vendors divided by total purchase:		
	Vendor A	57%	50%
	Vendor B	38%	30%
	Vendor C	5%	20%
		100%	100%
10.	Purchase price variances divided by budget purchases - favorable (unfavorable)	(4.1%)	(2%)
11.	Average lead time for critical components:		
	Part A	120D	120D
	Part B	180D	130D
	Part C	35D	40D
	Part D	50D	55D

11 key operating ratios, percentages, and measurements for management use.

MODEL REPORT #10-3

Key Use of Report:

Analyzes purchasing performance using a series of special ratios and measurements.

Suggested Routing:

Vice President Manufacturing, Purchasing Agent.

Frequency of Preparation:

Monthly.

Exhibit 10-4

PURCHASE ANALYSIS BY VENDOR

#	VENDOR NAME	AMOUNT CURRENT MONTH	RETURNS YEAR TO DATE	NET PURCHASES YEAR TO DATE	NET PURCHASES LAST YEAR TO DATE	INCREASE OR (DECREASE)
229	ABC Plastics	$103,540	$ 6,250	$ 97,290	$127,809	$(30,519)
382	Bartlett Supply	1,684		1,684	3,560	(1,876)
287	DuPont Chemical	38,340	1,580	36,760	31,410	5,350
333	Gulf Chemical	13,210		13,210	10,800	2,410
482	Marno Poly	3,876	520	3,356	5,210	(1,854)
297	Service Enterprise	1,580		1,580	2,650	(1,070)
610	Union Carbide	77,543	1,101	76,442	113,140	(36,698)
502	Watson Electric	8,261		8,261	6,150	2,111
		$248,034	$ 9,451	$238,583	$300,729	$(62,146)

Detailed purchasing information by individual supplier.

MODEL REPORT #10-4

Key Use of Report:

Documents the level of purchases from each supplier for planning and analysis purposes.

Suggested Routing:

Purchasing Manager.

Frequency of Preparation:

Monthly.

Exhibit 10-5

PURCHASED MATERIALS PLAN

	UNITS			REQUIRED PURCHASES		
	REQUIRED PRODUCTION UNITS	ADD ENDING INVENTORY	LESS BEGINNING INVENTORY	TOTAL UNITS	COST PER UNIT	TOTAL COST
Electro unit:						
July	410	110	150	370	$119.00	$ 44,030
Aug	540	145	110	575	119.00	68,425
Sept	610	120	145	585	119.00	69,615
2nd 1/4	1,650	410	120	1,940	119.00	230,860
3rd 1/4	1,900	375	410	1,865	123.00	229,395
4th 1/4	1,500	375	375	1,500	123.00	184,500
Capacitor:						
July	2,080	580	490	2,170	15.50	33,635
Aug	2,100	630	580	2,150	15.50	33,325
Sept	2,475	800	630	2,645	15.90	42,056
2nd 1/4	7,500	700	800	7,400	15.90	117,660
3rd 1/4	7,500	775	700	7,575	15.90	120,443
4th 1/4	6,800	775	775	6,800	16.00	108,800

Required material purchases for planned production by quarter and by product.

MODEL REPORT #10-5

Key Use of Report:

Aids in cash disbursement planning and matches purchasing requirements with production needs.

Suggested Routing:

Production Manager, Purchasing Manager.

Frequency of Preparation:

Quarterly.

Exhibit 10-6
WEEKLY PURCHASE BACKORDER REPORT

	BACKORDERED			EXPECTED DELIVERY			TOTAL UNITS AWAITING DELIVERY	TOTAL LAST REPORT	COMMENTS
	0-45 DAYS	46-90 DAYS	90 DAYS	WITHIN 30 DAYS	31-60 DAYS	60 DAYS			
Web tubing		$ 4,875		$ 4,875			195 ft.	195 ft.	Out of stock
Front panel		2,750			$ 2,750		20	20	Busy time of the year - heavy orders
Volt meter	$ 3,820			3,820			225	--	Parts shortage
Panel meter #1	8,532			5,000	3,532		115	160	Changing style slightly
Panel meter #4			$ 1,520			$ 1,520	10	15	Q.C. problem with two components
Crystals	4,870			4,870			900	1,000	Seems to be a normal delay lately
Leads 001 (special)		1,760		1,760			2,000	2,000	Out of stock - will be in by 7/10
Leads 093 (special)		950		950			770	770	Out of stock - will be in by 7/8
	$17,222	$10,335	$ 1,520	$21,275	$ 6,282	$ 1,520			

Analysis of backordered parts including expected delivery dates and reasons for delay.

MODEL REPORT #10-6

Key Use of Report:

Tracks the status of backordered production material.

Suggested Routing:

Purchasing Manager.

Frequency of Preparation:

Weekly.

PRODUCTION REPORTING

Production Reporting is a key ingredient in keeping smooth-flowing plant operations. It allows management to effectively forecast plant requirements (Exhibits 11-4 through 11-6) and monitor actual production to quickly pinpoint problem areas (Exhibits 11-1 through 11-3). A concise package of production reports, as these are, and a management that regularly scrutinizes them will undoubtedly lead to lower costs, increased cash flow, and ultimately a higher return on owner's investment.

Exhibit 11-1

DAILY PRODUCTION REPORT

EMPLOYEE	PRODUCT	SCHEDULED HOURS	ACTUAL HOURS	DOWNTIME	NET CHARGEABLE HOURS	UNITS MADE	UNITS SELECTED	% REJECTS	LABOR PER GOOD PIECE ACTUAL	LABOR PER GOOD PIECE STANDARD	LABOR PER GOOD PIECE VARIANCE+(−)
Ken Daly	Model 10	8	8		8	1,250	1,120	10%	.429 min	.37 min	(.059)min
John Moe	Model 10	8	8	.5	7.5	1,370	1,233	10%	.365	.37	.005
Bob Haller	Model C	10	10	1	9	3,810	3,499	8%	.172	.18	.008
Steve Wood	Model 40	8	8		8	125	125	--	3.840	3.5	(.34)
Al Beeler	Model 40	6	4		4	90	89	1%	2.697	3.0	.303

Daily production by employee by product including actual hours, downtime, units produced, rejects, and labor per good piece.

MODEL REPORT #11-1

Key Use of Report:
Analyzes activity of direct labor employees for cost control purposes.

Suggested Routing:
Production Supervisors.

Frequency of Preparation:
Daily.

Exhibit 11-2

STOCKOUT REPORT

PRODUCT #	DESCRIPTION	REASON FOR STOCKOUT				ANTICIPATED DATE OF RESTOCK	# OF DAYS OUT OF STOCK	# OF ORDERS BACKLOGGED	VALUE OF ORDERS BACKLOGGED
		COMPONENT PART DELAY	PRODUCTION DELAY	SALES IN EXCESS OF PLAN	OTHER				
316-21	Heater ring		X			6/10	9	3	$ 1,230
215-18	1/2" pulley	X				6/14	7	3	650
223-14	3/4" pulley	X				6/15	5	7	695
582-17	Repair kit-400A			X		6/18	15	21	3,975
550-13	Wheel bands		X			6/12	6	1	420
	TOTALS							35	$ 6,970

Analysis by product of reasons for stockout, anticipated date of restock, and orders backlogged.

MODEL REPORT #11-2

Key Use of Report:
    Inventory control.

Suggested Routing:
    Vice President Manufacturing, Production Manager, Sales Manager.

Frequency of Preparation:
    Weekly.

Exhibit 11-3

PRODUCTION MANAGEMENT REPORT

		CURRENT YEAR	PRIOR YEAR
1.	Direct materials cost divided by sales value of production	36%	35%
2.	Direct labor cost divided by sales value of production	21%	21%
3.	Production overhead divided by sales value of production	15%	14%
4.	Raw material stock divided by average daily purchases	35.2 days	41 days
5.	Finished goods divided by average daily value of production completed	14 days	13 days
6.	Direct labor cost divided by direct labor hours	$8.96	$8.42
7.	Total standard hours produced divided by actual hours worked	110%	114%
8.	Actual output divided by maximum output	74%	67%
9.	Maintenance divided by actual output	7%	6.2%
10.	Rework - rework hours divided by total hours	6%	4%

Ten key operating ratios and indicators for production management use.

MODEL REPORT #11-3

Key Use of Report:

Analyzes production performance using a series of special ratios and measurements.

Suggested Routing:

Vice President Manufacturing, Production Manager.

Frequency of Preparation:

Monthly.

Exhibit 11-4

FORECAST MATERIALS REQUIREMENTS

MONTH	MATERIAL REQUIREMENTS		INVENTORY LEVEL MONTH END
	MONTH	YEAR TO DATE	
January	164,000	164,000	164,000
February	142,000	306,000	85,000
March	145,000	451,000	85,000
April	140,000	591,000	85,000
May	155,000	746,000	90,000
June	170,000	916,000	100,000

Material: Plastic resin

Unit: Pounds

Date: December 10, 19xx

Raw material requirements by month and year-to-date, including expected month-end inventory levels.

MODEL REPORT #11-4

Key Use of Report:

Monitors the quantity of production material needed to attain planned activity levels.

Suggested Routing:

Production Manager, Purchasing Manager.

Frequency of Preparation:

Quarterly.

Exhibit 11-5

PROJECTED MACHINE HOUR REQUIREMENTS

PRODUCTS	BUDGETED UNIT SALES (CASES)				MACHINE HOUR REQUIREMENTS			
	1st QUARTER	2nd QUARTER	3rd QUARTER	4th QUARTER	1st QUARTER	2nd QUARTER	3rd QUARTER	4th QUARTER
Sport glasses	2,650	1,400	3,000	1,500	7,210	3,800	8,150	4,050
Buck bird	1,250	1,250	8,500	3,000	1,050	1,050	7,140	2,520
Torel embossing	3,500	4,000	6,000	5,000	3,000	3,350	5,000	4,150
Torel gunsling	1,750	2,000	7,000	6,000	5,000	5,700	20,000	17,100
Bull snap	1,000	1,000	1,500	1,000	125	125	190	125
TOTAL HOURS REQUIRED					16,385	14,025	40,480	27,945

Budgeted machine hour requirements by quarter needed to meet budgeted unit sales for the period by product type.

MODEL REPORT #11-5

Key Use of Report:

Itemizes the number of production machine hours required to meet the sales budget. This is a necessary planning report for the manufacturing department.

Suggested Routing:

Production Manager.

Frequency of Preparation:

Quarterly.

Exhibit 11-6

PROJECTED PRODUCTION AND INVENTORY PLAN

			IN UNITS		REQUIRED PRODUCTION		
		SALES	BEGINNING INVENTORY	ENDING INVENTORY	TOTAL	PER WEEK	PER DAY
AG - timer							
003825	Jan	2,420	1,700	2,550	3,270	755	151
	Feb	3,750	2,550	4,100	5,300	1,224	245
	Mar	5,240	4,100	3,850	4,990	1,152	231
	Apr	6,400	3,850	5,350	7,900	1,824	365
	May	6,000	5,350	6,270	6,920	1,598	320
	Jun	6,600	6,270	6,100	6,430	1,485	297
	3rd 1/4	17,500	6,430	4,000	15,070	1,159	232
	4th 1/4	12,400	4,000	3,000	11,400	877	175

Required production in total units needed to meet budgeted inventory levels by product, by month, and by quarter.

MODEL REPORT #11-6

Key Use of Report:

Matches production requirements with budgeted sales and inventory levels.

Suggested Routing:

Production Manager, Inventory Supervisor.

Frequency of Preparation:

Quarterly.

Exhibit 11-7

JOB ORDER PROJECT COST REPORT

PROJECT NO. _____   PERIOD ENDING _____

PROJECT DESCRIP. _____   PROJECT MGR. _____

PROJECT CATEGORIES	REG. HOURS	O/T HOURS	PREM. HOURS	TOTAL HOURS TO DATE	ESTIMATED HOURS REMAINING	ESTIMATED TOTAL JOB HOURS	JOB TO DATE DIRECT COSTS	ESTIMATED TOTAL JOB COSTS	BID JOB REVENUE	VARIANCE FAVORABLE (UNFAVORABLE)
Proposal preparation	94			94		94	$ 4,700	$ 4,700	$ 5,000	$ 300
Drafting	48	6		54	5	59	1,350	1,475	1,525	50
Design engineering	156			156	20	176	8,580	9,680	10,000	320
Testing	138	22	38	198	40	238	5,346	6,426	7,000	574
Report preparation	50		5	55	15	70	3,850	4,900	5,000	100
Other	10			10	10	10	250	250	--	(250)
Total labor	496	28	43	567	80	647	24,076	27,431	28,525	1,094
Billable expenses							4,320	4,320	3,800	(520)
TOTAL JOB	496	28	43	567	80	647	$28,396	$31,751	$32,325	$ 574

MODEL REPORT #11-7

Key Use of Report:

Evaluates the progress and profitability of a bid project for analysis and control purposes.

Recap of specific job—total hours to date, estimated hours remaining, job-to-date direct costs, and bid job revenue.

Suggested Routing:

Project Manager.

Frequency of Preparation:

Monthly.

PLANT CONTROL REPORTING

Plant Managers require a series of special reports to track overall plant activity. These include ones that cover current labor and overhead expenditures, shipments, maintenance and quality control performance, idle hours, backlog, plant capacity, and equipment utilization. Each report in this section covers a key component plant managers need to systematically control production flow and output efficiency. They are necessary tools for managers to exercise maximum control over plant costs.

Exhibit 12-1
DAILY PLANT CONTROL REPORT

	DAY					MONTH TO DATE				
	TOTAL OVERHEAD	FIXED OVERHEAD	VARIABLE OVERHEAD	STANDARD VARIABLE OVERHEAD	NET SAVINGS +(-)	TOTAL OVERHEAD	FIXED OVERHEAD	VARIABLE OVERHEAD	STANDARD VARIABLE OVERHEAD	NET SAVINGS +(-)
Indirect labor	$1,388	$ 410	$ 978	$1,000	$ 22	$ 7,120	$2,050	$5,070	$ 5,250	$ 180
Utilities	438	150	288	300	12	2,078	760	1,318	1,410	92
Repairs and maintenance	175	70	105	50	(55)	899	350	549	560	11
Insurance and taxes	97	97	--	--	--	510	510	--	--	--
Supplies	125	20	105	75	(30)	642	100	542	500	(42)
Samples	210	--	210	175	(35)	1,480	--	1,480	1,500	(20)
Depreciation	550	550	--	--	--	2,750	2,750	--	--	--
Other overhead	300	175	125	200	75	1,710	875	835	1,000	165
TOTAL	$3,283	$1,472	$1,811	$1,800	$ (11)	$17,189	$7,395	$9,794	$10,220	$ 386

	Day	Month	Year
Direct labor - actual	$2,980	$15,320	$181,500
Direct labor - standard	2,750	15,105	182,900
Savings - direct labor +(-)	(230)	(215)	1,400
Savings - overhead +(-)	(11)	386	1,710
Total savings	$ (241)	$ 171	$ 3,110
Shipments - budgeted	$20,900	$119,500	$1,955,000
Shipments - actual	18,410	116,000	1,720,000
Over (under) budget	$(2,490)	$ (3,500)	$ (235,000)
Returns	--	--	$ 18,250

MODEL REPORT #12-1

Key Use of Report:

Reveals plant activity for the day compared to budget. This report is an important planning and analysis tool for plant management.

Suggested Routing:

Plant Manager.

Frequency of Preparation:

Daily.

Daily and month-to-date overhead, direct labor, and shipments compared with budget.

Exhibit 12-2

MAINTENANCE PERFORMANCE REPORT

		CURRENT YEAR	PRIOR YEAR
1.	Maintenance dollar divided by cost of goods produced	1.6%	1.8%
2.	Unassigned time - actual maintenance hours divided by total hours worked	83%	87%
3.	Maintenance dollars divided by net property, plant and equipment	5.3%	4.6%
4.	% of maintenance man-hours on planned projects	79%	84%
5.	% of maintenance man-hours on emergency work	13%	7%

Five key operating ratios and measurements for management review.

MODEL REPORT #12-2

Key Use of Report:

Documents plant maintenance effectiveness.

Suggested Routing:

Plant Manager, Maintenance Supervisor.

Frequency of Preparation:

Quarterly.

Exhibit 12-3

QUALITY CONTROL PERFORMANCE REPORT

		CURRENT YEAR	PRIOR YEAR
1.	Quality Control costs divided by total cost of goods produced	7.5%	7.3%
2.	Scrap rate - scrapped units divided by total units produced	3.7%	4.0%
3.	Vendor orders rejected divided by total of vendor orders received	1.6%	1.2%
4.	Rework rate - number of items reworked divided by number of items produced	6%	6.8%
5.	Quality control costs divided by product warranty costs	27%	22%

Five key operating ratios and measurements for management review.

MODEL REPORT #12-3

Key Use of Report:

Summarizes quality control effectiveness.

Suggested Routing:

Plant Manager, Q.C. Supervisor.

Frequency of Preparation:

Quarterly.

Exhibit 12-4

ESTIMATED BACKLOG IN MAN-WEEKS OF WORK

| DEPARTMENT | UPCOMING MAN-WEEKS OF WORK | | | EMPLOYEES ON PAYROLL | MAN-WEEKS AVAILABLE |
	SCHEDULED	FORECASTED - NOT SCHEDULED	TOTAL		
Machine Shop	17	13	30	3	39
Electronic Assembly	35	10	45	4	52
Special Projects	14	20	34	3	39
Extrusion - Special	26	11	37	3	39
Sheeting - S/O	5	9	14	2	26
Blow Molding - F/R	3	12	15	2	26
Painting	1	4	5	1	13
R & D	13	13	26	2	26
Plant total	114	92	206	20	260

Projected utilization rate	Per the report	79.2%
(upcoming man-weeks ÷ man-weeks available)	Per annual plan	73.0%

Upcoming man-weeks of work compared to man-weeks available by department.

MODEL REPORT #12-4

Key Use of Report:

Measures backlog of work by department for planning purposes.

Suggested Routing:

Plant Manager, Production Manager.

Frequency of Preparation:

Bimonthly.

Alternative Reports:

Model Report #7-12.

Exhibit 12-5

REPORT OF UNFILLED SALES ORDERS

CUSTOMER	# OF DAYS ON BACKORDER	EXPECTED PRODUCTION COMPLETION DATE	VALUE OF ORDER	REASON FOR BACKORDER
G & X Poly	22	7/13	$3,875	Out of 032 Resin - coming on 7/12
Poly Port	20	7/13	15,760	Out of 032 Resin - coming on 7/12
Effram Industries	18	7/13	1,895	Waiting for special customer's package
Tassil Sack	15	7/15	975	Customer amending order - will consolidate shipment
Wisconsin Packaging	5	7/15	1,585	Resin problem - S/B run by the weekend
BCK Industries	3	7/15	3,760	Scheduling problem on line #2; will be run on 7/12
E. J. Nord	3	7/17	5,820	Scheduling problem on line #2; will be run on 7/12
City of Pittsville	2	7/20	9,950	Line #4 down for repair - order to be filled on 7/13

Analysis of unfilled sales orders showing number of days on backorder, expected production completion date, dollar value of order, and reasons for backorder.

MODEL REPORT #12-5

Key Use of Report:

Documents all customer backorders and the specific reasons for them. This is a vital report for not only plant management but also sales so they can head off potential customer problems.

Suggested Routing:

Sales Manager, Plant Manager, Production Manager.

Frequency of Preparation:

Weekly.

Exhibit 12-6

MASTER CAPACITY REPORT

	ORDERS (IN LBS.)			AVAILABLE CAPACITY	% OF CAPACITY
	DOMESTIC	EXPORT	TOTAL		
Week 1	48,220	16,295	64,515	83,500	77%
Week 2	63,807	10,820	74,627	83,500	89
Week 3	58,600	27,342	85,942	90,000	96
Week 4	49,950	28,950	78,900	90,000	88
Week 5	68,320	8,975	77,295	90,000	86
Week 6	64,270	16,850	81,120	83,500	97
Week 7	58,190	13,248	71,438	83,500	86
Week 8	62,195	14,890	77,085	83,500	92
(cont.)					

Running weekly total of orders in units compared to available plant capacity.

MODEL REPORT #12-6

Key Use of Report:

Tracks overall plant utilization on a weekly basis for planning and analysis purposes.

Suggested Routing:

Top Management, Plant Manager.

Frequency of Preparation:

Weekly.

Exhibit 12-7
EQUIPMENT USAGE REPORT

MONTH	TOTAL HOURS AVAILABLE	AVOIDABLE DELAYS	UNAVOIDABLE DELAYS	REPAIRS	SERVICING	UNASSIGNED	IN USE	% IN USE TO TOTAL HRS.
January	2,350	20	10	9	6	135	2,170	92%
February	2,475	11	5	6	14	97	2,342	95%
March	2,590	17	13	9	4	227	2,320	90%
April	2,550	22	11	4	22	197	2,294	90%
May	2,500	5	12	14	16	385	2,068	83%
June	2,575	9	13	8	12	291	2,242	87%
July								
August								
September								
October								
November								
December								

Running monthly analysis of total equipment hours available, in use hours, and reasons for downtime.

MODEL REPORT #12-7

Key Use of Report:
Evaluates the reasons for machine downtown for control purposes.

Suggested Routing:
Plant Manager, Production Manager.

Frequency of Preparation:
Monthly.

Alternative Reports:
Model Report #12-8.

Exhibit 12-8

SUMMARY OF IDLE MACHINE HOURS

MACHINE	TOTAL AVAILABLE HOURS	ACTUAL OPERATING HOURS	LOST HOURS	UTILIZATION %	REASON FOR LOST HOURS			
					LACK OF ORDERS	LACK OF MATERIAL	OPERATING DOWNTIME	OTHER
#1 Mill	2,000	1,790	210	90%	177	--	25	8
#2 Lathe	2,000	1,070	930	54	890	28	5	7
#2 Converter	4,050	3,725	325	92	225	49	37	14
#2 Winder	4,050	3,690	360	91	273	60	21	6
#3 Winder	3,800	3,240	560	85	491	11	42	16
TOTAL	15,900	13,515	2,385	85	2,056	148	130	51

Analysis by machine showing total available hours, actual operating hours, lost hours, utilization percentages, and reasons for lost hours.

MODEL REPORT #12-8

Key Use of Report:
Evaluates the reasons for machine downtime for control purposes.

Suggested Routing:
Plant Manager, Production Manager.

Frequency of Preparation:
Monthly.

Alternative Reports:
Model Report #12-7.

OPERATIONS REPORTS

Operations reporting provides management with an interpretation of the dynamics and interrelationships of the overall business. There is an endless supply of reports to accomplish this, and this section includes a sampling of the most appropriate ones. Exhibits 13-1 through 13-6, 13-11, and 13-12 are summary operating reports for the Board of Directors, President, and other top management. The remaining reports are more detailed and especially important for operating managers, department heads, and supervisors.

Exhibit 13-1
REPORT TO BOARD OF DIRECTORS

	ACTUAL	$ BUDGETED	ACTUAL OVER(UNDER) BUDGET
Net sales - current month	$ 585,000	$ 640,000	$ (55,000)
- year-to-date	3,200,000	3,490,000	(290,000)
Net income - current month	65,000	80,000	(15,000)
year-to-date	282,000	310,000	(28,000)
Net income as % of sales - current month	11%	13%	(2%)
- year-to-date	9%	9%	--
Cash	$ 110,000	$ 175,000	$ (65,000)
Receivables	460,000	550,000	(90,000)
Inventory	730,000	660,000	70,000
Current liabilities	855,000	810,000	45,000
Working capital	445,000	575,000	(130,000)
Current ratio	1.52	1.71	(.19)
Property additions - YTD	113,000	125,000	(12,000
Long-term debt - additions	85,000	70,000	15,000
pay-offs	39,000	45,000	(6,000)
Return on assets	10%	11%	(1%)
Return on investment	14%	15%	(1%)
Book value per share	$ 4.85	$ 5.00	$ (.15)
Market value per share	13.70	15.00	(1.30)
# of employees	95	91	4

Key income statement and balance sheet totals, ratios, and other financial measurements.

MODEL REPORT #13-1

Key Use of Report:

Summarizes top level, key operating and financial data for boardroom use.

Suggested Routing:

Board of Directors.

Frequency of Preparation:

Each board meeting.

Alternative Reports:

Model Reports #1-1, #1-3, #1-4, #1-5, #13-5.

Exhibit 13-2

PRESIDENT'S OPERATING REPORT

	MONTH ENDED		ACTUAL OVER(UNDER) BUDGET
	ACTUAL	BUDGETED	
Net sales	$6,532,000	$6,123,000	$ 409,000
Prime costs:			
Labor	410,000	396,000	14,000
Materials	2,700,000	2,545,000	155,000
Overhead	1,781,000	1,596,000	185,000
Selling, general and administrative	662,000	640,000	22,000
Operating profits	979,000	946,000	33,000
Non-operating items	162,000	146,000	16,000
N.I.B.T.	$ 817,000	$ 800,000	$ 17,000
Orders booked			
Backlog:			
Division A	$ 395,000	$ 440,000	$ 45,000
Division B	187,000	150,000	37,000
Cash summary:			
Beginning cash	$ 97,000	$ 97,000	--
Collections	587,000	520,000	67,000
Disbursements	(516,000)	(507,000)	(9,000)
Ending cash	$ 168,000	$ 110,000	$ 58,000
Receivables:			
Current	$ 399,000	$ 310,000	$ 89,000
Past due	205,000	235,000	(30,000)
Total	$ 604,000	$ 545,000	$ 59,000
Inventories	$ 795,000	$ 710,000	$ 85,000
Accounts payable	395,000	438,000	(43,000)
Head Count:			
Division A	49	45	4
Division B	67	70	(3)
Corporate	23	21	2
	139	136	3

Key income statement, balance sheet, and cash flow details plus important operating data about backlogs and headcounts.

MODEL REPORT #13-2

Key Use of Report:

Summarizes key operating and financial data for top management.

Suggested Routing:

CEO, Chief Operating Officer, Top Management.

Frequency of Preparation:

Monthly.

Alternative Reports:

Model Reports #1-1, #1-3, #13-5.

Exhibit 13-3

KEY DATA REPORT

		ACTUAL	BUDGET
Total assets		$7,750,000	$7,290,000
Asset turnover		2.17	2.12
Return on net sales		3.9%	3.9%
ROA		8.4%	8.3%
Employees		138	132
Unit sales per employee	$	316	$ 303
$ sales per employee		121M	117M
Order backlog (in weeks' production)		3.5	4.4
Machine utilization:			
Line 1		72%	82%
Line 2		68%	53%
Line 3		63%	58%
Line 4		71%	57%
Cash from operations:			
(net income + depreciation)	$	870,000	$ 790,000
Earnings per share	$	6.63	$ 6.17

Key operating and financial ratios and data for top management review.

MODEL REPORT #13-3

Key Use of Report:

Supplements monthly financial statements. It highlights other key information important in controlling and evaluating operations.

Suggested Routing:

Top Management.

Frequency of Preparation:

Monthly.

Exhibit 13-4

PERFORMANCE MEASUREMENT REPORT

	ACTUAL	BUDGET	VARIANCE+(-)
Net sales	$7,824,000	$7,423,000	$ 401,000
Net income	653,400	601,000	52,400
Total funded debt	1,350,000	1,050,000	(300,000)
Total equity	3,840,000	3,770,000	70,000
Return on assets	12.6%	12.5%	.1%
Return on equity	17.0%	16.0%	1.0%
Debt/equity ratio	35.0%	27.9%	(7.1)%
Marginal debt/equity ratio - 3 yrs	1.1 to 1		
Compound sales growth - 3 yrs	14.6%		
Compound income growth - 3 yrs	8.5%		
Compound asset growth - 3 yrs	10.7%		

(a) $1.10 in debt has been added for each $1.00 in equity for the last three year period.

Key financial data, ratios, and compounded growth rates for top management review.

MODEL REPORT #13-4

Key Use of Report:

Measures how strong a firm's performance was during the period.

Suggested Routing:

Board of Directors, Top Management.

Frequency of Preparation:

Annually.

Alternative Reports:

Model Reports #13-1, #13-2, #13-5.

Exhibit 13-5
KEY INDICATOR RELIABILITY REPORT

BUDGET ITEM	% OF BUDGET ATTAINED	COMMENTS
Sales	108%	New branch took off faster - little chance to forecast this
Cost of sales:		
Direct labor	103%	Higher union settlement than planned
Material	101%	Close
Overhead	105%	Maintenance & supervision were up
Gross profit	101%	Close
Selling expense	97%	Less T&E than planned
General and administrative expense	105%	Legal and other professional fees way up
Interest expense	105%	More short-term debt - has all been paid off
Net income	102%	Close
Cash	150%	Strong collection efforts
Receivables	94%	Close. Also, strong cash collections reduced receivables
Inventories	106%	Close
Funded debt	107% ⎫	Equipment loans to fund new addition in branch
Property additions	111% ⎭	

> Analysis of variances from budget for key income statement and balance sheet items.

MODEL REPORT #13-5

Key Use of Report:

Measures variances to plan using percentages rather than dollars. At a glance management can review key results.

Suggested Routing:

Top Management.

Frequency of Preparation:

Monthly.

Alternative Reports:

Model Reports #13-1, #13-2, #13-4.

Exhibit 13-6

BUDGETED PROFIT REPORT

```
Operating profit:
      Budgeted                                    $  625,385
      Actual                                         698,540
      Variance from budget (unfavorable)             73,155

Reasons for variance:
      1.  Sales volume                               22,350
      2.  Selling prices                             (2,850)
      3.  Product mix                                25,629
      4.  Selling expenses                           (3,950)
      5.  Purchased material prices                   2,430
      6.  Material usage                              4,950
      7.  Material mix                                5,820
      8.  Material yield                              4,232
      9.  Labor dollars                               7,230
     10.  Wage rates                                 (1,110)
     11.  Overhead spending                           5,948
     12.  Administration                              2,476
          Total                                   $   73,155


      1.  Actual sales - budgeted sales x budgeted price
      2.  Actual price - budgeted price x actual quantity
      3.  Actual product mix sales - budgeted product mix sales x budgeted price
      4.  Actual selling expenses - budgeted sales expenses
      5.  Actual price - budgeted price x actual purchased units
      6.  Actual material units used - budgeted material units used x budgeted cost
      7.  Actual material mix used - budgeted material mix used x budgeted cost
      8.  Actual output - standard output x standard mix x standard price
      9.  Actual hours - budgeted hours x budgeted labor rate
     10.  Actual labor rate - budgeted labor rate x actual hours
     11.  Actual overhead spending - budgeted overhead spending
     12.  Actual administrative costs - budgeted administrative costs
```

Detailed reconciliation of variance from budgeted profits.

MODEL REPORT #13-6

Key Use of Report:

Itemizes the specific reasons why actual profits varied from budgeted profits.

Suggested Routing:

Top Management.

Frequency of Preparation:

Monthly.

Alternative Reports:

Model Report #13-10.

Exhibit 13-7
DAILY EXPENSE REPORT

ITEM	DAY			MONTH TO DATE			YEAR TO DATE		
	BUDGET	ACTUAL	VARIANCE +(-)	BUDGET	ACTUAL	VARIANCE +(-)	BUDGET	ACTUAL	VARIANCE +(-)
Supervision	$ 250	$ 250	--	$ 2,250	$ 2,250	--	$ 22,000	$ 21,750	$ 250
Direct hourly	1,700	1,640	$ 60	15,500	15,820	$ (320)	141,000	142,500	(1,500)
Warehouse and delivery	155	155	--	1,395	1,395	--	13,200	13,200	--
Maintenance and repair	85	97	(12)	800	871	(71)	7,300	7,300	--
Overtime	42	68	(26)	325	349	(24)	3,000	3,650	(650)
Total labor	2,232	2,210	22	20,270	20,685	(415)	186,500	188,400	(1,900)
Heat, light, power	55	50	5	495	470	25	5,200	5,450	(250)
Repair parts	110	297	(187)	990	1,185	(195)	7,500	10,385	(2,885)
Vehicle operating expenses	32	53	(21)	288	310	(22)	3,000	2,805	195
Freight	900	831	69	8,400	8,925	(525)	80,000	82,735	(2,735)
Supplies	169	197	(28)	1,550	1,610	(60)	12,500	13,800	(1,300)
Scrap	510	784	(274)	4,700	5,200	(500)	40,000	43,892	(3,892)
Q.C. Samples	130	122	8	1,200	1,350	(150)	11,000	11,610	(610)
Other	210	380	(170)	1,900	1,742	158	17,000	12,817	4,183
	$ 4,348	$ 4,924	$ (576)	$ 39,793	$ 41,477	$ 1,684	$362,700	$371,894	$ 9,194

A daily, month-to-date and year-to-date factory expense analysis comparing actual expenditures against budgeted amounts.

MODEL REPORT #13-7

Key Use of Report:

Lists daily plant expenses compared with budgeted expenses for control purposes.

Suggested Routing:

Plant Manager.

Frequency of Preparation:

Daily.

Alternative Reports:

Model Report #8-4.

Exhibit 13-8

WEEKLY COST REPORT

PRODUCT	MATERIAL GAINS (LOSSES)			LABOR VARIANCES +(-)			SPENDING VARIANCE +(-)			TOTAL VARIANCE +(-)
	USAGE	MIX	YIELD	TOTAL	DOLLARS	RATE	TOTAL	SPENDING ALLOWANCE	ACTUAL	SPENDING VARIANCE
Sheeting	$1,430	$ (250)	$ 100	$1,280	$ (241)	--	$ (241)	$2,850	$3,150	$ (300)	$ 739
Balloon film	(620)	--	145	(475)	(79)	--	(79)	770	705	65	(489)
Packaging wrap	210	397	143	750	70	$ (85)	(15)	590	509	81	816
Trash bags	410	575	(205)	780	55	--	55	640	710	(70)	765
H.D. shrink wrap	958	1,625	385	2,968	(211)	(77)	(288)	2,175	1,980	195	2,875
L.D. shrink wrap	710	1,387	189	2,286	197	40	237	1,950	2,160	(210)	2,313
	$3,098	$3,734	$ 757	$7,589	$ (209)	$ 122	$ (331)	$8,975	$9,214	$ (239)	$7,019

Note: See Exhibit 13-6 for explanation of variance calculations.

Analysis of material, labor, and spending variances by product.

MODEL REPORT #13-8

Key Use of Report:

Summarizes manufacturing variances by product for analysis and control.

Suggested Routing:

Plant Manager, Production Manager.

Frequency of Preparation:

Weekly.

Exhibit 13-9

DEPARTMENTAL COST SUMMARY—ANALYSIS OF VARIANCES

| | ACTUAL DOLLARS | | OVER (UNDER) PLAN | |
	CURRENT MONTH	YTD	CURRENT MONTH	YTD
Controllable costs:				
Corporate office	$ 38,500	$ 192,340	$ 1,250	$ 6,850
Engineering	16,750	103,420	4,101	8,230
Sales	21,353	148,950	1,975	(3,725)
Marketing	12,620	84,830	(1,295)	4,238
Production	49,760	329,820	(3,842)	(6,954)
Total	$ 138,983	$ 859,360	$ 2,189	$ 8,639)
Fixed costs:				
Depreciation	17,400	109,250	550	1,280
Property taxes	5,500	38,250	--	
Other	6,200	49,800	4,375	13,784
Total	29,100	197,300	4,925	15,064
Direct labor - actual	63,720	327,420	3,784	6,854
Material purchases - actual	176,433	1,058,598	(5,982)	2,980
Total costs	$ 408,238	$2,442,678	$ 7,916	$ 33,537

Analysis of departmental cost categories (controllable costs, fixed costs, direct labor and material) comparing actual dollars to plan.

MODEL REPORT #13-9

Key Use of Report:

Summarizes company costs by department and types of expenses. This report evaluates costs by examining where they are incurred within the company.

Suggested Routing:

Top Management.

Frequency of Preparation:

Monthly.

Exhibit 13-10

RECONCILIATION OF OPERATING PROFITS (LOSSES)

Planned profit	$116,000
Actual profit	204,500
Difference - favorable (unfavorable)	$ 88,500
Reconciliation of difference:	
Items causing increase:	
1. Higher sales volume	69,870
2. Higher prices	19,400
3. Reduced material costs	3,459
Total items causing increases	92,759
Items causing decrease:	
1. Higher G&A expenses	2,150
2. More overtime	775
3. More travel & entertainment	1,220
4. Other	114
Total items causing decreases	4,259
Net change in profits - planned vs. actual	$ 88,500

Detailed analysis of difference between planned and actual profits.

MODEL REPORT #13-10

Key Use of Report:

Itemizes the specific reasons why actual profits vary from budgeted profits.

Suggested Routing:

Top Management.

Frequency of Preparation:

Monthly.

Alternative Reports:

Model Report #13-6.

Exhibit 13-11
EARNING POWER REPORT

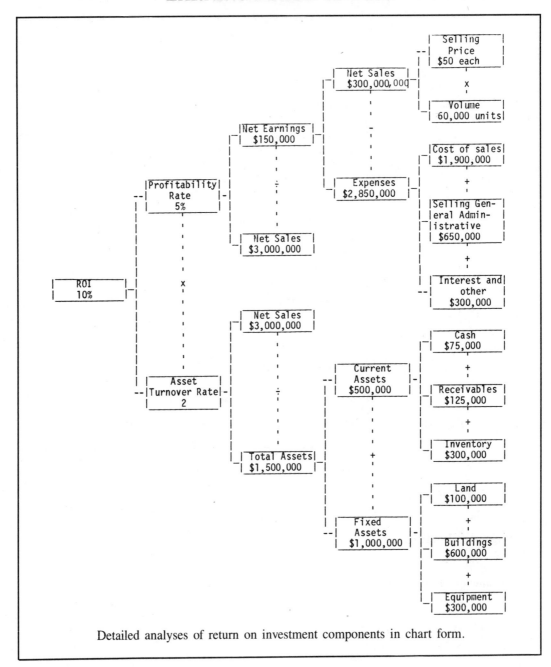

Detailed analyses of return on investment components in chart form.

MODEL REPORT #13-11

Key Use of Report:

Brings together various operating and financial ratios to determine a firm's profitability on assets.

Suggested Routing:

Top Management.

Frequency of Preparation:

Quarterly.

Exhibit 13-12

GROSS PROFIT ANALYSIS

PRODUCT	SALES ACTUAL	SALES PLANNED	COST OF SALES ACTUAL	COST OF SALES PLANNED	GROSS PROFIT ACTUAL $	%	GROSS PROFIT PLANNED $	%	VARIANCE +(-) $	% (1)
Catalog:										
Propellor	$ 62,300	$ 75,000	$ 30,200	$ 37,000	$ 32,100	52%	$ 38,000	51%	$ (5,900)	(16)%
Alert/Locator	48,550	50,000	22,750	24,000	25,800	53	26,000	52	(200)	(1)
Electric motor	73,842	70,000	34,700	34,200	39,142	53	35,800	51	3,342	9
Storage box	16,382	15,000	7,750	7,100	8,632	53	7,900	53	732	9
Subtotal	$201,074	$210,000	$ 95,400	$102,300	$105,674	53%	$107,700	51	$ (2,026)	(2)%
Store sales:										
Spool mono	18,450	18,000	9,920	9,200	8,530	46	8,800	49	(270)	(3)
Fuel rover	23,842	20,000	12,375	10,700	11,467	48	9,300	47	2,167	23
Balancing fan	8,452	15,000	5,010	7,850	3,442	41	7,150	48	(3,708)	(52)
Web belt	13,862	10,000	7,115	5,710	6,747	49	4,290	43	2,457	57
Subtotal	64,606	63,000	34,420	33,460	30,186	47	29,540	47	646	2
Total	$265,680	$273,000	$129,820	$135,760	$135,860	51%	$137,240	50%	$ (1,380)	(1)%

(1) Variance dollars -- planned gross profit dollars

Comparison of actual and planned gross profit by product.

MODEL REPORT #13-12

Key Use of Report:

Indicates what the gross profit contribution of each product was compared to budget for analysis and control purposes.

Suggested Routing:

Sales Manager, Plant Manager.

Frequency of Preparation:

Monthly.

Alternative Reports:

Model Report #4-7.

Exhibit 13-13
BREAKEVEN ANALYSIS

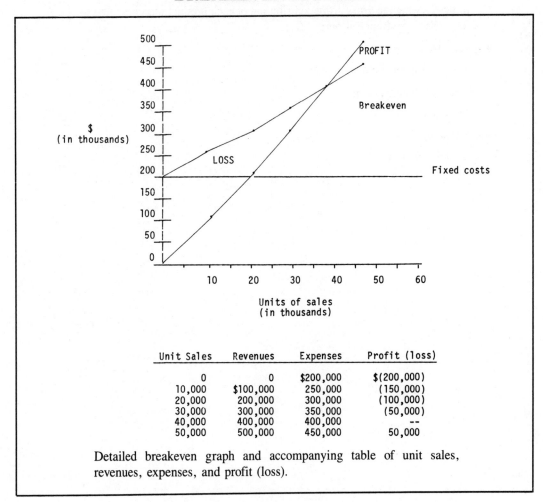

Unit Sales	Revenues	Expenses	Profit (loss)
0	0	$200,000	$(200,000)
10,000	$100,000	250,000	(150,000)
20,000	200,000	300,000	(100,000)
30,000	300,000	350,000	(50,000)
40,000	400,000	400,000	--
50,000	500,000	450,000	50,000

Detailed breakeven graph and accompanying table of unit sales, revenues, expenses, and profit (loss).

MODEL REPORT #13-13

Key Use of Report:

Indicates in graphic form the relationship of sales and production to profit levels.

Suggested Routing:

Top Management.

Frequency of Preparation:

Quarterly or whenever management desires to test a different cost or revenue assumption.

Alternative Reports:

Model Report #3-9, #14-9.

Exhibit 13-14

PRODUCT PROFITABILITY REPORT

	PRODUCTS		
	CRT	LOW BOY	ROTATING
Net Sales Price	$1,850	$795	$645
Variable costs:			
Manufacturing:			
Direct labor	185	62	69
Materials	497	112	104
Overhead	485	130	125
Total	1,167	304	298
Variances	(109)	40	5
Total manufacturing contribution	792	531	342
% to sales	43%	67%	53%
Operating expenses:			
Sales	89	42	39
Marketing	75	18	21
Administrative	195	120	129
Total	359	180	189
Total marginal contribution	433	351	153
% to sales	23%	44%	24%
Fixed costs:	384	139	142
Net income (loss)	49	212	11
% to sales	3%	27%	2%

A profit (loss) profile of each individual product.

MODEL REPORT #13-14

Key Use of Report:

Summarizes the contribution each product makes toward profits.

Suggested Routing:

Top Management, Product Managers.

Frequency of Preparation:

Monthly.

Alternative Reports:

Model Report #2-3, #2-5, #2-6, #5-2.

Exhibit 13-15

COST OF SALES BUDGET

```
Direct material:

    Material inventory, beginning of period    $  438,000
    Purchases                                   1,013,000
        Less purchase returns and allowances      (27,000)
    Material available for use                  1,424,000
        Less material inventory, end of period   (702,000)
        Direct materials consumed                            $  722,000

Direct labor                                                     329,000

Manufacturing expenses:

    Supervision                                    79,000
    Indirect labor                                114,000
    Fringe benefits                                39,000
    Repair and maintenance                         17,000
    Supplies                                       20,000
    Utilities                                     111,000
    Depreciation                                   62,000
    Real estate taxes                              31,000
    Rent                                           67,000
    Travel                                         18,000
    Miscellaneous                                  12,500
        Total manufacturing expenses                         $  570,500

Total manufacturing costs                                      1,621,500
    Add: work in process inventory, beginning of period         118,000
    Less: work in process inventory, end of period             (233,000)
Cost of goods manufactured                                    1,506,500
    Add: finished goods inventory, beginning of period          482,000
    Less: finished goods inventory, end of period              (593,000)
Cost of goods sold                                           $1,395,500
```

Detailed analyses of all components making up budgeted cost of sales.

MODEL REPORT #13-15

Key Use of Report:

Details all of the costs of sales components for planning purposes.

Suggested Routing:

Top Management, Plant Manager.

Frequency of Preparation:

As often as the profit and loss budget is redone.

Exhibit 13-16

REPORT OF SPENDING VARIANCES—CORPORATE, GENERAL, AND ADMINISTRATIVE

| | DEPARTMENT | | | | | | VARIANCES | | % OVER (UNDER) PLANNED |
	ACCOUNTING	FINANCE	TREASURY	EDP	PERSONNEL	OFFICE SERVICES	ACTUAL	PLANNED	VARIANCE
Salaries		1,220		460			1,680	1,450	16%
Payroll taxes	210	378	160	139			887	450	97
Employee benefits	360	295		103			758	300	152
Rent									
Utilities	195	110	100	190	35	50	680	500	36
Telephone	50	35	75	385	50	75	670	500	344
Repairs and maintenance	360			597			957	500	91
Insurance	125	50	50	50	50	50	375	100	275
Group insurance		110		145			255	200	28
Office supplies	(210)	15	35	110	(35)	110	25	100	(75)
Postage	103	35	42	(20)	(10)	37	187	100	87
Dues and subscriptions	50	185	(67)	(60)	(75)		33	100	(67)
Taxes and licenses	35	(75)	(80)			75	(45)	100	(145)
Auto expense	(195)	110	75	(100)			(110)	150	(173)
Contributions	(75)						(75)		--
Legal and audit	3,750	895	1,396	350	100	100	6,591	500	1,213
Leased equipment		295	205	762		172	1,434	200	617
Bank charges	50	175	50				275	50	450
Travel and entertainment	160	220	(50)	60	(65)		325	100	225
Continuing education	(325)	495		395	(100)	(50)	415	100	315
Total variances	4,643	4,548	1,991	3,566	(50)	619	15,317	5,500	178%
Planned variances	1,000	1,000	1,000	1,500	500	500	5,500	--	
% over(under) planned variance	364%	355%	99%	137%	(90)%	24%	178%		

Analysis of all actual expenses for each G&A department compared to plan.

MODEL REPORT #13-16

Key Use of Report:

Lists expense account variances compared with plan for analysis and control purposes.

Suggested Routing:

Administration and Finance Manager.

Frequency of Preparation:

Monthly.

Accounting Report Examples

Exhibit 13-17
TREND VARIANCE REPORT

EXPENSE ITEM	BUDGET ANNUAL	BUDGET MONTHLY	JAN	FEB	MAR	APR	MAY	JUN
Supervision	$136,000	$11,333	$12,000	$12,000	$12,200	$12,000	$12,000	$12,000
Indirect labor	148,000	12,333	11,650	12,100	11,900	12,200	13,100	11,500
Fringes	28,000	2,333	2,400	2,300	2,450	2,400	2,300	2,300
Supplies	22,000	1,833	500	750	1,450	2,600	1,700	1,750
Rent	52,000	4,333	4,333	4,333	4,333	4,333	4,333	4,333
Depreciation	38,000	3,167	3,167	3,167	3,167	3,167	3,167	3,167
Maintenance	19,000	1,583	550	750	1,200	925	975	1,110
Utilities	72,000	6,000	8,250	7,900	6,700	4,800	4,650	5,150
Miscellaneous	15,000	1,250	375	750	825	--	300	710
Total expenses	$530,000	$44,165	$43,225	$44,050	$44,225	$42,425	$42,525	$42,020
Variance for the period-- over (under) budget			(940)	(115)	60	(1,740)	(1,640)	(2,145)
Cumulative variance -- over (under) budget			(940)	(1,055)	(995)	(2,735)	(4,375)	(6,520)

Analysis of expense items by month comparing actual expenditures to budget and concluding with the variance for the period and year-to-date cumulative variance.

MODEL REPORT #13-17

Key Use of Report:
A user can spot spending trends at a glance while reviewing monthly results.

Suggested Routing:
Department Heads whose expenses are being "trended."

Frequency of Preparation:
Monthly.

CASH REPORTING

There is an old saying that a business only moves as fast as its cash flows. Thus, the importance of monitoring this key area cannot be overemphasized. Any cash system should have as its central focus an information flow that allows firms to optimally deploy their cash flow to maintain liquidity, finance operations, build profits, and pay for expansion. This section's reports emphasize monitoring actual cash flow (Exhibits 14-1 through 14-5) and establishing detailed cash flow budgets for planning purposes (Exhibits 14-6 through 14-8). Exhibit 14-9 depicts a cash breakeven graph that is extremely effective for financial presentations at management meetings.

Exhibit 14-1

DAILY CASH REPORT

Date	Beginning Cash	Cash Receipts	Cash Disbursements	Bank Loans + (-)	Investments + (-)	Ending Balance
1	$ 53,000	$ 18,200	$ 39,000	-	-	$ 32,200
2	32,200	58,670	23,410	-	-	67,460
3	67,460	110,950	3,400	-	(100,000)	75,010
4	75,010	19,570	28,200	-	-	66,380
5	66,380	27,470	82,550	-	-	11,300
6	11,300	8,250	87,350	-	100,000	32,200
7	32,200	24,375	162,570	150,000	-	44,005
8	44,005	38,010	52,000	-	-	30,015

Summary of cash activity by day—receipts, disbursements, bank loans, investments, and balances.

MODEL REPORT #14-1

Key Use of Report:

A control report for monitoring and managing cash balances.

Suggested Routing:

Treasurer, Cash Manager.

Frequency of Preparation:

Daily.

Alternative Reports:

Model Report #14-2.

Exhibit 14-2

DAILY CASH MOVEMENT REPORT

	1st National - General Disbur.			National City - Payroll				
	Book Balance	Collected Balance Per Bank	Float	Book Balance	Collected Balance Per Bank	Float	Lockbox #1 New York	Lockbox #2 Denver
June 1	$ 89,000	$107,060	$ 18,060	$ 5,000	$ 48,275	$ 43,275	$ 17,829	$ 5,897
2	77,540	89,820	12,280	5,000	47,390	42,390	22,546	9,542
3	135,000	149,327	14,327	5,000	23,542	18,542	38,297	10,762
4	107,840	119,820	11,980	5,000	17,685	12,685	14,620	29,760
5	97,233	118,438	21,205	5,000	12,975	7,975	18,211	8,762
6	-	-					19,760	5,554
7	-	-					5,231	6,976
8	137,860	81,540	(56,320)	5,000	7,354	2,354	19,821	22,650
9	152,820	178,235	25,415	5,000	5,977	977	48,760	5,982
10	99,820	162,720	62,900	5,000	5,977	977	30,211	1,876
11	137,685	168,940	31,255	5,000	5,432	432	5,962	2,953
12								
13								
14								
15								
(cont.)								

Book cash balances, collected cash balances per bank, and cash float by account by day.

MODEL REPORT #14-2

Key Use of Report:

Shows the amount of cash float in each of the company's bank accounts for cash planning purposes.

Suggested Routing:

Treasurer, Cash Manager.

Frequency of Preparation:

Daily.

Alternative Reports:

Model Report #14-1.

Exhibit 14-3
BANK BALANCE REPORT

Bank	Balance Per Books	Budgeted Balance	Above (Below) Plan	Balance Per Bank
Marquette:				
Regular	$ 85,000	$100,000	$(15,000)	$114,320
Payroll	16,500	16,500	-	21,320
Disbursement	73,250	100,000	(26,750)	44,890
1st National	8,770	10,000	(1,230)	9,950
Northern Trust	11,250	10,000	1,250	13,970
United Security	5,810	5,000	810	8,550
	$200,580	$241,500	$(40,920)	$213,000

Comparison of cash balances per book with balances per budget and per bank by bank account.

MODEL REPORT #14-3

Key Use of Report:

Compares actual cash balances with budgeted cash balances for planning and analysis purposes.

Suggested Routing:

Treasurer, Cash Manager.

Frequency of Preparation:

Monthly.

Exhibit 14-4
CASH FLOW HISTORICAL SUMMARY

	Previous week		Year to Date	
	Budget	Actual	Budget	Actual
Cash receipts	$ 135,000	$ 168,000	$1,100,000	$ 985,400
Cash disbursements:				
Payroll	27,500	29,000	400,000	412,800
Accounts payable	26,300	18,410	176,000	226,000
Property taxes	5,500	5,540	5,500	5,500
Group insurance premium	13,000	13,200	39,000	39,600
Bank note - interest	4,320	4,320	15,000	12,960
Lease payment - building	5,475	5,475	16,425	16,425
Lease payment - equipment	1,232	1,232	3,696	3,696
Rent - warehouse #2	6,897	6,897	20,691	20,691
Convention booth downpayment	-	4,500	-	4,500
Total disbursements	90,224	88,574	676,312	742,172
Net increase (decrease) in cash	$ 44,776	$ 79,426	$ 423,688	$ 243,228
Total bank borrowings	$ 200,000	$ 250,000		
Remaining borrowing availability	$ 500,000	$ 450,000		

Cash receipts and disbursements statement for the week and year to date both compared to budget. Also included are total bank borrowings and remaining borrowing availability.

MODEL REPORT #14-4

Key Use of Report:

Itemizes the ins and outs of cash for planning and control purposes.

Suggested Routing:

Treasurer, Cash Manager.

Frequency of Preparation:

Weekly.

Alternative Reports:

Model Report #14-6.

Exhibit 14-5

CASH FLOW SUMMARY

	1st Quarter		Last Year's
	Actual	Budget	Actual
Net income	$243,000	$275,000	$117,000
Depreciation	65,300	65,000	48,000
Short-term debt	125,000	75,000	350,000
New long-term debt	47,000	30,000	-
Total cash available	480,300	445,000	515,000
Property, plant & equipment purchase	79,000	50,000	39,000
Retirement of short-term debt	-	-	-
Retirement of long-term debt	38,500	40,000	43,650
Receivable requirements - increase/(decrease)	110,000	125,000	175,000
Inventory requirements - increase/(decrease)	187,000	200,000	190,000
Accounts payable - increase/(decrease)	(67,000)	(50,000)	15,000
Accrued expenses - increase/(decrease)	22,000	10,000	21,000
Total cash requirements	369,500	375,000	483,650
Net cash flow	$110,800	$ 70,000	$ 31,350
Total outstanding short-term debt	$150,000	$100,000	$350,000
Total available short-term debt	600,000	600,000	500,000
Net short-term debt still available	$450,000	$500,000	$150,000

Analysis of actual cash available and cash requirements for the quarter compared to budget and last year's actual.

MODEL REPORT #14-5

Key Use of Report:

Analyzes a company's net cash flow for liquidity planning purposes.

Suggested Routing:

Treasurer, Cash Manager.

Frequency of Preparation:

Quarterly.

Alternative Reports:

Model Report #1-7.

Exhibit 14-6
CASH FLOW BUDGET

		January	February	March	April	May	June
Planned Sales		$410,000	$385,000	$580,000	$600,000	$600,000	$625,000
Collections from sales:							
Cash sales	10%	41,000	38,500	58,000	60,000	60,000	62,500
One month ago	75%	375,000	307,500	288,750	435,000	450,000	450,000
Two months ago	10%	45,000	50,000	41,000	38,500	58,000	60,000
Three months ago	4%	18,000	18,000	20,000	16,400	15,400	23,200
Bad debts	1%						
	100%	479,000	414,000	407,750	549,900	583,400	595,700
Miscellaneous cash receipts		10,000	7,500	17,000	10,000	17,500	7,500
Beginning of month cash		74,500	(12,500)	41,600	31,650	36,850	80,250
Total available cash		563,500	409,000	466,350	591,550	637,750	683,450
Cash disbursements:							
Salaries and labor		138,000	145,000	150,000	125,000	140,000	150,000
Material		182,000	110,000	169,000	105,000	150,000	172,000
Operating costs		149,000	140,000	158,000	141,000	143,000	140,000
Selling costs		18,000	23,000	21,000	19,800	20,000	20,000
General and admin. costs		46,000	49,500	48,000	47,000	47,000	43,000
Income taxes		-	28,500	-	-	28,500	-
Capital equipment		28,000	5,200	21,200	-	13,000	4,800
Interest expense		15,000	16,200	17,500	16,900	16,000	14,300
Tot. cash disbursements		576,000	517,400	584,700	454,700	557,500	544,100
Ending cash balance (deficiency) before additional borrowings/(repayments) or (investments)/redemptions		12,500	108,400	118,350	136,850	80,250	139,350
Bank borrowings/(repayments)		-	150,000	150,000	(100,000)	80,250	139,350
(Investments)/redemptions		-	-	-	-	-	(100,000)
Ending cash balance		$(12,500)	$ 41,600	$ 31,650	$ 36,850	$ 80,250	$ 39,350

Detailed analysis of planned cash receipts and cash disbursements by month.

MODEL REPORT #14-6

Key Use of Report:

Itemizes all planned sources and uses of cash for the year. It is *the* crucial analysis for helping firms maintain adequate liquidity.

Suggested Routing:

Top Management, Treasurer, Cash Manager.

Frequency of Preparation:

Yearly or whenever the budgets are updated.

Alternative Reports:

Model Report #14-4.

Exhibit 14-7
PROJECTED PAYMENTS FOR MATERIAL PURCHASES

	Total	June	July	Aug	Payments 1st Quarter	2nd Quarter	3rd Quarter	4th Quarter	Payables Balance Next June 1
Beginning of fiscal year payables balance	$143,000	$ 89,000	$ 54,000		$ 143,000				
Budgeted purchases:									
June	227,000	10,000	175,000	42,000	227,000				
July	185,000		10,000	140,000	150,000	$ 35,000			
Aug	330,000			20,000	20,000	310,000			
1st Quarter	742,000	10,000	185,000	202,000	397,000	345,000			
2nd Quarter	830,000					389,000	$ 441,000		
3rd Quarter	900,000						436,000	$ 464,000	
4th Quarter	625,000							397,000	$ 228,000
Total purchases	3,097,000	10,000	185,000	202,000	397,000	734,000	877,000	861,000	228,000
Total	$3,240,000	$ 99,000	$ 239,000	$ 202,000	$ 540,000	$ 734,000	$ 877,000	$ 861,000	$ 228,000

Projected payments by month and quarter for all budgeted raw material purchases.

MODEL REPORT #14-7

Key Use of Report:

Establishes the plan for when budgeted material purchases will be paid for. It is a vital analysis whose results are used in a firm's overall cash receipts and disbursements budget.

Suggested Routing:

Cash Manager.

Frequency of Preparation:

Yearly or whenever the budgets are updated.

Exhibit 14-8

PROJECTED PAYMENTS FOR OPERATING EXPENSES

	Total	Payments							Payables Balance
		June	July	Aug	1st Quarter	2nd Quarter	3rd Quarter	4th Quarter	Next June 1
Beginning of the year operating expense payable balance	$ 97,000	$ 60,000	$ 37,000		$ 97,000				
Budgeted operating expenses:									
Electronics	342,000	22,000	32,000	$ 32,000	86,000	$ 82,000	$ 82,000	$ 82,000	$ 6,000
Machine shop	227,000	7,800	19,000	19,000	45,800	57,000	57,000	57,000	10,200
Fabrication	487,000	17,500	48,000	48,000	113,500	124,000	120,000	110,000	19,500
Total	1,056,000	47,300	99,000	99,000	245,300	263,000	259,000	249,000	35,700
Less noncash charges									
Depreciation	145,000	12,075	12,075	12,075	36,225	36,260	36,260	36,255	
Property tax accrual	42,000	3,500	3,500	3,500	10,500	10,500	13,000	8,000	
Vacation accrual	97,000	8,083	8,084	8,083	24,250	24,250	23,500	25,000	
	284,000	23,658	23,659	23,658	70,975	71,010	72,760	69,255	
Cash outflow	772,000	23,642	75,341	75,342	174,325	191,990	186,240	179,745	
Selling, gen. & admin.	398,000	19,000	34,000	33,000	86,000	99,000	100,000	98,000	15,000
Less noncash charges									
Depreciation	30,000	2,500	2,500	2,500	7,500	7,500	7,500	7,500	
Amortization	7,200	600	600	600	1,800	1,800	1,800	1,800	
Deferred compensation accrual	7,500	625	625	625	1,875	1,875	1,875	1,875	
Bad debts	5,000	450	450	450	1,350	1,225	1,225	1,200	
Vacation accrual	12,000	1,000	1,000	1,000	3,000	3,000	4,000	2,000	
	61,700	5,175	5,175	5,175	15,525	15,400	16,400	14,375	
Cash outflow	336,300	13,825	28,825	27,825	70,475	83,600	83,600	83,625	
Total cash outflow	$1,205,300	$ 97,467	$ 141,166	$ 103,167	$ 341,800	$ 275,590	$ 269,840	$ 263,370	$ 50,700

Projected payments by month and quarter for all budgeted operated expenses.

MODEL REPORT #14-8

Key Use of Report:

Establishes when budgeted operating expenses will be paid. Its results are used in a firm's overall cash receipts and disbursements budget.

Suggested Routing:

Cash Manager.

Frequency of Preparation:

Yearly or whenever the budgets are updated.

Exhibit 14-9

BREAKEVEN ANALYSIS—CASH

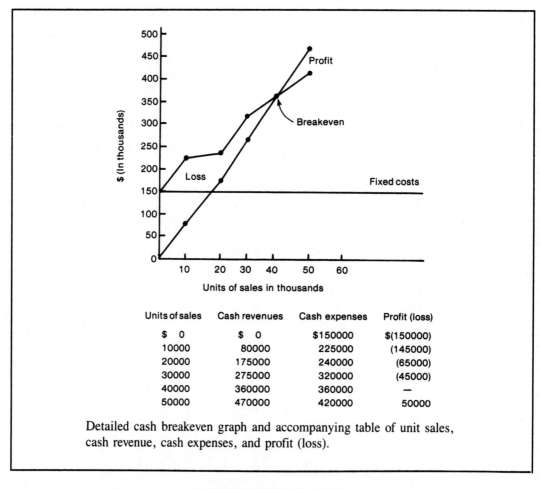

Units of sales	Cash revenues	Cash expenses	Profit (loss)
$ 0	$ 0	$150000	$(150000)
10000	80000	225000	(145000)
20000	175000	240000	(65000)
30000	275000	320000	(45000)
40000	360000	360000	—
50000	470000	420000	50000

Detailed cash breakeven graph and accompanying table of unit sales, cash revenue, cash expenses, and profit (loss).

MODEL REPORT #14-9

Key Use of Report:

Whereas normal breakeven analysis ignores cash, a cash breakeven removes all non-cash charges (depreciation, amortization, deferred expenses, etc.) from total costs and all non-cash sales from revenue. A firm's cash breakeven will in most cases be below its regular breakeven, and a firm can operate at this level.

Suggested Routing:

Top Management.

Frequency of Preparation:

Quarterly or whenever management desires to test different cash cost and revenue assumptions.

Alternative Reports:

Model Report #3-9, #13-13.

ACCOUNTS RECEIVABLE REPORTING

A major decision every firm must make is how liberal or restrictive to make their credit policy. Whatever policy is chosen, though, it is necessary that a reporting system be firmly in place to monitor activity. Exhibits 15-1 through 15-10 include both detailed and summary reports for credit department personnel as well as top management. Key information is highlighted in all reports that give users the analytical tools needed to control this significant part of a firm's balance sheet.

Exhibit 15-1

ANALYSIS OF RECEIVABLE COLLECTION TIMING DURING THE MONTH

July Collections by Day	Prior to May Sales	May Sales	June Sales	July Sales	Total	% of Month's Total
			Collections			
July 1	$ 1,580	$ 7,750	$ 62,500	$ -	$ 71,830	$ 8.9%
2	-	$ 1,400	6,930	-	8,330	1.0
3	-	-	2,420	-	2,420	.3
4	-	-	-	-	-	-
5	3,215	6,385	16,010	820	26,430	3.3
6	-	-	-	-	-	-
7	-	-	-	-	-	-
8	-	63,540	42,376	-	105,916	13.1
9	4,983	28,200	14,250	-	47,433	5.9
10	1,810	-	29,582	8,610	40,002	4.9
11	8,470	16,550	3,825	-	28,845	3.6
12	-	5,820	-	-	5,820	.7
13	-	-	-	-	-	-
14	-	-	-	-	-	-
15	-	13,950	58,327	-	72,277	8.9
16	-	-	8,150	-	8,150	1.0
17	-	16,750	16,642	-	33,392	4.1
18	-	27,888	8,210	-	36,098	4.5
19	-	8,620	-	-	8,620	1.1
20	-	-	-	-	-	-
21	-	-	-	-	-	-
22	-	8,543	69,582	8,003	86,128	10.5
23	-	-	38,762	-	38,762	4.8
24	-	-	85,710	-	85,710	10.6
25	-	9,300	1,007	500	10,807	1.3
26	-	1,420	16,342	-	17,762	2.2
27	-	-	-	-	-	-
28	-	-	28,550	-	28,550	3.5
29	-	-	-	-	-	-
30	-	-	38,200	-	38,200	4.8
31	-	-	8,420	-	8,420	1.0
	$ 20,058	$216,116	$555,795	$ 17,933	$809,902	$ 100.0%
Total Sales		$784,500	$649,200	$620,000		
% Collected		28%	86%	3%		

Analysis by day of cash receipts showing the month the sale originated.

MODEL REPORT #15-1

Key Use of Report:

Assists in planning for cash receipts during the month.

Suggested Routing:

Cash Manager, Credit Manager.

Frequency of Preparation:

Periodically to test timing of receivable collections.

Exhibit 15-2

SALES REPORT—COLLECTION BY MONTH

Month	Total Sales	Month of Collection Following Sale						Net Still Owing
		1	2	3	4	5	6	
January	$ 782,860	$ 283,400	$ 469,510	$ 9,870	$ 16,410	$ 3,670	$	$ -
February	892,500	199,410	629,340	23,810	9,840	18,740	5,500	5,860
March	1,364,800	341,820	841,950	125,360	22,340	18,240	10,675	4,415
April	1,290,540	260,480	793,590	110,510	120,305		5,655	
May	1,180,300	259,810	610,540	243,320	19,540	33,640		13,450
June	1,298,111	204,210	697,540	325,410	50,800	10,610		9,541
Total	$6,809,111	$1,549,130	$4,042,470	$838,280	$239,235	$84,900	$21,830	$33,266
%	100%	23%	59%	12%	4%	1%	-	1%

Note: Although this report shows only six months, many firms extend it for a full year by simply adding six more columns (7-12) and rows (July-December).

Analysis showing sales by month and the month of collection following the sale.

MODEL REPORT #15-2

Key Use of Report:
Analyzes accounts receivable collection trends for cash planning purposes.

Suggested Routing:
Cash Manager, Credit Manager.

Frequency of Preparation:
Semiannually.

Alternative Reports:
Model Report #15-9.

Exhibit 15-3

AVERAGE COLLECTION PERIOD OF RECEIVABLES

	BUDGET	ACTUAL	VARIANCE + (-)
Sale:			
Current Month	$ 797,200	$ 834,525	$ 37,325
Year-To-Date	1,982,700	2,389,950	407,250
Annualized	7,824,350	8,625,050	800,700
Average Daily Sales (Assume 360 Day Year)	21,734	23,958	2,224
Accounts Receivable	897,000	972,450	(75,450)
Average Collection Period in Days	41.3	40.6	

Comparison of actual number of days on the average it takes to collect receivables compared to budget.

MODEL REPORT #15-3

Key Use of Report:

Measures how many days accounts receivable on the average are outstanding. It is a means of evaluating the effectiveness of current credit policies and collection efforts.

Suggested Routing:

Top Management, Credit Manager.

Frequency of Preparation:

Monthly.

Exhibit 15-4
AGED TRIAL BALANCE OF RECEIVABLES

	Invoice #	Date	Current	1 to 30 Days	31-60 Days	61-90 Days	91 Over	Total Due	Date of Last Collection	Amount of Last Collection
Aaron Ltd. Credit Limit: $20,000	11639	11/17			$ 1,950					
	11745	11/18			1,320					
	12389	12/3		$ 750						
	12393	12/3		6,250						
	13750	12/5	$ 1,420							
	14820	12/10	3,789						11/13	$ 4,250
			$ 5,209	$ 7,000	$ 3,270			$15,479		
Barron Co. Credit Limit: $15,500	13600	12/4	1,820							
	14920	12/11	2,103						11/21	2,222
			3,923					3,923		
Cuttler Co. Credit Limit: $20,000	9582	9/6					3,150			
	*10720	10/25	5,814							
	13950	12/7	(1,490)			(820)				
	*13956	12/7	4,324						11/16	2,760
			4,324			(820)	3,150	6,654		
Denig Co. Credit Limit: $25,000	10970	10/27	1,582			2,150				
	13150	12/3	972							
	13620	12/4	2,554						10/11	1,590
						2,150		4,704		

Aged trial balance of receivables by customer by invoice number.

MODEL REPORT #15-4

Key Use of Report:
Used by collection personnel as a collection tool and by credit personnel as an aid in granting credit.

Suggested Routing:
Credit Manager and all credit and collection personnel.

Frequency of Preparation:
Monthly.

Exhibit 15-5

ACCOUNTS RECEIVABLE RUNNING SUMMARY REPORT

Month		Beginning Balance	New Invoicing	Collections	Credits & Adjustments	Ending Balance	% of Beginning Bal. Paid
January	Electronics	$ 397,000	242,000	$(268,000)	$(1,390)	$ 372,390	68%
	Plastics	658,350	385,000	(461,500)		581,850	70%
	Total	1,055,350	627,000	(729,500)	(1,390)	954,240	69%
February	Electronics	372,390	435,320	(288,880)		518,830	78%
	Plastics	581,850	426,305	(362,350)	3,654	649,459	62%
	Total	954,240	861,625	(651,230)	3,654	1,168,289	68%
March	Electronics	518,830	348,250	(401,360)		465,720	77%
	Plastics	649,459	501,250	(497,125)		653,584	77%
	Total	1,168,289	849,500	(898,485)		1,119,304	77%
April	Electronics	465,720	441,370	(355,340)		551,750	76%
	Plastics	653,584	401,580	(462,820)	(6,890)	585,454	71%
	Total	1,119,304	842,950	(818,160)	(6,890)	1,137,204	73%

Analysis of new invoicing, collections, credits/adjustments, and receivable balances by month and by product line.

MODEL REPORT #15-5

Key Use of Report:

Used as a tool by credit management to watch for any change in collection trends.

Suggested Routing:

Credit Manager.

Frequency of Preparation:

Monthly.

Exhibit 15-6
ACCOUNTS RECEIVABLE ANALYSIS

Month Ended	Sales $	Days Sales In Rec.	Total Rec.	$ Ageing Current-30 Days	$ Ageing 31-60 Days	$ Ageing 61+ Days	$ Collections (1) Current-30 Days	$ Collections (1) 31-60 Days	$ Collections (1) 61+ Days
June	$640,000	38	$ 810,000	$616,000	$180,000	$14,000	$486,000	$207,000	$ 5,900
July	592,000	40	780,000	578,000	186,000	16,000	539,000	162,000	8,000
August	520,000	39	680,000	503,000	148,000	29,000	462,000	158,000	12,000
September	630,000	36	765,000	597,000	147,000	21,000	411,000	131,000	18,200
October	795,000	37	975,000	748,000	205,000	22,000	501,000	129,000	13,000
November	897,000	37	1,120,000	833,000	268,000	19,000	610,000	161,000	14,000
December	695,000	44	1,015,000	652,000	327,000	36,000	727,000	230,500	8,900
January	385,000	52	662,000	369,000	264,000	29,000	542,000	289,000	19,900
February	350,000	44	510,000	335,000	151,000	24,000	301,000	227,000	18,000
March	480,000	39	617,000	462,000	148,000	7,000	289,000	137,000	13,750
April	500,000	48	805,000	472,000	303,000	30,000	358,000	133,000	-
May	550,000	37	683,000	527,000	148,000	8,000	400,000	238,000	21,600

(1) Collections of prior month's receivables

Running monthly analysis of sales, days sales in receivables, aged receivables, and collections.

MODEL REPORT #15-6

Key Use of Report:

Summary report of receivables aging and collections which is used to monitor credit department activity.

Suggested Routing:

Top Management, Credit Manager.

Frequency of Preparation:

Monthly.

Exhibit 15-7
CUSTOMER SALES AND PAYMENT RECORD

CUSTOMER	Year To Date Sales			Amount of Uncollected Past Due	Timing of Collections			
	Uncollected	Collected	Total		0-30 Days	31-45 Days	46-60 Days	>60 Days
Arnold Company	$13,400	$ 78,000	$91,400	$3,150	$ 8,275	$ 63,410	$ 6,315	$
Baker Partners	-	97,250	97,250		16,540	61,363	19,347	
Coleman Co.	1,250	34,230	35,480			34,230		
Dedrick Co.	5,820	1,390	7,210	2,975			975	415
Gaslow Ltd.	-	26,240	26,240		5,021	20,376	843	
Hughes Co.	3,960	18,270	22,230	1,920	397	14,280	3,593	
Jarvis Part.	520	8,270	8,790			8,270		
Total	$24,950	$263,650	$288,600	$8,045	$30,233	$201,929	$31,073	$415

Analysis by customer of year-to-date sales and timing of cash collections on those sales.

MODEL REPORT #15-7

Key Use of Report:
Used by credit personnel as an aid in granting credit.

Suggested Routing:
    Credit Manager.

Frequency of Preparation:
    Monthly.

Exhibit 15-8

CREDIT BALANCES IN ACCOUNTS RECEIVABLE

Customer	Age of Credit Balance	Dollars	Explanation
H. J. Charles Co.	5/3 *	$ 3,875	Returned old product per sales rep.
Marino Processors	6/7	1,670	Issued credit to correct inadvertent customer overbilling and subsequent payment.
Advanced Packaging	6/28	8,235	Returned unused product - will be upgrading within the month.
International Flavors	7/9	840	Double Payment.
Rogers Replacement	7/18	375	Correct Two Misbillings.
May Products	7/21 *	1,580	Double Payment.
Jerry's Packaging	8/3	2,760	Correct Misbillings,
Total		$19,335	

*Customer has requested payment.

Analysis of credit balances in accounts receivable by customer including age of credit balance, dollars, and explanation of balance.

MODEL REPORT #15-8

Key Use of Report:

Documents amounts owing customers as a result of credit balances. Used by credit personnel to analyze the cause and impact of these items.

Suggested Routing:

Credit Manager.

Frequency of Preparation:

Quarterly.

Exhibit 15-9

PROJECTED COLLECTION OF ACCOUNTS RECEIVABLE

	Sales	Reserve For Bad Debts	Net Collectible Balance	June	July	August	RECEIPTS 1st Quarter	2nd Quarter	3rd Quarter	4th Quarter	Receivables Balance Next June 1
Beginning of Fiscal Year Accounts Receivable Balance	$ 597,000	$25,000	$ 572,000	$473,000	$ 81,000	$ 18,000	$ 572,000	$	$	$	$
Budgeted Collections:											
June	496,000	1,000	495,000		360,000	113,000	473,000	22,000			
July	425,000	1,000	424,000		9,000	347,000	356,000	59,000	9,000		
August	581,000	1,000	580,000			18,000	18,000	562,000			
1st Quarter	1,502,000	3,000	1,499,000		369,000	478,000	847,000	643,000	9,000		
2nd Quarter	1,834,000	1,000	1,833,000					1,081,000	703,000	49,000	
3rd Quarter	2,100,000	1,000	2,099,000						1,260,000	783,000	56,000
4th Quarter	1,820,000	1,000	1,819,000							1,282,000	537,000
Total Collections	7,256,000	6,000	7,250,000	369,000	478,000	847,000	847,000	1,724,000	1,972,000	2,114,000	$593,000
Total	$7,853,000	$31,000	$7,822,000	$473,000	$450,000	$496,000	$1,419,000	$1,724,000	$1,972,000	$2,114,000	$593,000

Analysis of budgeted cash receipts by month and quarter.

MODEL REPORT #15-9

Key Use of Report:

Analyzes budgeted accounts receivable collections for the year as an aid in preparing the overall cash forecast.

Suggested Routing:

Cash Manager, Credit Manager.

Frequency of Preparation:

Annually or whenever the budgets are updated.

Alternative Reports:

Model Report #15-2.

Exhibit 15-10

DOUBTFUL ACCOUNT ANALYSIS

```
Bad Debt Reserve, Beginning of Year                   $100,000

Write-offs Against Reserve:
    Service Corporation              $ 8,200
    Wood Company                       1,500
    Cambridge Company                 12,100        (21,800)

Recovery of Accounts Previously
Written Off:
    York Brothers                                      3,150

Additions to Reserve                                  18,650
Bad Debt Reserve, End of Year                       $100,000
```

Reconciliation of bad debt reserve activity for a period, including write-offs against reserve, recovery of acccounts previously written-off, and additions to reserve.

MODEL REPORT #15-10

Key Use of Report:

Monitors the bad debt reserve level, making sure it is adequate based on the current level of receivables.

Suggested Routing:

Treasurer, Controller.

Frequency of Preparation:

Monthly.

INVENTORY REPORTING

To maintain proper control of inventories and avoid overstocks, production interruptions, shortages, and obsolescence, firms must establish comprehensive reporting guidelines. This includes not only detailed reports on usage, receipts, balances, and obsolescence such as shown in Exhibits 16-1 through 16-5, but also inventory budget requirements as shown in Exhibits 16-6 through 16-8. Inventories need as much if not more attention than any asset group on a firm's balance sheet. Without key information highlighted the way exhibits in this section are, proper inventory management becomes a strenuous assignment.

Exhibit 16-1

WEEKLY STOCK STATUS

Part #	Description	Unit of Measure	Remaining On-Hand Qty.	On-Order Qty.	Usage Average Monthly	Usage Current Mo. For.	Current Mo. Act.	Current Mo. Issue Freq.	ABC Code	Unit Price
H189	Helmet	Ea	850	–	250	300	350	14	B	$ 38.50
B629	Frame	Ea	210	250	185	200	225	8	B	176.40
B297	Seat	Ea	364	100	330	300	250	6	B	48.75
C840	Chain	Ea	310	150	240	200	170	12	A	58.00
C230	Exhaust System	Ea	587		122	150	130	11	C	95.50
B320	Custom Wheel	Ea	1,382	700	820	650	720	19	A	113.40
D840	Batteries	Ea	3,750		985	1,100	1,350	17	C	39.60

Analysis of inventory by part on a weekly basis showing quantity on hand, quantity on order, usage, and unit prices.

MODEL REPORT #16-1

Key Use of Report:

Analyzes inventory usage so adequate inventory levels can be maintained to meet sales demand.

Suggested Routing:

Inventory Supervisor, Materials Manager, Stockroom Supervisor.

Frequency of Preparation:

Weekly.

Alternative Reports:

Model Report #6-3, #16-2.

Exhibit 16-2
MANAGEMENT INVENTORY CONTROL REPORT

Part #	Description	ABC Code	Unit Price	Unit of Measure	Beginning of Month Balance	Receipts	Usage	On-Hand Qty.	On-Order Qty.	Current Mo. Issue Freq.	Average Monthly Usage	On-Hand Qty. In Dollars
H189	Helmet	B	$ 38.50	Ea	820	150	490	480	600	20	250	$ 18,480
B629	Frame	B	176.40	Ea	240	-	200	40	500	10	185	7,056
B297	Seat	B	48.75	Ea	310	200	375	135	400	10	330	6,581
C840	Chain	A	58.00	Ea	390	-	170	220	150	16	240	12,760
C230	Exhaust System	C	95.50	Ea	700	275	200	775	-	16	122	74,013
B320	Custom Wheel	A	113.40	Ea	1,420	350	925	845	500	24	820	95,823
D840	Batteries	C	39.60	Ea	4,280	-	1,890	2,390	1,500	21	985	94,644
										Total Dollars		$ 309,357

Analysis of inventory by part showing unit receipts and usage, quantity on hand and on order, and quantity on hand in dollars.

MODEL REPORT #16-2

Key Use of Report:

Analyzes inventory activity so proper inventory levels can be maintained to meet sales demand.

Suggested Routing:

Inventory Supervisor, Materials Manager, Stockroom Supervisor.

Frequency of Preparation:

Monthly.

Alternative Reports:

Model Report #6-3, #16-1.

Exhibit 16-3
MATERIAL OBSOLESCENCE REPORT

Part #	Description	Last Usage Date	Unit of Measure	On-Hand Qty.	Unit Price	Total $
3820	Marble Vanity	1/13/81	EA	149	$ 89	$ 13,261
6215	Hot Water Heater	11/26/81	EA	10	233	2,330
3420	Solar Closet	2/03/82	EA	16	384	6,144
2350	Auto Maid	4/08/82	EA	113	16	1,808
3214	Tub Enclosine	6/16/83	EA	77	110	8,470
3951	Standard Steamist	7/14/83	EA	342	12	4,104
4251	Fitprice Pump	7/17/83	EA	176	86	15,136
1997	Comtel Hose Heater	7/31/83	EA	60	169	10,140
	Total Obsolete Material					$ 61,393

> Note: Companies should set this report up by selecting
> the last usage date that they feel denotes a part
> is obsolete. In the above report, the company
> felt any last usage date 7/31/83 or prior meant
> obsolete parts.

Obsolete inventory on hand ranked by last usage dates and including
on-hand quantity, unit price, and total dollars.

MODEL REPORT #16-3

Key Use of Report:

Itemizes obsolete inventory for analysis and planning purposes.

Suggested Routing:

Top Management, Sales Manager, Inventory Supervisor, Stockroom Supervisor.

Frequency of Preparation:

Quarterly.

Exhibit 16-4
INVENTORY ANALYSIS REPORT

	Beginning of Year	End of Previous Month	End of Current Month	Current Month Over (Under) Beginning of Year $	%	Current Month Over (Under) End of Previous Month $	%	Budget - End of Current Month	Current Month Actual Over (Under) Budget $	%
Electronics:										
Raw materials	$ 463,000	$ 397,000	$ 407,000	$ (56,000)	(12%)	$ 10,000	3%	$ 433,000	$(26,000)	(6%)
Work in process	382,580	329,000	348,500	(34,080)	(9)	19,500	6	372,500	(24,000)	(6)
Finished goods	627,380	572,520	529,600	(97,780)	(16)	(42,920)	(8)	500,000	29,600	6
Total	1,472,960	1,298,520	1,285,100	(187,860)	(13)	(13,420)	(1)	1,305,500	(20,400)	(2)
Inventory turnover annualized (a)	7.6									
Extrusion:										
Raw materials	649,050	562,000	503,000	(146,050)	(23)	(59,000)	(11)	462,000	41,000	9
Work in process	203,000	234,000	267,000	64,000	32	33,000	14	125,000	142,000	114
Finished goods	168,300	97,500	114,000	(54,300)	(32)	16,500	17	142,000	(28,000)	(20)
Total	$1,020,350	$ 893,500	$ 884,000	$(136,350)	(13)	$(9,500)	(1)	$ 729,000	$155,000	21
Inventory turnover annualized (a)	8.3									

(a) Annualize cost of sales and divide by end of current month inventory.

Beginning of year, end of previous month, and end of current month inventories by department compared to budget.

MODEL REPORT #16-4

Key Use of Report:

Analyzes inventory levels compared to budget for evaluating the effectiveness of inventory management.

Suggested Routing:

Inventory Supervisor.

Frequency of Preparation:

Monthly.

Exhibit 16-5

REPORT OF AVERAGE INVESTMENT PERIOD IN INVENTORY

Description	Inventory Dollars			Inventory Age in Days		
	Actual	Budget	Variance + (-)	Actual	Budget	Variance + (-)
Jan.						
Raw material	$ 462,430	$ 425,000	$ (37,430)	42 (a)	40	(2)
Work in process	197,820	260,000	62,180	9 (b)	10	1
Finished	397,155	420,000	22,845	27 (c)	30	3
Total	1,057,405	1,105,000	47,595	78	80	2
Feb.						
Raw material	510,897	500,000	(10,897)	43	41	(2)
Work in process	236,140	220,000	16,140	12	10	(2)
Finished	409,800	430,000	20,200	28	31	3
Total	1,156,837	1,150,000	25,443	83	82	(1)
Mar.						
Raw material	497,820	500,000	2,180	43	41	(2)
Work in process	221,520	220,000	(1,520)	10	10	
Finished	438,270	475,000	36,730	31	30	(1)
Total	1,157,610	1,195,000	37,390	84	81	(3)

(a) Raw materials issued to manufacturing divided by raw material ending inventory = raw material turnover; 360 days divided by raw material turnover = number of days' raw material inventory

(b) Work in process finished divided by work in process ending inventory = work in process turnover; 360 days divided by work in process turnover = number of days' work in process inventory

(c) Finished goods sold divided by finished goods inventory = finished goods turnover; 360 days divided by finished goods turnover = number of days' finished inventory

Inventory dollars and inventory age in days compared to budget.

MODEL REPORT #16-5

Key Use of Report:

Measures if inventory levels are in line with budget and if inventory control procedures are working.

Suggested Routing:

Top Management, Inventory Supervisor.

Frequency of Preparation:

Monthly.

Exhibit 16-6

INVENTORY BUDGET WORKSHEET

Item Description: Marine Alert Signal
Item Number   : 3019804

	Inventory Item	Formula For Calculating	Inventory Quantity
1.	Lead time quantity	Lead time in weeks x Weekly usage (units/wk)	1,200
2.	Reorder point quantity	Lead time quantity + Minimum stock quantity	1,400
3.	Order-up-to quantity	Reorder point quantity + Reorder quantity	2,600 (a)
4.	Maximum stock quantity	Order-up-to quantity - Lead time quantity	1,400 (b)
5.	Average expected inventory level	Reorder point quantity - Lead time quantity + 1/2 reorder quantity	800

(a) Order-up-to quantity will often change during the year as a company decides to build or reduce its inventory levels.

(b) In this example maximum stock quantity equals reorder point quantity. This will not be the case when a company decides to build or reduce its inventory levels by adjusting its order-up-to quantity.

Analysis by inventory item of budgeted lead time quantity, reorder point quantity, order-up-to quantity, maximum stock quantity, and average expected inventory level including formulas for calculating.

MODEL REPORT #16-6

Key Use of Report:

Documents how many of each key inventory item must be on hand to meet sales requirements. By analyzing needs using the five different formulas in this report, a firm can best walk the tightrope between having excessive inventories on hand or crippling stockouts.

Suggested Routing:

Inventory Supervisor, Purchasing Manager.

Frequency of Preparation:

Annually or whenever a firm decides to change inventory levels.

Exhibit 16-7

CUMULATIVE INVENTORY REQUIREMENTS

Week #	Product	Unit Projected Sales (1)	Safety Stock Budget Errors (a) (2)	Safety Stock One Week Supply (3)	Total Safety Stock (4)	Cumulative Inventory Requirements
1	A	3,800	250	500	750	
	B	8,510	700	1,450	2,150	
	C	1,325	100	120	220	
	D	1,500	50	110	160	
		15,135	1,100	2,180	3,280	18,415
2	A	2,700	100	140	240	
	B	4,000	250	400	650	
	C	2,500	100	175	275	
	D	1,500	50	110	160	
		10,700	500	825	1,325	27,160 (b)
3	A	3,000	125	200	325	
	B	5,000	300	520	820	
	C	3,000	150	280	430	
	D	1,500	50	110	160	
		12,500	625	1,110	1,735	40,070 (c)

(a) Cushion for budgeting errors.

(b) 15,135 + 10,700 + 1,325 = 27,160.

(c) 15,135 + 10,700 + 12,500 + 1,735 = 40,070.

Analysis of unit projected sales, safety stock, and cumulative inventory requirements by product by week.

MODEL REPORT #16-7

Key Use of Report:

Provides cumulative inventory requirements so management can project unit and safety stock needs. Firms often convert this report to dollars to analyze purchasing and production requirements.

Suggested Routing:

Inventory Supervisor, Purchasing Agent.

Frequency of Preparation:

Monthly.

Exhibit 16-8
SEASONAL INVENTORY BUILDUP NEEDS

Month	(1) Unit Sales Demand	(2) Sales Minus Max. Plant Capacity (a)	(3) Inventory Accumulation (b)
Dec.	11,200	(3,800)	--
Nov.	8,400	(6,600)	--
Oct.	17,800	2,800	2,800
Sept.	23,500	8,500	11,300
Aug.	20,000	5,000	16,300
July	14,000	(1,000)	15,300
June	13,000	(2,000)	13,300
May	12,000	(3,000)	10,300
April	17,500	2,500	12,800
March	7,000	(8,000)	4,800
Feb.	7,000	(8,000)	--
Jan.	7,000	(8,000)	--

(a) 15,000 units per month.
(b) Step i : Locate first month when demand exceeds capacity - October.
    Step ii : Enter inventory demand in inventory accumulation column
              - 2,800 units.
    Step iii: Add to / (Reduce) the total by the amount in column (2)
              for each month until the quantity in column (3) becomes
              negative.

Schedule of needed inventory buildup to meet seasonal sales demand.

MODEL REPORT #16-8

Key Use of Report:

Analyzes seasonal inventory needs for planning and cash flow purposes.

Suggested Routing:

Inventory Supervisor, Purchasing Agent, Cash Manager.

Frequency of Preparation:

Annually or whenever sales are forecast.

CAPITAL EXPENDITURES AND OTHER FINANCING DECISIONS

Capital expenditure decisions are among the most complex and far reaching a firm has to make. Any business intent on controlling the large dollars that are usually associated with fixed assets requires access to the type of reports included in this section. Whether it is a summary of activity (Exhibits 17-1 through 17-3, 17-7, and 17-8), a capital request (Exhibit 17-4), a decision analysis (Exhibits 17-5, 17-6, 17-9, 17-10, 17-13, 17-14, and 17-15), or capital budgets (Exhibits 17-11 and 17-12), the key information must be presented in a clear, succinct manner for management to thoroughly evaluate. All of these exhibits accommodate this need.

Exhibit 17-1

SUMMARY OF FIXED ASSET TRANSACTIONS

Acct. #	Description	Asset Balance 12/31	Addition	(Disposals)	Balance 12/31	Reserve Balance 12/31	Depreciation Expense	(Disposals)	Balance 12/31
1811	Machinery & equipment	$189,000	$ 26,500	$ (2,900)	$212,600	$ 83,000	$ 14,200	$ (2,900)	$94,300
1831	Office furniture	63,000	5,200		68,200	29,000	7,100		36,100
1841	Land	40,500			40,500	--			--
1845	Land improvements	13,700	2,400		16,100	4,800	1,850		6,650
1850	Buildings	495,300			495,300	161,000	32,200		193,200
1851	Automobiles	23,000	11,250	(10,425)	23,825	14,250	4,650	(10,425)	8,475
1860	Equipment deposits	14,000	2,300	(14,000)	2,300	--	--	--	--
		$838,500	$47,650	$(27,325)	$858,825	$292,050	$60,000	$(13,325)	$338,725

Fixed asset activity for the period—additions, disposals, and depreciation expense by account number.

MODEL REPORT #17-1

Key Use of Report:

Summarizes fixed asset activity for the period for management review. Aids in preparing a working capital and cash flow statement.

Suggested Routing:

Top Management, Controller.

Frequency of Preparation:

Quarterly.

Exhibit 17-2

CAPITAL EXPENDITURE MANAGEMENT SUMMARY

	Current Year	198_	198_	198_	198_
Land	$ 40,500	--	--	--	--
Buildings	175,000	385,000	--	--	--
Building improvements	82,000	59,000	27,000	--	--
Machinery & equipment	143,000	58,000	72,000	80,000	80,000
Office equipment	10,500	5,000	5,000	13,500	5,000
Automobiles	--	23,800	--	25,000	14,000
Contingency	20,000	35,000	20,000	20,000	20,000
	$471,000	$565,800	$124,000	$138,500	$119,000
Projected net income	$362,000	$409,000	$475,000	$530,000	$570,000
Add: depreciation	160,000	195,000	210,000	189,000	175,000
Cash flow from operations	522,000	604,000	685,000	719,000	745,000
Capital expenditure as a % of operational cash flow	90%	94%	18%	19%	16%
Planned financing:					
Internal operations	60%	50%	100%	90%	100%
External debt	40	50		10	
External equity					
	100%	100%	100%	100%	100%

Five-year capital budget, ratio of projected capital expenditures to operational cash flow, and planned financing techniques for capital purchases.

MODEL REPORT #17-2

Key Use of Report:

Summarizes capital needs for the next five years for planning purposes. It also details how the additions will be financed which is a crucial concern of management.

Suggested Routing:

Top Management.

Frequency of Preparation:

Annually.

Exhibit 17-3

REPORT OF CAPITAL EXPENDITURES

Property Description	Expenditures Month			Year-to-Date		
	Actual	Budget	Variance + (-)	Actual	Plan	Variance + (-)
Buildings	--	--		--	--	
Building Improvements	--	$11,500	$11,500	$19,560	$27,870	$8,310
Equipment	$23,575	28,350	4,775	129,650	163,582	33,932
Furniture & Fixtures	5,827	2,950	(2,877)	6,730	5,890	(840)
Leasehold Improvements	9,540	13,360	3,820	23,820	22,980	(840)
Tooling	6,750	5,400	(1,350)	8,560	15,700	7,140
Automobiles	10,800	--	(10,800)	10,800	18,260	7,460
Total	$56,492	$61,560	$5,068	$199,120	$254,282	$55,162

Analyses of capital expenditures by category by month and year to date compared to budget.

MODEL REPORT #17-3

Key Use of Report:

Monitors capital spending compared with budget for control purposes.

Suggested Routing:

Top Management.

Frequency of Preparation:

Monthly.

Exhibit 17-4
CAPITAL APPROPRIATION REQUEST

```
Project
Location:                                        Date:
Project Description:
        _____
        _____
        _____
        _____

Reason For Request:
        _____ Unavoidable Replacement        _____ Economically Desirable
        _____ To Meet Volume Increases       _____ Required To Meet Contractual
        _____ To Cut Costs                         Arrangement
        _____ Competitively Obsolete         _____ Regulatory Demand
        _____ Change In Product Style and Design  _____ Nondeferrable(Carry forward Of
        _____ Deversification                      Prior Year's Project)
        _____ Research And Development       _____ Discretionary

Project Justification
    Cost:
        Purchase price            $
        Freight
        Less: Salvage Value On Replaced
            Equipment             _____   _____ Estimated Economic Life
        Internal Material                      _____ Depreciation Method
            - Labor                            _____ Salvage Value
            - Overhead            _____    _____ Payback Period
        Cost To Be Capitalized   $_____    _____ Discount Rate
        Additional Working Capital             _____ ROI -- Discounted Cash Flow
        Other                    _____
                                 $_____
                                 ==========
    Timing And Amount of Cash
        Outlays:
        _____   _____   _____
        Year    Quarter   Amount

Replaced Equipment:
    Description_____ Original Cost        _____
    Location_____ Current Net Book Value_____




Approval and Comments:              Approved   Rejected   Comments
    Requested By:        _____  _____    _____     _____
    Department Manager:  _____  _____    _____     _____
    Division Manager:    _____  _____    _____     _____
    Appropriations Committee:_____  _____    _____     _____
        (Requests > $10,000)
    Board of Directors:  _____  _____    _____     _____
        (Requests > $25,000)
```

Project description, reason for capital request, and project justification.

MODEL REPORT #17-4

Key Use of Report:

Documents all of the reasons and justifications for making a capital expenditure.

Suggested Routing:

See approval section of the Capital Request.

Frequency of Preparation:

For any capital request.

Exhibit 17-5

CAPITAL INVESTMENT SUMMARY FOR DECISION ANALYSIS

```
Cost of new equipment (per invoice)              $138,250

Add:  Freight                                        2,325
      Installation costs                             1,820
      Other
            Total cost                             142,395


Less: Trade-in allowance                          (27,800)
      Salvage recovery net of income taxes   (a)   (2,975)
      Costs avoided on old equipment, net
        of income taxes:
          Repairs                                  (1,750)
          Maintenance                              (2,900)
          Wage reduction                           (4,460)
          Other                                       --
                                                   102,510


Add:  Additional working capital needed
      Cash                                           7,500
      Receivables                                   15,800
      Inventory                                     20,000


Net investment for decision analysis             $145,810


      (a)  Sale of peripheral equipment not needed with new
           equipment.
```

Reconciliation between cost of capital equipment and true investment for decision analysis purposes.

MODEL REPORT #17-5

Key Use of Report:

Documents the cost of an investment for decision analysis. This report starts with the investment accounting cost and reconciles to the cost of the investment for decision-making purposes.

Suggested Routing:

Head of Department planning the capital investment.

Frequency of Preparation:

Each time a significant capital investment is planned.

Exhibit 17-6

CAPITAL EXPENDITURE FINANCIAL EVALUATION

		1st year	2nd year	3rd year	4th year	5th year	5-year average
1	Summary of investment:						
2	Land	$95,000					
3	Buildings	138,000					
4	Machinery & equipment	7,200	6,300				
5	Other: removal of old equip.		975				
6	Total new funds requested	240,200	7,275				
7	Less: salvage value old equip.	(19,800)	(1,105)				
8	Net project cost	220,400	6,170				
9							
10	Funds used:						
11	Net project cost	220,400	226,570	226,570	226,570	226,570	
12	Deduct cum. depreciation	(11,000)	(33,385)	(55,770)	(78,155)	(100,540)	
13	Total capital funds used	209,400	193,185	170,800	148,415	126,030	
14	Cash	7,500	10,000	12,500	15,000	16,000	
15	Receivables	58,000	65,000	72,000	79,000	84,000	
16	Inventory	48,500	55,000	60,000	65,000	69,000	
17	Less: current liabilities	(57,000)	(62,000)	(69,000)	(77,000)	(85,000)	
18	Total working funds	57,000	68,000	75,500	82,000	84,000	
19	Total new funds used	266,400	261,185	246,300	230,415	210,030	242,866
20							
21	Profit & loss:						
22	Net sales						
23	Cost of sales						
24	Gross profit						
25	S.G.&A expenses						
26	Interest						
27	Other						
28	Profit B4 taxes						
29	Taxes						
30	Profit after taxes	4,000	35,000	52,000	70,000	89,000	50,000
31	Cumulative profit	4,000	39,000	91,000	161,000	250,000	
32	Deferred taxes	1,000	6,000	9,000	7,000	8,000	
33	Cumulative deferred tax	1,000	7,000	16,000	23,000	31,000	
34	New funds to repay						
35	(31 + 33 - 19)	$(261,400)	$(215,185)	$(139,300)	$(46,415)	$70,970*	
36							

* Payback year

Average return on new
funds used (30 divided by 19)   20.6%

Analysis of net capital project cost, funds used on the project, and profit and loss resulting from the project.

MODEL REPORT #17-6

Key Use of Report:

Provides information on return of invested funds and the payback period for justifying a capital expenditure.

Suggested Routing:

Top Management, Head of Department planning the capital expenditure.

Frequency of Preparation:

Whenever a significant capital expenditure is planned.

Exhibit 17-7

CAPITAL PROJECT SUMMARY STATUS REPORT

Project	Date Authorized	Amount Authorized	Spent or Committed	Balance	
Rail siding installation	3/13	$55,000	$46,200	$8,800	(1)
Cement slabs	4/15	16,000	16,000	--	
Silos	4/15	17,900	17,900	--	
Conveying system	5/20	66,500	72,000	(5,500)	(2)
Line #1	7/1	142,000	110,000	32,000	(1)
Line #2	7/1	67,800	16,800	51,000	(1)
Line #3	8/1	29,250	5,500	23,750	(1)
Modulators	8/10	5,210	5,300	(90)	
Winder #2	7/1	13,600	3,000	10,600	(1)
Winder #6	9/13	8,250	2,500	5,750	(1)

(1) On budget at this stage
(2) Additional work was authorized

Analysis by project of amounts authorized and amounts spent or committed to date.

MODEL REPORT #17-7

Key Use of Report:

Keeps management informed on the current status of capital projects planned or in progress.

Suggested Routing:

Top Management.

Frequency of Preparation:

Monthly.

Exhibit 17-8

CAPITAL PROJECT STATUS REPORT

Location	Project Description	Completion Date A = Actual E = Expected		Original Budget	Actual Costs To Date	Outstanding POs	Estimated Completion Costs	Total Project Cost	(Over) Under Budget	Comments
Plant	Site work	A	5/14	$17,500	$17,500	--	--	$17,500	--	
	Concrete	A	6/28	38,800	42,350	--	$1,000	43,350	(4,550)	Underestimated
	Rail siding	E	8/15	68,250	15,300	$52,950	--	68,250	--	
	Air-conditioning	E	7/10	125,000	79,700	38,620	7,500	125,820	(820)	Underestimated
	Electrical	E	7/10	27,000	21,100	6,000	3,000	30,100	(3100)	
	Plumbing	E	7/10	13,850	5,800	6,360	500	12,660	1,190	
	Line conversion	E	8/15	86,275	38,700	3,900	50,000	92,600	(6,325)	Problem in removing old towers
	Contingency fund	E	8/30	25,000	6,750	2,000	8,000	16,750	8,250	
				$401,675	$227,200	$109,830	$70,000	$407,030	$(5,355)	

Original project capital budget compared to estimated actual project costs.

MODEL REPORT #17-8

Key Use of Report:

Keeps management informed on the current status of significant individual capital projects.

Suggested Routing:

Top Management, Project Manager.

Frequency of Preparation:

Monthly.

Alternative Reports:

Model Report #17-9.

Exhibit 17-9

CAPITAL EXPENDITURE PROJECT FLASH REPORT

Project:	Refurbish Warehouse Conveying System Line #3	Approved Cost Estimate	Spent/ Committed	Balance
Capital expenditures:				
Automatic rollers		$32,000	$32,000	--
Slides		8,250	4,000	$4,250
Neutral picker		28,675	18,000	10,675
Other expenditures:				
Preparation of site		4,700	4,400	300
Rearrangement of machinery		6,520	3,800	2,720
Expenses		13,600	8,590	5,010
		$93,745	$70,790	$22,955

Funds spent/committed   76%
Project physically complete 69%

Comments: Project proceeding as anticipated as far as dollars go. Completion date will be one week late due to illness of two key foremen.

Analysis of individual capital expenditure project showing approved cost estimate and funds spent/committed to date.

MODEL REPORT #17-9

Key Use of Report:

Keeps management informed on a regular basis on the current status of significant capital projects.

Suggested Routing:

Top Management, Project Manager.

Frequency of Preparation:

Bimonthly.

Alternative Reports:

Model Report #17-8.

Exhibit 17-10

CAPITAL FUNDING CAPACITY REPORT

```
Operating cash flow:
      Net earnings (loss)                              $390,000
      Plus depreciation and amortization               110,000
      Plus/(Minus) net reduction or (investment)
         in noncash working capital            (1)     (89,000)
            Total operating cash flow                  411,000

            (-)
Fixed funding requirements:
      Debt service                                     175,000
      Dividends                                         40,000
            Total fixed funding requirements           215,000

            (+)
Other funding sources and uses:
      Cash balance beginning of period                 $53,000
      Sale of fixed assets                              10,500
      Borrowing capacity                               250,000
      New equity capacity                      (2)     400,000
                                                       713,500

Total capital funding capacity                        $909,500


(1)                     Last period   This period
      Current assets     $1,100,000   $1,280,000
      Current liabilities   785,000      876,000
      Working capital    $  315,000   $  404,000
                                         315,000
                                      $   89,000
```

(2) New equity capacity is at best an estimate for most smaller companies and
    is often left off this particular report.

Analysis of sources of funds available for capital expansion.

MODEL REPORT #17-10

Key Use of Report:

Measures a firm's dollar capacity to add capital projects during the year. This is a vital report for building the capital budget.

Suggested Routing:

Top Management.

Frequency of Preparation:

Annually.

Exhibit 17-11

ANNUAL CAPITAL EXPENDITURE BUDGET

Location	Project Description	Return on Investment	Total Appropriation	Current Year's Budget				Total	Expended in Prior Years
				1st Quarter	2nd Quarter	3rd Quarter	4th Quarter		
Plant	Expansion								
	Thickness gauge	7.9%	$10,700		$10,700			$10,700	
	10" shears	10.8%	1,400		400	$1,000		1,400	
	Replacement								
	Hydraulic press	16.9%	34,400	$16,000		14,400		30,400	$4,000
	Coolant system	10.0%	1,385			1,385		1,385	
	Tool block	7.0%	975				$975	975	
Hq.	Replacement								
	Copy machine	--	5,953			5,953		5,953	
	Other (Contractual)								
	Automobile	--	13,850				13,850	13,850	
			$68,663	$16,000	$11,100	$22,738	$14,825	$64,663	$4,000

Analysis of planned capital expenditures showing total appropriations, current year's budget by quarter, and estimated return on investment.

MODEL REPORT #17-11

Key Use of Report:

Details approved capital expenditures for the year for cash and operational planning purposes.

Suggested Routing:

Top Management, Department Heads.

Frequency of Preparation:

Annually.

Exhibit 17-12

FIVE-YEAR CAPITAL BUDGET

Location	Project Description	Authorized Amount	1985	1986	1987	1988	1989
Plant	Servo-shift lathe	$23,500	$3,500	$20,000			
	Lincoln tig	8,620		8,620			
	52" shear	9,300		3,100	$6,200		
	Drill press	19,550			19,550		
	2500 # hopper	23,650				$23,650	
		84,620	3,500	31,720	25,750	23,650	--
Warehouse	Conveying line	167,500	20,000	102,500	45,000		
	Portable bins (150)	22,500		12,500	10,000		
	Platform skid	8,000			8,000		
	Scales (2)	23,500			12,000		$11,500
	Forklift	19,200				19,200	
		240,700	20,000	115,000	75,000	19,200	11,500
Hdq.	Copy machine	6,000		6,000			
	Automobile	12,000		12,000			
	Office furniture	8,500			4,000	2,500	2,000
	Micro computer (8)	30,000	11,250	7,500	7,500	3,750	
		56,500	11,250	25,500	11,500	6,250	2,000
	Contingency fund	60,000	12,000	12,000	12,000	12,000	12,000
		$441,820	$46,750	$184,220	$124,250	$61,100	$25,500

Authorized capital expenditure by year by location.

MODEL REPORT #17-12

Key Use of Report:

Details capital spending plans for a five-year period for long-range planning purposes.

Suggested Routing:

Top Management, Department Heads.

Frequency of Preparation:

Annually.

Exhibit 17-13

CAPITAL EXPENDITURE SAVINGS ANALYSIS REPORT

	(Annual Basis)		
	Current	Proposed	Planned Savings/(Loss)
Expense Category			
Direct labor	$53,000	$49,000	$4,000
Supervision	17,500	17,500	--
Overtime	4,150	--	4,150
Downtime	2,120	2,000	120
Maintenance-labor	3,800	1,500	2,300
Fringe benefits	12,100	10,500	1,600
Supplies	2,750	2,750	--
Maintenance-non labor	2,900	1,000	1,900
Scrap/rework	26,500	18,300	8,200
Overhead:			
Utilities	41,000	39,000	2,000
Occupancy - space, taxes, insurance	20,000	25,800	(5,800)
Other specify	5,000	4,500	500
Total cash expenses	190,820	171,850	18,970
Depreciation	23,500	29,000	(5,500)
Total expenses	$214,320	$200,850	$13,470

Proposed savings on an annual basis by detailed expense category.

MODEL REPORT #17-13

Key Use of Report:

Itemizes planned savings as a result of a capital expenditure. This is a crucial capital expenditure planning aid.

Suggested Routing:

Top Management, Head of Department planning the capital expenditure.

Frequency of Preparation:

Whenever a significant capital expenditure is planned.

Exhibit 17-14

MAKE OR BUY ANALYSIS

```
Purchasing:
    Machine cost                              $109,250
    Freight in                                   4,825
    Other costs:
        Training                                 1,000
        Warranty contract                        2,550
    Total purchase price            1          117,625

Production:
    Variable costs:
    Machine shop  - material                    33,500
                  - direct labor                18,640
                  - overhead                    27,960
                      Total         2           80,100
    Electronics   - material                     9,720
                  - direct labor                 4,260
                  - overhead                     5,751
                      Total         3           19,731

    Fixed costs:
    Machine shop                                19,600
    Electronics                                  7,250
            Total                   4           26,850
    Total production costs  2 + 3 + 4 = 5      126,681

Excess of production costs over
purchase price                      5-1        $ 9,056
```

Detailed analysis of production costs versus purchase costs for a capital project.

MODEL REPORT #17-14

Key Use of Report:

Evaluates from a cost standpoint whether it is more advantageous to purchase a capital item or make it.

Suggested Routing:

Department head planning the capital expenditure.

Frequency of Preparation:

Each time the make or buy decision comes up.

Exhibit 17-15
LEASE OR PURCHASE DECISION REPORT

| | Leasing | | Purchase/Borrow | | | | | Present | Discounted Cash Flow (c) | |
| | | Net After- | | | | Investment | Net After- | Value | | |
Year	Lease Payments (1)	Tax Cash Flow (a) (2)	Loan Payments (3)	Interest Expense (4)	Depreciation Expense (5)	Tax Credit (6)	Tax cash Flow (b) (7)	Factor (8)	Leasing (9)	Purchase (10)
0	--	--	$5,000			$6,000		--		$(1,000)
1	$14,844	$7,422	16,056	$8,246	$9,000		$7,433	.877	$6,509	6,519
2	14,844	7,422	16,056	6,926	13,200		5,993	.769	5,708	4,609
3	14,844	7,422	16,056	5,331	12,600		7,090	.675	5,010	4,786
4	14,844	7,422	16,056	3,461	12,600		8,025	.592	4,394	4,751
5	14,844	7,422	16,056	1,316	12,600		9,098	.519	3,904	4,722
6	3,000	1,500						.456	684	
	$77,220	$38,610	$85,280	$25,280	$60,000	$6,000	$37,639		$26,209	$24,387

	Lease Proposal	Purchase Proposal
Cost of silos	$60,000	$60,000
Terms of payment	6 years	5 years
Interest rate	14%	16%
Downpayment	--	$5,000
Monthly payments	$1,237	$1,338
Investment credit	Lessor keeps it	10%
Depreciation	--	5 year recovery
Residual purchase price	5%	--
Corporate tax bracket	50%	50%
Cost of capital	14%	14%

(a) Column 1 x .50
(b) Column 3 minus .50 (Column 4 + 5)
(c) The purchase proposal has the lowest discounted cash flow cost and should be chosen over the leasing proposal.

Detailed analysis of leasing costs compared to purchase costs for a capital project.

MODEL REPORT #17-15

Key Use of Report:

Evaluates from a cost standpoint whether it is more advantageous to purchase a capital item or lease it.

Suggested Routing:

Departmental head planning the capital expenditure.

Frequency of Preparation:

Each time the lease or purchase decision comes up.

OTHER ASSETS REPORTING

It is important that management can obtain a detailed analysis of all accounts on the balance sheet. The two most effective ways to do this, which are demonstrated in this section, are through the use of: (1) a detailed listing of what makes up an account at the end of a reporting period (Exhibits 18-1 and 18-2), and (2) a reconciliation showing the prior period ending balance, current period additions and reductions, and current period ending balance. Because insurance coverages are a significant need of all businesses, three supplementary reports (Exhibits 18-3 through 18-5) documenting premiums, losses, and adequacy of coverages are included in this section.

Exhibit 18-1
TEMPORARY INVESTMENT REPORT

Description	Purchase Date	Maturity Date	Interest Rate	Face Value	Purchase Price	Premium = P (Discount = D)	Accrued Interest Earned
Treasury Bill	8/11/83	8/9/84	10.6757% Y	325,000	$293,059.00	$(31,941.00) D	$12,340.65
Treasury Note	8/19/82	2/29/84	15.125%	100,000	100,000.00	(1) 4,312.50 P	5,125.71
Federal Farm Credit	7/18/83	1/03/84	9.6%	100,000	99,968.75	(31.25) D	4,438.18
Federal Farm Credit	8/8/83	2/01/84	9.9%	100,000	99,906.25	(93.75) D	4,058.26
Treasury Bill	8/11/83	2/09/84	10.23539% Y	110,000	104,672.46	(5,327.54) D	4,225.92
Federal Farm Credit	8/18/83	5/01/84	10.10%	150,000	149,953.13	(46.87) D	5,678.91
				$885,000	$847,559.59	$(37,440.41) D	$35,867.63

Net premium/(discount)
4,312.50 P
$(33,127.91) D

Y = Equivalent yield

(1) Amortized premium of $5,593.80

Analysis of temporary investments including purchase date, maturity, interest rate, face value, purchase price, premiums (discounts), and accrued interest earned.

MODEL REPORT #18-1

Key Use of Report:

Summarizes all short-term investments as an aid in managing a firm's temporary excess funds.

Suggested Routing:

Treasurer.

Frequency of Preparation:

Whenever additions or deletions take place in short-term investments.

Exhibit 18-2

PREPAID INSURANCE SUMMARY

Insurance Company	Policy #	Policy Description	Amount of Coverage	Term	Prepaid Balance 12/31/–	Additions	Expense	Prepaid Balance 12/31/–
Hartford	83421	Comprehensive Liability	$2,500,000	6/1 - 5/31	$ 4,900	$ 9,000	$ (8,650)	$ 5,250
Chubb	21002	Property	3,000,000	6/1 - 5/31	8,600	14,500	(14,640)	8,460
Chubb	5290	Automobile	500,000	6/1 - 5/31	1,200	2,500	(2,240)	1,460
Hartford	37214	Umbrella Liability	3,000,000	6/1 - 5/31	1,000	1,200	(1,500)	700
					$15,700	$27,200	$(27,030)	$15,870

Analysis of insurance activity for the period, including additions, expense, and prepaid balance.

MODEL REPORT #18-2

Key Use of Report:

Aids in monitoring insurance activity for the period. It is the standard report outside auditors use when they review prepaid insurance.

Suggested Routing:

Insurance Manager.

Frequency of Preparation:

Annually.

Exhibit 18-3

MONTHLY INSURANCE REPORT

Month	Inventories	Buildings	Mach. & Equip.	Furn. & Fix.	Vehicles	Estimated Replacement Value Adjust.	Total Insurable Value	Amount of Coverage	Percent of Coverage to Value
Jan.	1,250,500	1,680,290	962,540	29,580	38,750	148,000	4,109,660	4,000,000	97%
Feb.	1,103,620	1,680,290	949,610	29,580	32,540	145,000	3,940,640	4,000,000	101
Mar.	970,580	1,730,540	981,340	29,580	32,540	150,000	3,894,580	4,000,000	103
April	1,234,645	1,730,540	984,650	30,620	32,540	150,000	4,162,995	4,250,000	102
May	1,582,390	1,730,540	997,000	30,620	32,540	150,000	4,523,090	4,500,000	99
June									
July									
Aug.									
Sept.									
Oct.									
Nov.									
Dec.									

Running monthly analysis of asset carrying values and replacement values for insurance purposes compared to amount of insurance coverages actually in force.

MODEL REPORT #18-3

Key Use of Report:

Monitors insurance coverage to make sure it equals or exceeds total company insurable values.

Suggested Routing:

Insurance Manager.

Frequency of Preparation:

Monthly.

Alternative Reports:

Model Report #18-4.

Exhibit 18-4

MONTHLY INSURED VALUE REPORT

Description	Location 1	Location 2	Insured Values at Replacement Cost Location 3	Location 4	Total
Inventory	$175,000	$ 84,500	$233,000	$ 417,000	$ 909,500
Supplies	32,000	15,000	13,500	43,700	104,200
Building & Improvements	154,000	-	135,000	610,900	899,900
Machinery & Equipment	125,000	76,000	59,000	507,000	767,000
Leasehold Improvements	-	97,000	-	-	97,000
Furniture & Fixtures	18,000	13,200	19,420	25,310	75,930
Molds, Tools, Dies & Patterns	68,200	-	-	138,950	207,150
Total Insurable Value	572,200	285,700	459,920	1,742,860	3,060,680
Insurance in Force at Month End	600,000	300,000	500,000	1,900,000	3,300,000
Insurance Over (Under) Insurable Value	$ 27,800	$ 14,300	$ 40,080	$ 157,140	$ 239,320

Summary of insured values at replacement cost by location compared to insurance in force at month end.

MODEL REPORT #18-4

Key Use of Report:

Monitors insurance coverage by location to make sure it exceeds insurable values.

Suggested Routing:

Insurance Manager.

Frequency of Preparation:

Monthly.

Alternative Reports:

Model Report #18-3.

Exhibit 18-5

ANNUAL COMPARATIVE PREMIUM AND LOSS SUMMARY

Type of Insurance	Policy Year	Premium	Losses Incurred	# of Loss Occurrences	Loss Ratio
Workers Compensation	79-80	$23,100	$ 700	7	.03
	80-81	28,900	13,250	23	.46
	81-82	45,200	104,000	30	2.30
	82-83	39,600	3,820	11	.10
	83-84	55,300	28,700	5	.52
	84-85	65,500	23,950	18	.36
Package (Auto, General Liability, etc.)	79-80	34,300	13,850	12	.40
	80-81	43,800	15,000	22	.34
	81-82	45,700	21,500	24	.47
	82-83	44,700	12,500	20	.28
	83-84	40,500	17,400	18	.43
	84-85	38,800	13,800	14	.36
Property	79-80	8,200	7,420	3	.90
	80-81	9,700	580	1	.06
	81-82	13,200	6,500	4	.49
	82-83	16,000	1,090	2	.07
	83-84	15,300	8,950	7	.59
	84-85	14,500	17,820	4	1.23

Analysis of premium, losses incurred, number of loss occurrences, and loss ratios for each insurance type.

MODEL REPORT #18-5

Key Use of Report:

Helps spot loss trends by policy type. It is a useful aid for a firm's risk manager to have when evaluating the effectiveness of loss prevention programs.

Suggested Routing:

Insurance Manager.

Frequency of Preparation:

Annually.

Exhibit 18-6

OTHER ASSETS REPORT AND ANALYSIS

Description	Balance Beg. of Year	Additions	Reductions	Balance End of Year
Non-compete agreements	$ 87,000		(A) $ (10,875)	$ 76,125
Acquired customer lists	22,500		(A) (4,500)	18,000
Prepaid royalty	-	$ 3,422		3,422
Deposits	13,375	2,180	(5,300)	10,255
Minimum lease payments	7,900	1,700		9,600
	$ 130,775	$ 7,302	$ (20,675)	$ 117,402

(A) Amortization

Activity analysis of other assets for the period.

MODEL REPORT #18-6

Key Use of Report:

Monitors activity in other asset categories for planning and control purposes.

Suggested Routing:

Controller.

Frequency of Preparation:

Monthly.

LIABILITIES AND SHAREHOLDERS' INVESTMENT REPORTS

When businesses close their books each month, they normally generate a detailed listing of payables and other liabilities. Seldom, though, are these reports aged, which can be a valuable tool for monitoring upcoming cash requirements. Exhibits 19-1 and 19-2 show liability agings.

Borrowings and limitations under borrowing agreements are also key information every firm needs at its fingertips. Exhibits 19-4 and 19-5 demonstrate an efficient way to present this data.

This section concludes with two reports that analyze changes in equity accounts and highlights key shareholder information. This data is essential in monitoring owners' activity during the year.

Exhibit 19-1
AGED TRIAL BALANCE OF ACCOUNTS PAYABLE

Vendor Name	Current			61 – 90 Days	Over 90 Days	Past Due			Future	Total	Last Payment	
	1 to 15 Days	16 – 30 Days	31 – 60 Days			1 to 30 Days	31 – 60 Days	Over 60 Days			Date	Amount
American Carpet	$ 2,550		$ 1,400			$ 950				$ 4,900	4/07	$ 2,500
Carlson Sales	14,375	$ 8,210		$ 550						23,135	4/15	13,200
Devcon		4,875	3,250						$ 95	8,220	3/01	4,013
Engler Co.	2,820	1,750				1,710	$ 150			6,430	4/10	1,300
Federal Printers		13,270				5,840				19,110	3/01	5,825
Green Thumb		4,320	2,150							6,470	3/08	1,500
J & L Co.	8,750				$ 310					9,060	1/15	5,320
LeMars									2,410	2,410	12/15	1,580
Mason Ltd.							682			682	4/10	520
	$ 28,495	$ 32,425	$ 6,800	$ 550	$ 310	$ 8,500	$ 832		$ 2,505	$ 80,417		

Detailed aging of payables by vendor.

MODEL REPORT #19-1

Key Use of Report:

Helps to monitor and plan for cash disbursements. It is a strong cash management tool.

Suggested Routing:

Treasurer, Accounts Payable Supervisor.

Frequency of Preparation:

Weekly.

Exhibit 19-2

ACCRUED LIABILITIES AGING

Vendor Name	Current 1 to 15 Days	16 - 30 Days	Over 30 Days	Past Due	Future	Total	Last Payment Date	Amount
Rent - Warehouse #3	$ 5,650					$ 5,650	6/01	$ 5,650
Sales tax	6,380					6,380	3/05	2,875
Property taxes		$ 14,280				14,280	10/03	13,760
Employee bond deductions		2,750				2,750	5/28	2,450
Profit sharing fees				$ 1,285		1,285	11/18	1,425
Unemployment taxes	5,805					5,805	4/10	7,850
Deferred compensation	2,720				$ 15,386	18,106		-
	$ 20,555	$ 17,030		$ 1,285	$ 15,386	$ 54,256		

Detailed aging of accrued liabilities by vendor.

MODEL REPORT #19-2

Key Use of Report:

Helps to monitor and plan for cash disbursements. It aids a firm's cash manager plan upcoming requirements.

Suggested Routing:

Treasurer, Accounts Payable Supervisor.

Frequency of Preparation:

Weekly.

Exhibit 19-3

DEBIT BALANCES IN ACCOUNTS PAYABLE

Customer	Amount	Comments
Am Arbor Co.	$1,150	Awaiting customer check
Berkley	782	Checking into this one
Mason Co.	3,825	Corrected customer invoice will offset this
Patell Co.	400	Accidental overpayment
Satelite Co.	110	Disputed amount
Universal Co.	650	Requested payment from customer
	$6,917	

Listing of debit balances in accounts payable by customer including comments about each amount.

MODEL REPORT #19-3

Key Use of Report:

Documents amounts owing the company resulting from credit balances. Used by accounts payable personnel to analyze the cause and disposition of these items.

Suggested Routing:

Accounts Payable Supervisor.

Frequency of Preparation:

Quarterly.

Exhibit 19-4

SHORT-TERM BANK BORROWINGS

Date of Borrowings	Amount		Outstanding Borrowings	
	Borrowed	Prepaid		
11/12/82	$200,000		$200,000	
11/13/82	100,000		300,000	
11/20/82	100,000		400,000	
12/3/82		$100,000	300,000	Balance 12/31/82
1/29/83	200,000		500,000	
3/12/83		100,000	400,000	
7/6/83	100,000		500,000	
7/14/83	100,000		600,000	
10/27/83		300,000	300,000	Balance 12/31/83
1/8/84	100,000		400,000	
1/13/84	100,000		500,000	
1/17/84	200,000		700,000	
2/8/84	100,000		800,000	
5/10/84		200,000	600,000	
6/11/84		150,000	450,000	
9/8/84		250,000	200,000	
12/10/84		100,000	100,000	Balance 12/31/84

Prime Interest Rate Changes

Date of Change	Interest Rate
10/13/82	12%
2/25/83	11
8/8/83	12
10/8/83	12 1/4
1/5/84	12 1/2
2/14/84	12 3/4
4/10/84	13
6/15/84	12 3/4
7/20/84	13
9/1/84	13 1/4
11/6/84	13 1/2
11/12/84	14
12/6/84	14 1/4

Analysis of short-term borrowings showing amounts borrowed and repaid and a running outstanding balance. Also, a schedule of interest rate changes is included.

MODEL REPORT #19-4

Key Use of Report:

Details short-term borrowing activity for cash planning and control purposes.

Suggested Routing:

Treasurer.

Frequency of Preparation:

Continually updated as borrowing activity takes place.

Exhibit 19-5

SCHEDULE OF LIMITATIONS UNDER BANK AGREEMENT

Bank Limitation	Compliance				
	1st Quarter	2nd Quarter	3rd Quarter	4th Quarter	Prior End of Year
1. Maintain current assets to current liabilities ratio of not less than 1.4 to 1	Yes	No	No	Yes	Yes
2. Maintain debt to worth ratio of not more than 2 to 1	Yes	Yes	Yes	Yes	Yes
3. Company shall deliver to the Bank within 45 days after the end of each fiscal quarter a balance sheet and income statement	Yes	No	Yes	No	Yes
4. Acquire capital assets with an aggregate value in excess of $50,000 in any one fiscal year	Yes	Yes	Yes	Yes	Yes
5. Increase the compensation of any officer by greater than 10% in any one year	Yes	Yes	Yes	Yes	Yes

List of all limitations (covenants) under a borrowing agreement and a schedule to note whether a company is in compliance with each one.

MODEL REPORT #19-5

Key Use of Report:

Lists all bank loan covenants and serves as a checklist to ensure the company remains in compliance with them.

Suggested Routing:

Treasurer.

Frequency of Preparation:

Whenever a new loan is added, an old one is deleted or an existing one is changed.

Exhibit 19-6

SHAREHOLDERS' EQUITY REPORT

	Common Stock	Paid-In Capital	Retained Earnings	Treasury Stock
Balance, beginning of year, as previously reported	$185,000	$410,000	$797,000	$(52,000)
Deduct cumulative effect of change in accounting for leases			(62,500)	
Balance, beginning of year, as restated	185,000	410,000	734,500	(52,000)
Net earnings			183,740	
Cash dividends of $1.00 per share			(77,500)	
Exercise of stock options	11,100	15,650		
Conversion of debt	18,350	26,110		
Purchase of treasury stock				(43,790)
Balance, end of year	$214,450	$451,760	$840,740	$(95,790)

Analysis of changes in each equity account during the period.

MODEL REPORT #19-6

Key Use of Report:

Documents all changes in equity accounts for planning and control purposes. If a firm is audited each year, this type of analysis must be shown as part of the audited financials.

Suggested Routing:

Treasurer.

Frequency of Preparation:

Quarterly.

Exhibit 19-7

MAJOR SHAREHOLDER REPORT

Name & Address	Phone #	Last Transaction B = Bought S = Sold	Quantity	Transaction Date	Total Shares Owned	% Ownership
J. B. Hollands 9501 James Ave. Minneapolis, MN 55420	612-871-9235	S	5,500	10/1/83	127,385	18.2%
Leroy Johnson 210 Sutliff Ave. New York, NY 10005	212-888-8000	B	3,900	5/1/84	62,820	9.0%
John Garnett 11 Pine Street Chicago, IL 60606	312-521-5231	B	5,350	5/7/84	61,500	8.8%
Sy McMillon 2000 National Plaza Chicago, IL 60670	312-945-3702	B	4,120	12/3/84	39,720	5.7%

Note: Report includes shareholders having greater than 3% ownership.

Listing of major shareholders plus date and amount of last transaction, total shares owned, and percent of ownership.

MODEL REPORT #19-7

Key Use of Report:

Documents significant shareholders to determine where control of the company lies and any changes in ownership.

Suggested Routing:

Treasurer.

Frequency of Preparation:

Monthly or more often if there is a high level of shareholder activity.

RESEARCH AND DEVELOPMENT REPORTS

Research and development costs are discretionary budget items that are often difficult to control. Projects may span several accounting periods, and the department may be headed by technical people with little financial background. But just like any other corporate program there needs to be authorization to spend funds, a budget for how it will be spent, and performance and project status reports. This section includes the type of reports necessary for management to key on important R & D departmental activities.

Exhibit 20-1

R & D ANNUAL PROJECT AUTHORIZATION REPORT

Project Title: Modified 40-A Measuring Gauge   Date: October 15

Project Number: 83   Estimated Completion Date: July 1

Project Description: Redesign microcircuitry to speed up processing of data by
                      25%

Project Justification: Comments
                      $6,900   Estimated Cost (1)
                      8 1/2 Mos. Estimated Project
                                  Life
                                  Personnel:
                      1 1/2   Existing   Use existing lab personnel
                      -           New
                                  Capital Equipment:
                      $3,800   Existing
                      $3,980   New

Background Information: Customer demands for high speed processing of thickness
                       profiles make this project crucial. Should have been
                       started 4 Mos. ago, but we're waiting for new lab equipment
                       before we can proceed

Approval: Principal Contact:
    Requested by: J. Johnson   J. Johnson
    Department Manager Don Page
    Divisional Manager Doug Hart

(1) Estimated cost must be supported by detail schedules showing a breakdown of
     dollars by professionals, technicians, materials, direct and indirect costs.

     Detailed justification for an R & D project including project description,
     project costs, and background information.

MODEL REPORT #20-1

Key Use of Report:

Documents the justification for each R & D project.

Suggested Routing:

Divisional or Department Manager, R & D Manager.

Frequency of Preparation:

For each R & D request.

Exhibit 20-2

R & D PROJECT REVIEW FORM

```
Project Title:        Modified 40-A Measuring Gauge     Date: March 15

Project Number:       83

Estimated Cost:                        $6,900
Actual Costs this Reporting Period       850
Total Actual Costs to Date             4,720

% of Actual to Estimated Costs         68.4%
% of Estimated Work Complete            55%

Financial Comments:        Materials are 85% complete while labor and other costs
                           are 40% complete.  Still on target for July 1 and at
                           estimated cost of $6,900


General Review Comments:   Looks like data processing will even be faster than 25% -
                           closer to 40%.  Should make marketability much stronger.
                           Material content in production units will be 10% less than
                           anticipated (about $150).


Approval:
     Project Manager      J. Johnson
     Department Manager   Don Page
     Divisional Manager   Doug Hart
```

R & D project status report that compares estimated costs with actual costs to date and has space for both financial comments and general review comments.

MODEL REPORT #20-2

Key Use of Report:

Keeps management informed on the current status of significant individual R & D projects.

Suggested Routing:

Divisional or Department Manager, Project Manager.

Frequency of Preparation:

Monthly.

Alternative Reports:

Model Report #20-3, #20-4.

Exhibit 20-3

R & D PERFORMANCE REPORT

Project #	Description	Actual Hours to Date	Planned Contract Hours	% of Actual Hrs to Planned	Estimated % of Completion	Comments
139	Model 10A – new product introduction	75	375	20%	20%	Receiving full attention of one engineer now; preliminary testing complete and we are awaiting production evaluation
152	Complete prototype	175	590	30%	20%	Slight delay waiting for prototype parts but everything is going fine
157	Complete budgets for S.I.C. value engineering	29	50	58%	60%	On target
167	Complete patent search	31	40	78%	80%	Will be complete by Aug. 15 as planned
169	Develop information to standardize department cost accounting	43	75	57%	45-50%	Looks like will spend 10-15 hours more than planned due to difficulty in decoding some previous years allocations
	Project estimates prepared this month		4			
	Backlog of unapproved estimates		5			
	Total departmental hours available		606			
	Actual hours charged to projects		510			
	% of actual hours to available hrs.		84%			
	Budgeted % of actual hrs. to available hrs.		77%			

Analysis by R & D project showing actual hours to date, planned hours, percent of actual hours to planned, and estimated percentage of completion.

MODEL REPORT #20-3

Key Use of Report:

Keeps management informed on the current status of all R & D projects.

Suggested Routing:

Divisional or Department Manager, Project Manager.

Frequency of Preparation:

Monthly.

Alternative Reports:

Model Report #20-2, #20-4.

Exhibit 20-4

MONTHLY R & D PROJECT STATUS REPORT

Project 79: Superpressure Balloon

	Budgeted Dollars	Expenditures This Month	Expenditures To Date	Outstanding Purchase Commitments	Total Activity To Date	Budget Remaining
Research:						
Payroll	$ 4,700	$ 830	$ 995		$ 995	$ 3,705
Fringe benefits	595	105	126		126	469
Utilities	1,230	250	310		310	920
Supplies	3,250	1,250	1,635	$ 485	2,120	1,130
Occupancy	1,250	375	460	310	770	480
Other	975	185	185	150	335	640
	12,000	2,995	3,711	945	4,656	7,344
Development:						
Payroll	6,840	475	475		475	6,365
Fringe benefits	730	51	51		51	679
Utilities	1,490	110	110		110	1,380
Supplies	2,975	940	1,138	1,520	2,658	317
Occupancy	1,420	297	297		297	1,123
Other	2,620	340	340	610	950	1,670
	16,075	2,213	2,411	2,130	4,541	11,534
Legal:						
Patent search	2,310	1,640	1,930		1,930	380
Patent application	1,110	220	220	950	1,170	(60)
Other	350	100	100		100	250
	3,770	1,960	2,250	950	3,200	570
Administrative	3,600	730	887		887	2,713
Total	$35,445	$7,898	$9,259	$4,025	$13,284	$22,161

Individual project analysis showing activity to date—budgeted dollars, expenditures, outstanding purchase commitments, and budget remaining.

MODEL REPORT #20-4

Key Use of Report:

Keeps management informed on the current status of significant R & D projects.

Suggested Routing:

Divisional or Department Manager, Project Manager.

Frequency of Preparation:

Monthly.

Alternative Reports:

Model Report #20-2, #20-3.

Exhibit 20-5

DIVISIONAL R & D PROGRAM BUDGET

Division	Product Improvements			Cost Reductions			New Products			Total		
	Current Year	Prior Year	Change +(-)	Current Year	Prior Year	Change +(-)	Current Year	Prior Year	Change +(-)	Current Year	Prior Year	Change +(-)
Engineering	$ -	$ -	$ -	$ -	$ -	$ -	$18,000	$12,000	$ 6,000	$ 18,000	$ 12,000	$ 6,000
Extrusion	22,000	10,000	12,000	10,000	5,000	5,000	30,000	20,000	10,000	62,000	35,000	27,000
Electronics	49,000	40,000	9,000	17,000	13,000	4,000	25,000	25,000	-	91,000	78,000	13,000
Machining	-	-	-	8,000	3,000	5,000	-	-	-	8,000	3,000	5,000
Sheeting	5,000	5,000	-	5,000	15,000	(10,000)	10,000	7,500	2,500	20,000	27,500	(7,500)
	$76,000	$55,000	$21,000	$40,000	$36,000	$ 4,000	$83,000	$64,500	$18,500	$199,000	$155,500	$43,500

R & D budgets by division showing amounts allocated for product improvements, cost reductions, and new products.

MODEL REPORT #20-5

Key Use of Report:
Summarizes planned R & D expenditures by type for management review and approval.

Suggested Routing:
Top Management, R & D Manager.

Frequency of Preparation:
Annually.

SUPPORT DEPARTMENTS—EDP, PERSONNEL REPORTING, CUSTOMER SERVICE

Support departments are playing an ever-increasing role within organizations. Because these areas are commanding larger budgets each year, there is an important need to closely scrutinize their contribution. It is often a fine line between satisfying increasing user demands yet remaining cost justifiable. The reports in this section offer management the means to judge the effectiveness of these support departments. They include not only key information necessary for management to evaluate daily activities but also data on how closely budgets are being adhered to.

Exhibit 21-1

HEADCOUNT BY DEPARTMENT

	Month's Budget	Week #1	#2	#3	#4
Direct labor:					
Machine Shop	6	6	5	5	5
Electronic Production	35	33	34	34	35
Electronic Assembly	10	10	10	10	10
Total direct labor	51	49	49	49	50
Indirect labor:					
Shipping/Rec.	1	1	1	1	1
Purchasing	1	1	1	1	1
Engineering	2	2	2	2	2
Draftsmen	2	1	2	2	2
Janitors	1	1	1	1	1
Total indirect labor	7	6	7	7	7
Selling, general & admin.					
Accounting	5	5	5	5	5
Marketing	2	2	2	2	2
Sales	6	5	6	6	6
Secretarial	3	3	3	3	3
Officers	4	4	4	4	4
Total S, G, & A	20	19	20	20	20
Total employees	78	74	76	76	77

Number of employees by department compared to budget.

MODEL REPORT #21-1

Key Use of Report:

Monitors the number of employees compared with budget for evaluation and control purposes.

Suggested Routing:

Top Management.

Frequency of Preparation:

Monthly.

Alternative Reports:

Model Report #21-2, #21-3.

Exhibit 21-2
WORKFORCE REPORT

		Beginning Employees	New Hires	Terminated	Ending Employees
Machine Shop	- Actual	6			6
	- Budget	6			6
Warehousing	- Actual	8	2	1	9
	- Budget	8	1		9
Production	- Actual	48	5	3	50
	- Budget	48	5	2	51
Sales	- Actual	12	2		14
	- Budget	12	4	2	14
Administrative	- Actual	11			11
	- Budget	11	1		12
Total	- Actual	85	9	4	90
	- Budget	85	11	4	92

Analysis of new hires and terminations by department compared to budget.

MODEL REPORT #21-2

Key Use of Report:

Itemizes workforce increases and decreases compared to budget for management evaluation.

Suggested Routing:

Top Management.

Frequency of Preparation:

Monthly.

Alternative Reports:

Model Report #21-1, #21-3.

Exhibit 21-3

EMPLOYEE TURNOVER REPORT

Month	Beginning Work Force	New Hires (Replacements)	Turnover Rate	New Hires (Increases)	Employees Reductions	Ending Work Force	Planned Work Force	Variance
Jan	160	5	3%	1	(3)	163	161	(2)
Feb	163	2	1%	-	(4)	161	160	(1)
Mar	161	1	1%	1	(1)	162	160	(2)
Apr	162	-	-	-	(1)	161	160	(1)
May	161	3	2%	-	(2)	162	161	(1)
June								
July								
Aug								
Sept								
Oct								
Nov								
Dec								

Reconciliation of beginning and end of month employee totals compared to plan.

MODEL REPORT #21-3

Key Use of Report:

Tracks additions and deletions to the workforce during the period for management review and evaluation.

Suggested Routing:

Top Management.

Frequency of Preparation:

Monthly.

Alternative Reports:

Model Report #21-1, #21-2.

Exhibit 21-4

PERSONNEL MANAGEMENT EFFECTIVENESS REPORT

		Current Year	Prior Year
1.	Personnel costs divided by average number of employees	$300	$265
2.	Absentee man-days divided by number of man-days worked	2.6%	2.8%
3.	Employee turnover - number of employees leaving divided by average number of employees	4.8%	6.3%
4.	Recruiting costs divided by recruits selected	$2142	$928
5.	Benefit costs as a percent of compensation	21%	20.1%
6.	Employee suggestions received	58	29
7.	Employee suggestions accepted	40	21

Seven key ratios and other measurements for management review.

MODEL REPORT #21-4

Key Use of Report:

Analyzes the effectiveness of personnel management.

Suggested Routing:

Vice President Administration.

Frequency of Preparation:

Quarterly.

Exhibit 21-5

DATA PROCESSING EFFECTIVENESS REPORT

	Current Year	Prior Year
1. Utilization rate (application hours used divided by application hours available)	77%	72%
2. Usage rate (production hours divided by total hours staffed)	68%	73%
3. Effectiveness (application hours minus rerun hours divided by application hours)	96%	93%
4. Reliability (downtime divided by hours staffed)	7%	9%
5. Scheduling reliability (number of reports prepared on time divided by number of reports prepared)	89%	92%
6. Quality of output (number of reports produced error free divided by number of reports)	90%	91.5%
7. Data processing costs divided by sales	3.4%	3.2%

Seven key operating ratios for management review.

MODEL REPORT #21-5

Key Use of Report:

Analyzes the effectiveness of the data processing department.

Suggested Routing:

Vice President Administration.

Frequency of Preparation:

Quarterly.

Exhibit 21-6

SYSTEMS AND PROGRAMMING DEPARTMENTAL STATUS

Project Description	Scheduled Dates Start	Completion	Actual Dates Start	Estim. Compl.	Programming People	Man Days	Systems People	Man Days	Hours Budgeted	Actual	% Complete	Estim. Hrs. to Complete
Purge Mobile Office Systems	9/15	9/19	9/15	9/17	1	1/2	1	1/2	8	10	100%	-
Customer Service Adjustments	9/17	9/22	9/18	9/20	1	1	1	1/2	12	11	100	-
Integrate O.E. to G.L. System	9/21	10/5	9/21	10/10	1	4	2	8	96	90	90	10
A.P. System Program Maintenance	9/25	9/27	9/25	9/29	1	1	2	1/2	12	15	100	-
Modify Online Branch Input Program	10/6	10/17	10/6	10/15	1	4	1	2	48	29	75	11
Review Master Update Select Program	9/30	10/2	9/30	10/1	1	1	1	1	8	8	100%	-

Analysis by project of start date, estimated completion date, and manpower requirements.

MODEL REPORT #21-6

Key Use of Report:

Serves as a master schedule for all data processing department project activity.

Suggested Routing:

EDP Manager.

Frequency of Preparation:

Bimonthly.

Exhibit 21-7

DATA PROCESSING REPORT SCHEDULE

Report #	Description	Due Date - Input	Date Input Received	Due Date - Proof	Proof Received	Due Date - Report	Actual Run Date	Rerun #1	Rerun #2	Date Distributed
A/R 1089	A/Rec Cash Update	5/2	5/2			5/4	5/5	5/6		5/7
A/R 107	A/Rec Monthly Cash Rec.					5/5	5/6			5/7
A/R-M	A/Rec Monthly Aging					5/11	5/11	5/12		5/12
J/E 100	J/E Single Entry	5/10	5/8			5/11	5/11			5/11
P/L 107	Budget P & L Summary					5/13	5/14			5/15
P/L 109	P & L - Profit Center					5/13	5/14			5/15
B/S 100	Balance Sheet - Corporate					5/13	5/14			5/15
P/L 3087	R & D Manufacturing					5/13	5/14			5/15
P/L 4089	T & E Detail					5/14	5/15			5/15
P/L 1070	Branch Sales Analysis					5/14	5/15			5/15
P/L 1175	Product Division P & L					5/13	5/14			5/14
A/P 300	A/P Check Register					5/10	5/10			5/10
A/P 315	A/P Checks					5/10	5/10			5/10
A/P-V	Vendor Master List	5/3	5/2	5/4	5/4	5/5	5/5	5/6		5/8
P/R-M	P/R Master Listing	5/3	5/3	5/4	5/4	5/5	5/5			5/8

Detailed calendar of report deadlines showing input due dates and actual run dates.

MODEL REPORT #21-7

Key Use of Report:

Serves as the master schedule for computer operations to use to meet monthly report demands.

Suggested Routing:

EDP Manager, Head of EDP Operations.

Frequency of Preparation:

Monthly.

Exhibit 21-8

CUSTOMER SERVICE PERFORMANCE REPORT

| Week Ended | Performance Criteria | | | | |
	Billing Errors	Stockouts	Customer Refusals	Customer Returns	Total
Jan 12	4	2	1	3	10
Jan 19	8	3	-	1	12
Jan 26	5	-	1	4	10
Feb 2	3	-	-	2	5
Feb 9	3	-	-	1	4
Feb 16	4	-	-	2	6
Feb 23					
March 2					
March 9					
March 16					

Running weekly analysis of customer service performance criteria—billing errors, stockouts, and customer refusals.

MODEL REPORT #21-8

Key Use of Report:

Measures the performance of the company in servicing customers.

Suggested Routing:

Administrative Manager, Sales Manager, Customer Service Manager.

Frequency of Preparation:

Weekly.

Alternative Reports:

Model Report #21-9.

Exhibit 21-9

CUSTOMER COMPLAINT REPORT

Month Ended	Billing Errors	Defective Merchandise	Non Delivery	Wrong Quantity	Late Delivery	Other	Total	Last Year
Jan – Month	7	4	-	-	2	-	13	6
– YTD	7	4	-	-	2	-	13	6
Feb – Month	5	1	2	-	-	1	9	8
– YTD	12	5	2	-	2	1	22	14
Mar – Month	10	-	-	1	1	-	12	5
– YTD	22	5	2	1	3	1	34	19
Apr – Month	2	-	1	-	1	-	4	10
– YTD	24	5	3	1	4	1	38	29
May – Month	3	2	-	1	1	1	8	4
– YTD	27	7	3	2	5	2	46	33
June – Month								
– YTD								
July – Month								
– YTD								
Aug – Month								
– YTD								
Sept – Month								
– YTD								
Oct – Month								
– YTD								
Nov – Month								
– YTD								
Dec – Month								
– YTD								

Analysis of customer complaints by type on a running monthly and year-to-date basis.

MODEL REPORT #21-9

Key Use of Report:

Measures company performance in properly servicing customers.

Suggested Routing:

Top Management, Administrative Manager.

Frequency of Preparation:

Monthly.

Alternative Reports:

Model Report #21-8.

FINANCIAL EFFICIENCY AND EFFECTIVENESS REPORTS

A company's financial health can best be monitored by a series of reports that examine working capital, liquidity ratios, returns on debt and equity, and the overall nature of the long-term financial condition. This section contains four reports that cover these essential areas. They specifically measure a company's ability to meet its short-term obligations, the contribution of the owners in comparison with other financing, and how effectively a firm is using its financial resources.

Exhibit 22-1

WORKING CAPITAL STATUS REPORT

		Actual	Planned	Variance + (-)
Current Assets				
Cash	(1)	$117,000	$182,000	$(65,000)
Receivables	(2)	489,000	510,000	(21,000)
Inventories		810,000	830,000	(20,000)
Other		30,000	25,000	5,000
Total	(3)	1,446,000	1,547,000	(101,000)
Current Liabilities				
Notes payable		$350,000	$500,000	$(150,000)
Accounts payable		275,000	300,000	(25,000)
Accrued expenses		105,000	85,000	20,000
Current portion of				
long-term debt		175,000	150,000	25,000
Income taxes		75,000	90,000	(15,000)
Other		10,000	15,000	(5,000)
Total	(4)	990,000	1,140,000	(150,000)
Net Working Capital		$456,000	$407,000	$ 49,000
Current Ratio (3) divided by (4)		1.46	1.36	
Quick Ratio (1) + (2) divided by (4)		.61	.61	

Analysis of actual current assets and current liabilities compared to budget including net working capital, current ratio, and quick ratio calculations.

MODEL REPORT #22-1

Key Use of Report:

Measures the ability of a firm to meet its current obligations. It is a crucial report in monitoring a firm's liquidity.

Suggested Routing:

Chief Financial Officer, Treasurer.

Frequency of Preparation:

Monthly.

Alternative Reports:

Model Report #22-2.

Exhibit 22-2

CORPORATE LIQUIDITY STATUS REPORT

	Current Year		Prior
	Actual	Planned	Year
1. Current ratio Calculation: current assets divided by current liabilities. Indicates: degree of safety short-term creditors will have extending credit to the firm.	1.6 to 1	1.7 to 1	1.75 to 1
2. Quick ratio Calculation: cash + receivables + temporary investments divided by current liabilities. Indicates: dollars of current assets that are immediately available to pay short-term creditors.	.9 to 1	.9 to 1	1 to 1
3. Vulnerability ratio Calculation: fixed overhead divided by total overhead. Indicates: vulnerability of profits during an economic slowdown; the higher the ratio the higher the current ratio should be.	35%	37%	38%
4. Average collection period of receivables Calculation: average accounts receivable divided by net credit sales x 365. Indicates: how liquid and collectable receivables are.	44 days	41 days	40 days
5. Inventory turnover Calculation: cost of goods sold divided by average inventory. Indicates: how rapid inventories are being sold and replaced.	63 days	58 days	56 days

Five key liquidity ratio calculations and a discussion of what each indicates.

MODEL REPORT #22-2

Key Use of Report:

Measures the extent of corporate liquidity using five recognized ratios and calculations.

Suggested Routing:

Chief Financial Officer, Treasurer.

Frequency of Preparation:

Monthly.

Alternative Reports:

Model Report #22-1.

Exhibit 22-3

TRADING ON EQUITY REPORT

	Items	Computation	This Year	Last Year
	10 1/2% bank note payable		$350,000	$650,000
	9 % sinking fund debenture		610,000	750,000
	10% building mortgage bonds		375,000	375,000
	Total debt		1,335,000	1,775,000
a	Total shareholders' equity		2,378,000	2,051,000
b	Total debt & shareholders' equity		$3,713,000	$3,826,000
c	Income before interest charges		$635,000	263,000
d	Interest charges		129,150	143,280
	Net income for shareholders		$505,850	$119,720
e	Return on debt and shareholders' equity	c divided by b	17.1%	6.9%
f	Return on shareholders' equity	d divided by a	21.2%	5.8%

> If e is greater than f, trading on equity is unprofitable for the year
> If f is greater than e, trading on equity is profitable for the year

Note: trading on equity involves the use of borrowed funds in the
expectation that a return higher than the interest cost will
be earned.

Comparison of return on debt and shareholders' equity and return on shareholders' equity to see if the use of debt by a firm has been profitable.

MODEL REPORT #22-3

Key Use of Report:

Measures how effective a company is employing leverage (the use of borrowed funds to finance a portion of a company's asset needs).

Suggested Routing:

Chief Financial Officer, Treasurer.

Frequency of Preparation:

Quarterly.

Exhibit 22-4

ANALYSIS OF LONG-TERM FINANCIAL CONDITION

		Current Year		Prior Year
		Actual	Planned	Year

1.	Stockholders' equity ratio
	Calculation: stockholders' equity
	  divided by total assets.
	Indicates: Measure of relative financial
	  strength and reflection of long-term
	  solvency by showing presence or absence
	  of long-term liability pressure.
		62%	60%	57%

2.	Liability liquidity ratio
	Calculation: current assets divided
	  by total liabilities
	Indicates: higher the ratio the more
	  working capital there is to pay off
	  long-term liabilities.
		122%	115%	120%

3.	Fixed obligation security ratio
	Calculation: fixed assets divided by
	  long-term liabilities.
	Indicates: when fixed assets are pledged
	  on long-term liabilities, this ratio
	  indicates the protection afforded long-
	  term creditors and the possibility of
	  long-term debt expansion based on avail-
	  able security.
		196%	190%	187%

4.	Book value of common stock
	Calculation: shareholders' equity
	  divided by number of outstanding
	  shares of common stock.
	Indicates: dollar equity in corporate
	  capital of each share of stock.
		$11.50	$11.00	$10.60

5.	Earnings ratio
	Calculation: net income divided by
	  shareholders' equity.
	Indicates: reflects the extent
	  satisfactory profits are being earned.
		6.7%	6%	6%

6.	Times fixed interest charges have been
	earned
	Calculation: net income after taxes,
	  before deduction for fixed interest
	  divided by interest on long-term
	  liabilities.
	Indicates: margin of safety afforded
	  long-term creditors.
		5.8	5.5	5.5

Six key long-term financial condition ratio calculations and a discussion
of what each indicates.

MODEL REPORT #22-4

Key Use of Report:

Monitors the long-term financial strength of a firm using six recognized ratios and
calculations.

Suggested Routing:

Chief Financial Officer, Treasurer.

Frequency of Preparation:

Monthly.

INFLATION REPORTING

The purchasing power of a dollar in one year is not the same as those in other years, and when financial results intermingle dollars of different purchasing power, the results can be misleading. For example, by expressing assets in terms of dollars paid at different dates in the past, the balance sheet fails to provide any indication of their current value to the firm. The reports in this section adjust all data to a current price basis using the consumer price index. These price level adjusted financial statements are extremely useful when making interperiod comparisons especially in times of rapid inflation. For instance, in a three-year review of operating results, a firm showing a 25% increase in sales dollars may be categorized as a strong performer. But could the same thing be said if during this same period prices escalated 40%? Price-adjusted reporting such as this section contains, would highlight this effect.

Exhibit 23-1

PRICE LEVEL ADJUSTED BALANCE SHEET

	Nominal Dollars (1)	Restatement Ratio	Constant December 31, 1985 Dollars
Assets			
Current Assets:			
Cash	$158,000	235/235	$158,000
Receivables	749,000	235/235	749,000
Inventories (fifo)	1,250,500	235/233.7	1,257,456
Total current assets	2,157,500		2,164,456
Property, plant and equipment, net	1,978,350	EXHIBIT 23-3	2,547,979
Total assets	4,135,850		$4,712,435
Liabilities and shareholders' equity			
Current Liabilities:			
Accounts payable	$899,000	235/235	$899,000
Accrued expenses	521,500	235/235	521,500
Total current liabilities	1,420,500		1,420,500
Bonds payable	850,000	235/235	850,000
Deferred income taxes	365,000	235/235	365,000
Shareholders' equity:			
Common stock	210,000	235/160	308,438
Additional paid-in capital	338,000	235/160	496,438
Retained earnings	952,350	PLUG	1,272,059
Total shareholders' equity	1,500,350		2,076,935
Total liabilities & shareholders' equity	$4,135,850		$4,712,435

(1) Nominal dollars are the current balances from the general ledger.

MODEL REPORT #23-1

Key Use of Report:

Measures the impact of inflation on the historical balance sheet (from the general ledger) by adjusting all dollars to their current value (current purchasing power/constant dollars).

Suggested Routing:

Top Management.

Frequency of Preparation:

Quarterly.

Alternative Reports:

Model Reports #1-4, #1-8.

Exhibit 23-2

PRICE LEVEL ADJUSTED PROPERTY AND EQUIPMENT REPORT

	Nominal Dollars	Restatement Ratio	Constant December 31, 1985 Dollars
Net sales	$8,420,600	235/232	$8,529,487
Cost of sales	6,295,000	EXHIBIT 23-5	6,397,961
Gross profit	2,125,600		2,131,526
Selling, general and administrative	710,000	235/232	719,181
Depreciation	267,000	EXHIBIT 23-4	337,025
Interest	284,000	235/232	287,672
Other income - gain on sale of equipment	(38,000)	(a)	(20,223)
Pretax income	902,600		807,871
Income taxes	406,170	235/232	411,422
Net income	$496,430		$396,449

(a) Sales price: $143,000 x 235/231 = $145,476
     Book value :   cost $211,000
                   a/Dep (106,000)
                          $105,000 x 235/197 =   125,253
     Price adjusted gain $ 20,223

MODEL REPORT #23-2

Key Use of Report:

Measures the impact of inflation on the historical income statement (from the general ledger) by adjusting all dollars to their current value (current purchasing power/constant dollars).

Suggested Routing:

Top Management.

Frequency of Preparation:

Quarterly.

Alternative Reports:

Model Reports #1-1, #1-3, #1-9.

Exhibit 23-3

PRICE LEVEL ADJUSTED DEPRECIATION REPORT

Year Acquired		Nominal Dollars		Restatement Ratio	Constant December 31, 1985 Dollars	
		Cost	Acc. Dep.		Cost	Acc. Dep.
1975	Land	$ 125,000	--	235/162	$ 181,327	--
1976	Building	1,300,000	$ 409,000	235/173	1,765,896	$555,578
1976	Equipment	496,000	400,000	235/174	669,885	540,229
1977	Equipment	343,000	256,000	235/181	445,331	332,375
1979	Equipment	712,000	185,650	235/197	849,340	221,460
1981	Equipment	325,000	72,000	235/208	367,188	81,346
		$3,301,000	$1,322,650		$4,278,967	$1,730,988
		(1,322,650)			(1,730,988)	
		$1,978,350			$2,547,979	

MODEL REPORT #23-3

Key Use of Report:

Restates general ledger property costs to their current value (current purchasing power/constant dollars) as a measure of inflation's impact.

Suggested Routing:

Top Management.

Frequency of Preparation:

Quarterly.

Exhibit 23-4

PRICE LEVEL ADJUSTED INCOME STATEMENT

Year Acquired		Nominal Dollars	Restatement Ratio	Constant December 31, 1985 Dollars
1976	Building	$43,000	235/173	$58,410
1976	Equipment	62,000	235/174	83,736
1977	Equipment	37,000	235/181	48,039
1979	Equipment	89,000	235/197	106,167
1981	Equipment	36,000	235/208	40,673
		$267,000		$337,025

MODEL REPORT #23-4

Key Use of Report:

Restates actual depreciation dollars to their current value (current purchasing power/constant dollars) as a measure of inflation's impact.

Suggested Routing:

Top Management.

Frequency of Preparation:

Quarterly.

Exhibit 23-5

PRICE LEVEL ADJUSTED COST OF SALES REPORT

	Nominal Dollars		Restatement Ratio	Constant December 31, 1985 Dollars
Beginning inventory	$930,400	(a)	235/229	$954,777
Purchases Goods available for sale	6,615,100		235/232	6,700,640
Less ending inventory Cost of goods sold	(1,250,500) $6,295,000	(b)	235/233.7	(1,257,456) $6,397,961

(a) Assume all inventory was purchased evenly during the last
     quarter.   228 + 229 + 230 divided by 3 = 229

(b) Same assumption as (a). 233 + 233 + 235 divided by 3 = 233.7

For Exhibits 23-1 through 23-5, the reports show data adjusted to a
current price basis (constant dollars) using the consumer price index for
the adjustment factor.

MODEL REPORT #23-5

Key Use of Report:

Restates cost of sales dollars from actual to their current value (current purchasing
power/constant dollars) as a measure of inflation's impact.

Suggested Routing:

Top Management.

Frequency of Preparation:

Quarterly.

Exhibit 23-6

CONSUMER PRICE INDEX FOR VARIOUS DATES

Date	Index
May 1975 (corporation formed)	160
June 1975 (land was acquired)	162
April 1976 (building was acquired)	173
May 1976 (equipment acquired)	174
Feb. 1977 (equipment acquired)	181
July 1979 (equipment acquired)	197
May 1981 (equipment acquired)	208
December 1981	212
December 1982	216
December 1983	221
October 1984	228
November 1984	229
December 1984	230
May 1985 (equipment sold)	231
October 1985	233
November 1985	233
December 1985	235
Average 1985	232

Running history of changes in the consumer price index.

MODEL REPORT #23-6

Key Use of Report:

Lists the consumer price index for each date needed to restate the historical dollars in Model Reports #23-1–#23-5. Consumer price index data is available at any library reference desk near you.

CONTRACTOR REPORTING

Construction contract accounting is a reporting specialty. Because construction contracts often extend for months and even years, companies need a satisfactory method of accumulating: costs as the job progresses, billings, projected costs to complete, and the anticipated gross profit on the contract. Exhibits 24-1 through 24-5 incorporate the most popular alternatives for accomplishing this. Exhibits 24-6 through 24-9 involve another crucial aspect of construction accounting—the contract bid. The overall success of any contractor starts with the bidding process, and these reports detail an effective method for contractors to use.

Exhibit 24-1

CONTRACTOR JOB STATUS REPORT

```
Job Number              _____
Billing Method          _____   Start Date        _____
Project Manager         _____   Completion Date   _____
```

                           _____ Contract Price _____

	Original Contract	Change Orders	Current Contract
Labor	$97,000	--	$97,000
Material	148,000	13,000	161,000
Subcontractors	62,000		62,000
Total	$307,000	$13,000	$320,000

                           _____ Estimated Costs _____

	Original Estimate	Change Orders	Cost Revisions	Total Estimate
Labor	$85,000			$85,000
Material	133,200	11,500		144,700
Subcontractors	51,800		(1,000)	50,800
Total	$270,000	$11,500	$(1,000)	$280,500

                           _____ Costs Incurred _____

	Current Month	Prior Month Year-to-Date	Prior Year Job-to-Date	Total Costs Incurred $	%
Labor	$4,600	$18,200	$2,000	$24,800	29.17%
Material	62,000	12,200	6,900	81,100	56.04%
Subcontractors	2,500	--		2,500	4.92%
Total	$69,100	$30,400	$8,900	$108,400	38.64%

                           _____ Revenue Recognized _____

```
Current estimate due        75,000
Received to date            62,000
Retention                    8,000
   Total billed to date    145,000 - - - - - - - - - - - - -  $145,000
Remaining to bill          175,000
Current contract total    $320,000
% complete                  38.64%
Revenue recognized         123,648 - - - - - - - - - - - -     123,648
Over (Under) billing                                         $ 21,352
```

Analysis of a construction job showing contract price, estimated costs, costs incurred, billings to date, and revenue recognized.

MODEL REPORT #24-1

Key Use of Report:

Measures actual activity on a construction job as a means of evaluating whether the job is ahead or behind schedule and by how much.

Suggested Routing:

Project Manager.

Frequency of Preparation:

Monthly.

Alternative Reports:

Model Report #24-2.

Exhibit 24-2

ANALYSIS OF CONTRACT IN PROCESS

```
Contract Name:                     Manufacturing Company
Contract Number:                   1105


Amount billed to date:
   Accounts receivable:
      Current                           $175,000
      Retention                            7,000
      Total                              182,000
   Cash collected                        120,000
   Total billed to date         1        302,000

Remaining to be billed                    73,000

Total estimated contract amount  2      $375,000

Costs incurred to date:
   Accounts payable:
      Trade accounts                   $ 58,000
      Subcontracts:
         Current                         62,000
         Retention                        9,000
         Total                           71,000
   Accrued payrolls                      14,000
   Paid                                 105,000
   Total costs incurred to date  3      248,000

Additional costs to be incurred          82,000

Total estimated costs            4      $330,000

Estimated gross profit           5     $ 45,000    2 - 4
Percentage completed             6         75.2%   3 divided by 4
Revenue recognized               7     $282,000    2 x 6
Costs recognized                 8     $248,160    4 x 6
Gross profit recognized          9     $ 33,840    7 - 8
Over (under) billings                  $ 20,000    1 - 7
```

Analysis of a specific contract job showing amount billed to date, remaining to be billed, contract amount, costs incurred to date, additional expected costs, and contract gross profit.

MODEL REPORT #24-2

Key Use of Report:

Measures activity to date on a contract in process as a means of evaluating progress compared to plan.

Suggested Routing:

Project Manager.

Frequency of Preparation:

Monthly.

Alternative Reports:

Model Report #24-1.

Exhibit 24-3

SUMMARY ANALYSIS OF CONTRACTS IN PROCESS— PERCENTAGE OF COMPLETION METHOD

	1	2	3	4	5	6	7	8	9	10	11	12
	Progress Billings to Date	Remaining to be Billed	Total Estimated Contract Amount	Costs Incurred to Date	Estimated Additional Costs	Total Estimated Costs	Estimated Gross Profit	% Completed	Revenue Recognized	Costs Recognized	Gross Profit Recognized	Over (Under) Recognized Billings
			1 + 2			4 + 5	3 - 6	4 divided by 6	3 x 8	6 x 8	9 - 10	1 - 9
Contracts overbilled:												
Contract 1000	$245,000	$38,000	283,000	190,000	$55,000	$245,000	$38,000	77.55%	$219,467	$189,998	$29,469	$25,533
Contract 2000	438,200	59,000	497,200	375,000	70,000	445,000	52,200	84.27%	418,990	375,002	43,988	19,210
Contract 3000	79,350	125,000	204,350	70,000	150,000	220,000 (a)	(15,650)	31.82%	65,024	80,674 (a)	(15,650) (a)	14,326
	762,550	222,000	984,550	635,000	275,000	910,000	74,550		703,481	645,674	57,807	59,069
Contracts underbilled:												
Contract 1500	183,000	110,000	293,000	160,000	70,000	230,000	63,000	69.56%	203,811	159,988	43,823	(20,811)
Contract 1600	140,500	27,500	168,000	125,000	20,000	145,000	23,000	86.20%	144,816	124,990	19,826	(4,316)
	323,500	137,500	461,000	285,000	90,000	375,000	86,000		348,627	284,978	63,649	(25,127)
Total – all contracts	$1,086,050	$359,500	$1,445,550	$920,000	$365,000	$1,285,000	$160,550		$1,052,108	$930,652	$121,456	$33,942

(a) Anytime estimated gross profit is negative the entire amount must be accrued in colum 11.

Analysis of contracts in process showing billings, costs, percentages complete, and gross profit recognized.

MODEL REPORT #24-3

Key Use of Report:

A summary of contracts in progress that recognizes income as work on a contract is completed, instead of all at the end of a job.

Suggested Routing:

Top Management.

Frequency of Preparation:

Monthly.

Exhibit 24-4

SUMMARY ANALYSIS OF CONTRACTS IN PROCESS— COMPLETED CONTRACT METHOD

	1	2	3	4	5	6	7	8	9
	Progress Billings to Date	Remaining to be Billed	Total Estimated Contract Amount	Costs Incurred to Date	Estimated Additional Costs	Total Estimated Costs	Estimated Gross Profit	% Completed	Costs Over (Under) Billings
			1 + 2			4 + 5	3 - 6	4 divided by 6	1 - 4
Contracts on which billings exceed costs:									
Contract 5000	$340,000	$70,000	$410,000	$325,000	$50,000	$375,000	$35,000	94.66%	$(15,000)
Contract 6000	110,000	50,000	160,000	75,000	55,000	130,000	30,000	57.69%	(35,000)
	450,000	120,000	570,000	400,000	105,000	505,000	65,000		(50,000)
Contracts on which costs exceed billings:									
Contract 5500	$510,000	$130,000	$640,000	$540,000	$60,000	$600,000	$40,000	90%	$30,000
Contract 6500	230,000	60,000	290,000	235,000	15,000	250,000	40,000	94%	20,000
	740,000	190,000	930,000	775,000	75,000	850,000	80,000		50,000
Total - all contracts	$1,190,000	$310,000	$1,500,000	$1,175,000	$180,000	$1,355,000	$145,000		$ --

Analysis of contracts in process showing billings, costs, percentages complete, and estimated gross profits.

MODEL REPORT #24-4

Key Use of Report:

A summary of contracts in progress that recognizes income only when a job is completed. It is a method that is more exact than the percentage-of-completion method because it is based on the final results of a contract and not periodic estimates along the way.

Suggested Routing:

Top Management.

Frequency of Preparation:

Monthly.

Exhibit 24-5

SUMMARY ANALYSIS OF COMPLETED CONTRACTS

-- Job --		Contract Revenues	Contract Costs	Gross Profit Amount	Gross Profit Percentage
Contract	300	$375,000	$372,000	$3,000	--
Contract	350	628,000	582,000	46,000	7.3%
Contract	400	410,000	391,000	19,000	4.6%
Contract	450	83,000	74,000	9,000	10.8%
Contract	500	197,000	210,000	(13,000)	--
Contract	550	320,000	284,000	36,000	11.3%
		$2,013,000	$1,913,000	$100,000	5.0%

Analysis of contract revenues, costs, gross profits, and gross profit percentages by contract.

MODEL REPORT #24-5

Key Use of Report:

Summarizes the profitability of completed contracts for management review and analysis.

Suggested Routing:

Top Management.

Frequency of Preparation:

Monthly.

Exhibit 24-6

CONTRACT BIDDING SUMMARY

```
Customer   _____
Location   _____
Date       _____
                                                        %          $

    1   Direct labor cost      1 divided by 5        23.5     $147,000

    2   Indirect labor cost    2 divided by 5         2.9       18,000

    3   Material cost          3 divided by 5        47.5      297,000

    4   Subcontract cost       4 divided by 5        26.1      163,000
                                                    _____   _____
    5   Prime cost                                  100.0      625,000

        Overhead application:

            (1) x    17  % = $24,990
            (2) x    17  % = $ 3,060
            (3) x     3  % = $ 8,910
            (4) x     3  % = $ 4,890                             41,850

    6   Total prime costs plus overhead                        666,850

    7   Profit (6 x   6   %)                                     40,011

    8   Subtotal                                               706,861

    9   Other costs:
            Bond and insurance      2,500
            Gross receipts tax     10,200                        12,700

   10   Contract price                                        $719,561

        Profit:
   11       Contract price                                     719,561
   12       Contract costs                                     679,550
   13       Contract profit                                     40,011
   14       Markup %          13 divided by 12                    5.9%
   15       Profit %          13 divided by 11                    5.6%
```

Worksheet that analyzes all the component costs of a contract bid.

MODEL REPORT #24-6

Key Use of Report:

A worksheet used to compile the various components of a contract bid.

Suggested Routing:

Project Manager.

Frequency of Preparation:

Every job requiring a bid.

Exhibit 24-7

MATERIAL COST BIDDING SUMMARY

```
Customer     _____
Location     _____
Date         _____


_____ Type of Work _____          $

             Carpentry                          75,000

             Masonry                            32,000

             Concrete - outside                 64,000

                      - inside                  13,000

             Electrical                         79,000

             Roofing                            34,000

             Roofing                          $297,000
```

Summary of material costs in an individual bid by type of work.

MODEL REPORT #24-7

Key Use of Report:

A worksheet used to compile the labor portion of a contract bid.

Suggested Routing:

Project Manager.

Frequency of Preparation:

Every job requiring a bid.

Exhibit 24-8

LABOR COST BIDDING SUMMARY

```
Customer     _____
Location     _____
Date         _____

Craft    Carpenters                        Foreman      Journeyman

         Direct labor cost:
           Base rate                        $11.30       $10.00

         Fringe benefits                      1.20         1.04

         Payroll taxes @ 7.25%                 .82          .73

         Workmen's compensation @ 1.7%         .19          .17

         Total rate per hour                 13.51        11.94

         Number of hours                       400        1,670

         Total direct labor cost           $5,404      $19,940

         Combined total direct labor
           cost                            $25,344

         Indirect cost:
           Room      40 days x $22           $880      $    --

         Board       40 days x $21            840           --

         Travel                               695           --

         Other    _____

                  _____        _____

         Total indirect cost              $2,415      $     --

         Combined total indirect
           cost                           $2,415
```

Note: Proposals should contain a labor cost bidding
      summary for each different craft anticipated
      on the job.

Summary of direct labor costs, fringe benefits, and indirect costs
associated with labor (travel, room, etc.) to be used in a contract bid.

MODEL REPORT #24-8

Key Use of Report:

A worksheet used to compile the material portion of a contract bid.

Suggested Routing:

Project Manager.

Frequency of Preparation:

Every job requiring a bid.

Exhibit 24-9
UNIT COST REPORT

Description		1 Units	2 Bid Units	3 Actual Units to Date	4 % 2 divided by 3	5 Bid Labor	6 Bid Labor To Date 4 x 5	7 Actual Labor to Date	8 Actual Labor Over (under) Budget 6 - 7	9 Bid Labor Per Unit 5 divided by 2	10 Actual Labor Per Unit 7 divided by 3
Gravel		CY	900	900	100%	3,625	3,625	3,400	(225)	4.03	3.78
Sand		CY	1,050	1,050	100%	4,250	4,250	4,000	(250)	4.05	3.81
Blacktop		CY	490	--	0	3,900	--	125	125	7.96	--
Edging		LF	8,350	2,700	32.3%	8,345	2,695	2,950	255	1.00	1.09
Finishing		SF	42,300	8,140	19.2%	10,942	2,101	2,460	359	.26	.30

Analysis of bid units and bid labor per unit by project type.

MODEL REPORT #24-9

Key Use of Report:

Monitors actual versus bid labor per unit (pounds, square feet, cubic feet, height, and so on). It is a useful management control report.

Suggested Routing:

Project Manager.

Frequency of Preparation:

Monthly.

RETAILER REPORTING

Retail accounting is also a specialty calling for its own unique set of reports. Fundamentally, retailing management is concerned with merchandise planning and control. Total inventory investment, stock depth, and breadth of choice go into a merchandise budget that in turn goes into various operating reports and ultimately the financial statements. The 11 reports in this section highlight the key information retailers need to control operations most effectively. They are essential not only for top management, but also department managers, merchandise managers, and buyers.

Exhibit 25-1

MONTHLY OPERATING PLAN

	Current Month			Year to Date		
	Actual	Budget	Variance +(-)	Actual	Budget	Variance +(-)
Gross sales	$743,000	$765,000	$(22,000)	$2,143,000	$2,250,000	$(107,000)
Number of transactions	27,300	--	--	82,107	--	--
Average gross sale	27.22	--	--	26.10	--	--
Markdown & allowances	(17,900)	(18,500)	600	(56,700)	(60,000)	3,300
Employee discounts	(8,375)	(9,000)	625	(14,350)	(13,000)	(1,350)
Returns	(13,500)	(15,000)	1,500	(32,500)	(33,500)	1,000
Net sales	703,225	722,500	(19,275)	2,039,450	2,143,500	104,050
Retail purchases at cost	331,500	337,000	5,500	960,000	1,009,780	49,780
Cash discounts	(3,950)	(4,500)	(550)	(8,320)	(9,000)	(680)
Inventory shortage & shrinkage	(9,230)	(10,000)	(770)	(14,650)	(15,750)	(1,100)
Retail stock-B.O.P. at cost	862,000	862,000	--	1,076,970	1,076,970	--
Retail stock-E.O.P. at cost	(750,500)	(742,000)	8,500	(750,500)	(742,000)	8,500
Cost of sales	429,820	442,500	12,680	1,263,500	1,320,000	56,500
Gross profit	273,405	280,000	(6,595)	775,950	823,500	(47,550)
Space charges - stores	18,500	18,000	(500)	50,500	52,000	1,500
- warehouse	9,430	10,000	570	26,000	24,000	(2,000)
Taxes and insurance	3,400	4,000	600	9,550	9,000	(550)
Maintenance	6,250	5,000	(1,250)	19,500	21,000	1,500
Newspaper advertising	44,000	45,000	1,000	120,000	110,000	(10,000)
Advertising preparation	4,850	3,000	(1,850)	15,000	14,300	(700)
Windows	2,500	3,000	500	7,675	8,000	325
Other publicity	2,150	2,000	(150)	4,835	3,000	(1,835)
Receiving and marking	3,705	3,000	(705)	10,250	11,000	750
Delivery	750	1,000	250	1,285	2,000	715
Direct selling	3,852	3,000	(852)	9,550	10,000	450
Stock and clerical	6,358	6,500	142	18,550	17,500	(1,050)
Mail and telephone orders	1,430	1,500	70	2,956	2,000	(956)
Cashier	10,810	10,000	(810)	33,500	30,000	(3,500)
Packaging	7,825	8,000	175	25,200	25,000	(200)
Buying expenses	7,380	9,000	1,620	14,820	13,000	(1,820)
Returns to vendor	3,950	3,000	(950)	10,100	9,000	(1,100)
Other	6,520	2,000	(4,520)	8,230	6,500	(1,730)
Total controllable expenses	143,660	137,000	(6,660)	387,501	367,300	(20,201)
Fixed expenses	63,500	63,500	--	190,500	190,500	--
Total expenses						
Net profit	$66,245	$79,500	$(13,255)	$197,949	$265,700	$(67,751)

Monthly actual profit and loss compared to budget, formatted using reporting conventions unique to a retailing operation.

MODEL REPORT #25-1

Key Use of Report:

Shows actual operating results of each merchandising department for management review and corrective action if necessary.

Suggested Routing:

V.P. Merchandising, Department Managers, Buyers.

Frequency of Preparation:

Monthly.

Exhibit 25-2

MERCHANDISE PLAN—VERSION I

Current Year Budget	Sales	End of Period Inventory	Markdowns $	Markdowns %	Shrinkage $	Shrinkage %	Allowance & Discounts $	Allowance & Discounts %	Purchases	Initial Markup Percent %	Gross Margin $	Gross Margin %
June - Dec.	$1,400,000	$325,000	$70,000	5%	$15,400	1.1%	$21,000	1.5%	$1,650,000	40%	$518,000	37%
July - Jan.	1,200,000	199,000	72,000	6%	12,000	1	18,000	1.5	1,325,000	40	408,000	34
Aug. - Feb.	985,000	190,000	59,100	6%	9,850	1	14,775	1.5	1,040,000	40	344,750	35
Sept. - Mar.	960,000	210,000	57,600	6%	9,600	1	14,400	1.5	1,025,000	40	336,000	35
Oct. - April	1,040,000	260,000	62,400	6%	10,400	1	15,600	1.5	1,110,000	40	364,000	35
Nov. - May	1,065,000	310,000	63,900	6%	10,650	1	15,975	1.5	1,120,000	40	383,400	36

MODEL REPORT #25-2

Key Use of Report:

Furnishes budgeted purchases and estimated gross margins for management planning and review.

Suggested Routing:

Department Manager, Buyer.

Frequency of Preparation:

Monthly.

Alternative Reports:

Model Report #25-3.

Current merchandise plan in six-month intervals showing sales, inventory levels, markdowns, shrinkage, allowances and discounts, purchases, markups, and gross margins.

Exhibit 25-3

MERCHANDISE PLAN—VERSION II

		Sept.	Oct.	Nov.	Dec.	Seasonal Total
1.	Budgeted beginning inventory	$118,000	$165,000	$230,000	$432,000	$118,000
2.	Budgeted sales	410,000	685,000	1,350,000	730,000	3,175,000
3.	Budgeted reductions:					
	Employee discounts	1,200	2,850	4,875	3,760	12,685
	Shortages	2,650	3,900	5,010	4,460	16,020
	Markdowns	1,650	2,975	3,850	14,375	22,850
	Total	5,500	9,725	13,735	22,595	51,555
4.	Budgeted ending inventory	165,000	230,000	432,000	400,000	400,000
5.	Budgeted retail purchases	462,500	759,725	1,565,735	720,595	3,508,555
	2+3+4-1					
6.	Purchases at cost (65%)	300,625	493,821	1,017,727	468,386	2,280,559
	5 x .65					
7.	Cumulative markup	161,875	265,904	548,008	252,209	1,227,996
	5 - 6					
8.	Budgeted gross profit	156,375	256,179	534,273	229,614	1,176,441
	7 - 3					

Current merchandise plan by month showing inventory levels, sales, budgeted reductions, purchases, markups, and gross profit.

MODEL REPORT #25-3

Key Use of Report:

Provides monthly budgeted purchases and estimated gross profit for management planning and review.

Suggested Routing:

Department Manager, Buyer.

Frequency of Preparation:

Monthly.

Alternative Reports:

Model Report #25-2.

Exhibit 25-4

SUMMARY STOCK REPORT

```
  1. Planned end-of-month stock                    $168,540
  2. Open to buy planned sales                       362,500
  3.        Total (1 + 2)                             531,040
  4. Actual sales for the month                       148,120
  5. Stock on hand today                              143,220
  6. Outstanding orders as of today                   232,400
  7.        Total (4 + 5 + 6)                          523,740

        Overbought _____ Open to buy  ✔  for
        the month (3 - 7)                               7,300

     Planned sales for the month                       362,500
     To reach planned sales daily sales for
        balance of month must average                   13,400
     Last year's month-to-date sales                   127,150
     Deliveries since last report                      298,200
     Deliveries current month-to-date                  148,120
     Planned markup % on current month purchases         50%
     Actual markup % on current month sales             48.3%
     Actual markup % on last year's current
        month sales                                     49.1%
     Current month actual markdowns                      2,980
     Last year current month actual markdowns            4,620



              (All figures are at retail)
```

Analysis of inventory on hand, orders, planned sales, deliveries, markups, and markdowns.

MODEL REPORT #25-4

Key Use of Report:

Itemizes inventory (at retail prices) activity for the period which is a vital piece of information in operating an effective retail business.

Suggested Routing:

Department Manager, Buyer.

Frequency of Preparation:

Monthly.

Exhibit 25-5

STOCK TURNOVER RATE

Department	Stockturn	Percentage of Sales Total	Sales in Dollars	Average Stock at Retail
A	8.0	17%	$58,275	$7,285
B	7.5	11%	39,100	5,213
C	5.1	13%	46,520	9,122
D	9.0	12%	42,390	4,710
E	4.3	19%	68,123	15,843
F	7.8	28%	97,840	12,543
	6.4	100%	$352,248	$54,716

Analysis by department showing how many times inventory turned over, sales dollars, and average stock at retail.

MODEL REPORT #25-5

Key Use of Report:

Measures the degree of balance between inventory and sales. It shows the number of times during a given period that inventory is sold and replaced.

Suggested Routing:

Department Manager, Buyer.

Frequency of Preparation:

Monthly.

Exhibit 25-6
SLOW MOVING MERCHANDISE REPORT

Class	Less Than 3 Months			3-6 Months			More Than 6 Months			Total		
	Beginning $ of Season on Hand	Currently on Hand	% Reduction	Beginning $ of Season on Hand	Currently on Hand	% Reduction	Beginning $ of Season on Hand	Currently on Hand	% Reduction	Beginning $ of Season on Hand	Currently on Hand	% Reduction
Warmup jackets	$6,250	$3,945	37%	$2,970	$1,270	57%	$1,420	$382	73%	$10,640	$5,597	47%
Sweat suits	7,320	4,860	34	3,742	1,210	68	580	195	66	11,642	6,265	46
Singlets	5,235	3,902	26	1,838	810	56	395	--	100	7,468	4,712	37
Running shorts - Class A	3,890	2,750	29	2,430	975	60	295	--	100	6,615	3,725	44
Running shorts - Class B	2,970	1,260	58	1,638	1,110	32	575	230	60	5,183	2,600	50
Running shorts - Class C	4,265	1,290	70	2,050	720	65	960	385	60	7,275	2,395	67
Gloves	1,395	540	61	420	155	63	55	--	100	1,870	695	63
Sweaters	2,760	1,207	56	897	350	61	640	410	36	4,297	1,967	54
	$34,085	$19,754	42%	$15,985	$6,600	59%	$4,920	$1,602	67%	$54,990	$27,956	49%

Ageing by product showing beginning-of-the-season inventory and remaining inventory currently held.

MODEL REPORT #25-6

Key Use of Report:

Itemizes slow-moving inventory for management analysis and planning.

Suggested Routing:

Department Manager, Buyer.

Frequency of Preparation:

Monthly.

Exhibit 25-7

RETAIL INVENTORY METHOD REPORT

Item	1 Cost	2 Retail	3 Markup
1. Beginning inventory (lines 11 & 13 from preceding month's statement)	$86,000	$145,000	$59,000
2. Net purchases	690,000	1,100,000	410,000
3. Freight in	32,500		(32,500)
4. Additional markups	--	22,300	22,300
5. Total goods available for sale (1+2+3+4)	$808,500	1,267,300	$458,800
6. Net sales		1,030,000	
7. Net markdowns		72,500	
8. Employee discounts		8,220	
9. Total retail deduction (6+7+8)		1,110,720	
10. Ending inventory at retail (col. 2, item 5 less item 9)		$156,580	
11. Ending inventory at estimated cost $156,580 x 63.8% ($808,500 divided by $1,267,300)	$99,898		
12. Cost of goods sold (col. 1, item 5 less item 11)	$708,602		

Traditional retail inventory calculation showing total goods available for sale, ending inventory at retail, and cost of goods sold.

MODEL REPORT #25-7

Key Use of Report:

Provides an efficient means of valuing a retailer's ending inventory. It permits a realistic valuation of the ending inventory without going through the time and expense of taking a physical inventory. Instead the valuation is done by applying cost percentages to the book inventory at retail.

Suggested Routing:

V.P. Merchandising, Department Manager.

Frequency of Preparation:

Monthly.

Exhibit 25-8

OPEN-TO-BUY REPORT

Description	Total	Class A	Class B	Class C
Budgeted closing inventory	$496,500	$135,000	$263,000	$98,500
Budgeted sales	666,000	213,000	295,000	158,000
Total stock required	1,162,500	348,000	558,000	256,500
Opening inventory on hand	486,630	149,250	223,000	114,380
Budgeted purchases	675,870	198,750	335,000	142,120
Outstanding orders	525,355	143,550	248,970	132,835
Open to buy	$150,515	$55,200	$86,030	$9,285

Summary by department of budgeted closing inventory, sales, stock requirements, budgeted purchases, outstanding orders, and open to buy.

MODEL REPORT #25-8

Key Use of Report:

Shows outstanding purchase orders and the current unspent balance in the purchases account (open to buy). This report is commonly used to help regulate purchases.

Suggested Routing:

Buyers.

Frequency of Preparation:

Weekly.

Exhibit 25-9

OPEN-TO-ORDER CONTROL REPORT

Merchandise Classification	Planned Quarterly Sales	Planned Stock Beg. of Qua.	Planned Stock End of Qua.	Total Planned Purchases	Planned Purchases By Month May	June	July
A	$862,000	$381,000	$176,000	$657,000	$395,000	$200,000	$62,000
B	529,000	340,000	210,000	399,000	265,000	79,000	55,000
C	610,000	367,500	205,000	447,500	310,000	95,000	42,500
D	322,000	132,500	98,000	287,500	155,000	95,000	37,500
E	142,000	162,000	50,000	30,000	20,000	10,000	--
F	101,000	75,000	40,000	66,000	35,000	20,000	11,000
	$2,566,000	$1,458,000	$779,000	$1,887,000	$1,180,000	$499,000	$208,000

Planned sales, stock levels, and monthly purchases by merchandise classification.

MODEL REPORT #25-9

Key Use of Report:

Analyzes total planned purchases by month as a means of budgeting and monitoring purchasing activity.

Suggested Routing:

V.P. Merchandising, Department Manager, Buyer.

Frequency of Preparation:

Monthly.

Exhibit 25-10
STOCK STATUS REPORT

Dept.	Mfg.	Price	Style	Weeks In Stock	Weeks Since Last Receipt	Current Season	Previous 2 Periods 2	Previous 2 Periods 1	Current Period	Today	On Hand	On Order
							Sales					
10	167	9.95	2110	6	4	48	3	8	10	2	42	—
10	167	9.95	2320	2	5	52	16	14	5	—	11	40
10	167	13.95	2620	3	4	73	10	18	27	1	28	30
10	167	16.95	2695	5	3	25	5	9	3	1	16	45
10	124	22.00	980	2	5	38	7	8	15	2	12	50
10	124	24.50	1020	5	6	47	10	12	11	1	38	20
10	124	29.90	1145	5	6	62	12	18	16	—	47	—
10	124	29.90	1165	4	6	40	5	9	17	1	52	—
10	124	32.50	1325	6	2	25	6	5	6	—	60	—

Analysis of unit inventory including stock on hand, sales, and outstanding orders.

MODEL REPORT #25-10

Key Use of Report:

Provides inventory unit control and tracks stock activity within each department.

Suggested Routing:

Buyer.

Frequency of Preparation:

Weekly.

Exhibit 25-11
PRICE LINE REPORT

Dept.	Class	Price	Store #	Current Year Sales		Prior Year Sales				On Hand	Merchandise On Order	Total
				Last Month	Current Month to Date	Current Month	Next Month	Month After Next	Total			
10	32	19.50	1	58	27	47	53	68	168	89	60	149
			2	73	38	61	67	61	189	67	100	167
			3	37	25	52	41	39	132	105	--	105
				168	90	160	161	168	489	261	160	421
10	32	29.95	1	42	56	48	50	42	140	114	--	114
			2	29	38	42	51	56	149	105	--	105
			3	28	18	32	20	27	79	82	50	132
				99	112	122	121	125	368	301	50	351
10	32	32.95	1	17	25	28	32	33	93	85		85
			2	23	13	21	16	39	76	69	50	119
			3	20	27	21	20	25	66	29	80	109
				60	65	70	68	97	235	183	130	313

Summary of current year sales, prior year sales, and merchandise on hand and on order.

MODEL REPORT #25-11

Key Use of Report:

Segregates unit sales activity by sales price as a means of monitoring which priced merchandise sells the best and adjusting future inventory "buys" to accommodate the trend.

Suggested Routing:

Department Manager, Buyers.

Frequency of Preparation:

Monthly.

SERVICE COMPANY REPORTING

Service company accounting is a third specialty relying on its own singular set of reports. In service organizations the main emphasis is on controlling the performance of employees. Their utilization—i.e., chargeability to clients—is the foremost factor in determining a service firm's profitability. The exhibits in this section focus on how to monitor this critical requirement as well as how to construct an operating statement, budgets, and a summary staffing analysis.

Exhibit 26-1

OPERATING STATEMENT

Description	Current Month			Year to Date		
	Actual	Budget	Variance + (-)	Actual	Budget	Variance + (-)
Net billings	$262,000	$290,000	$(28,000)	$1,120,000	$1,165,000	$(45,000)
Cost of billings - standard	146,720	162,400	15,680	492,800	512,600	19,800
Standard Gross profit	115,280	127,600	(12,320)	627,200	642,400	(25,200)
Fee gain / (loss)	(3,950)	(1,500)	(2,450)	(8,420)	(6,000)	(2,420)
Project budget variances	11,200	5,000	6,200	5,200	10,000	(4,800)
Project expenses written off	(2,250)	(2,500)	250	(3,150)	(4,200)	1,050
Actual gross profit	120,280	128,600	(8,320)	620,830	652,200	(31,370)
Expenses - professional time:						
Vacation	3,950	3,000	(950)	11,075	12,500	1,425
Sick pay	1,100	750	(350)	2,200	4,000	1,800
Business promotion	12,500	10,000	(2,500)	38,550	40,000	1,450
Training	5,950	6,000	50	23,100	24,000	900
Professional development	8,300	7,500	(800)	29,750	26,000	(3,750)
Unassigned time	2,000	3,500	1,500	9,900	12,000	2,100
Other	1,400	1,000	(400)	7,325	5,000	(2,325)
	35,200	31,750	(3,450)	121,900	123,500	1,600
Expenses - administrative:						
Office salaries	6,750	6,750	--	27,000	27,000	--
Office supplies	1,250	1,500	250	7,040	6,000	(1,040)
Occupancy	8,310	8,300	(10)	34,050	35,000	950
Office services	6,275	6,700	425	26,875	27,500	625
Other	1,215	1,000	(215)	6,980	4,000	(2,980)
	23,800	24,250	450	101,945	99,500	(2,445)
Distributable income	$61,280	$72,600	$(11,320)	$396,985	$429,200	$(32,215)

Monthly and year-to-date profit and loss statements compared to budget formatted, using reporting conventions unique to service companies.

MODEL REPORT #26-1

Key Use of Report:

Shows actual operating results of a service company for management evaluation and action if necessary.

Suggested Routing:

Top Management.

Frequency of Preparation:

Monthly.

Exhibit 26-2

EMPLOYEE PERFORMANCE REPORT

| Employee | Hours | | | Chargeable % | | Billing Rate | Fees Generated | Monthly Salary | Utilization Rate (a) |
	Standard	Actual	Chargeable	Nonchargeable	To Standard	To Total				
S. Pederson	80	77	65	12	81%	84%	$40	$2,600	$3,250	.80
W. Meyers	80	75	71	4	89	95	40	2,840	3,200	.89
T. Cass	80	80	50	30	63	63	37	1,850	2,500	.74
E. Mason	80	80	63	17	79	79	35	2,205	2,300	.96
P. Larson	80	80	43	37	54	54	33	1,419	2,000	.71
S. Richards	50	50	38	12	76	76	28	1,064	1,125	.95
	450	442	330	112	73%	75%	$36.30	$11,978	$14,375	.83

(a) Fees divided by monthly salary

Analysis by employee showing chargeable and nonchargeable hours, billing rates, fees generated, monthly salary, and utilization rate.

MODEL REPORT #26-2

Key Use of Report:

Measures the overall performance of employees as a means of evaluating staffing needs, productivity, and effectiveness.

Suggested Routing:

Top Management.

Frequency of Preparation:

Monthly.

Exhibit 26-3

TASK BUDGET

Task	Partner	Man Hours Required Manager	Senior	Junior	$ Budget (1)
General audit administration	3	6			$720
Correspondence	1	2	4		420
Internal control		1	3	14	625
Workpaper review	4	8	10		1,410
Audit procedures:					
Cash			1	2	105
Receivables			1	4	165
Inventories		1	8	24	1,150
Liabilities			6	20	870
Stockholders' equity		1	5	1	325
Income statement			7	10	615
Report preparation	2	3	16	4	1,250
Conferences	2	4	6	5	900
	12	26	67	84	$8,555

(1) Partner $100 hr.
(2) Manager   70 hr.
(3) Senior   45 hr.
(4) Junior   30 hr.

Manhours required by job task for each employee level (partner, manager, senior, junior) and total budget dollars by task.

MODEL REPORT #26-3

Key Use of Report:

Details total budgeted hours and dollars for a specific job. It is used to monitor and evaluate progress on a project.

Suggested Routing:

Top Management.

Frequency of Preparation:

Each time a job is planned.

Exhibit 26-4
STAFFING TABLE

Employee	Total Available Hours	Less: Estimated Time Off	Net Available Hours	Estimated Chargeable Rate	Chargeable Hours	Cost per Hour Salary	Overhead	Total	Hourly Billing Rate	Total Billing Value
Al Haman	2,080	175	1,905	65%	1,238	$68	$10	$78	$105	$129,990
Robert Sheman	2,080	140	1,940	75%	1,455	50	10	60	75	109,125
Gayle Allen	2,080	85	1,995	75%	1,496	48	10	58	70	104,720
Bob Johnson	2,080	80	2,000	80%	1,600	28	10	38	60	96,000
Tom Olson	975	5	970	90%	873	20	10	30	30	26,190
Harold Solberg	550	5	545	90%	491	20	10	30	30	14,750
			9,355	77%	7,153				$67	$480,755

MODEL REPORT #26-4

Key Use of Report:

Summary of net available hours, estimated chargeable percentage, chargeable hours, cost per hour, and total billing value by employee.

Provides staffing availability for the upcoming year. It is used as a planning aid in staffing the year's workload.

Suggested Routing:

Top Management.

Frequency of Preparation:

Annually.

Exhibit 26-5

MONTHLY PROJECT BUDGET REPORT

Task	Budgeted Dollars	% Complete	Earned Dollars	Cost of Billings	Contract over (under) Budget
Initial data gathering	$ 5,000	100%	$ 5,000	$ 5,600	$600
Field interviews	4,250	95%	4,038	4,250	212
Financial modeling	14,850	40%	5,940	5,800	(140)
Package design	11,275	10%	1,128	1,150	22
Field testing	7,825	3%	235	200	(35)
Documentation	8,900	2%	178	100	(78)
Modification	4,000	--	--		
Training	3,900	--	--	350	350
Final evaluation	2,850	--	--		
Field implementation	8,500	--	--		
Cleanup	3,000	--	--		
Followup review/meetings	4,000	--	--		
	$78,350		$16,519	$17,450	$931

Budgeted dollars, earned dollars, cost of billings, and percent complete by job task.

MODEL REPORT #26-5

Key Use of Report:

Measures activity to date on a specific contract as a means of evaluating progress compared to plan.

Suggested Routing:

Project Manager or Partner.

Frequency of Preparation:

Monthly.

Exhibit 26-6

REPORT OF BUDGET CHARTING RATES

Employee Classification	Job Rates Per Hour			
	Salary	Fringes	Overhead (a)	Total
Intern	$6	$1	$7	$14
Trainee	9	1	10	20
Junior	10	1	10	21
Senior	12	2	12	26
Supervisor	16	2	15	33
Manager	20	2	18	40
Shareholder - Junior	27	3	25	55
Shareholder - Senior	46	5	42	93

(a) Includes administrative expenses and billing profit.

Buildup of job rates per hour by employee classification.

MODEL REPORT #26-6

Key Use of Report:

Itemizes hourly pay rates of employees to be used for bidding jobs during the current period.

Suggested Routing:

Top Management.

Frequency of Preparation:

Updated anytime salaries, fringes, or overhead changes.

MISCELLANEOUS REPORTS

Every firm from time to time has various miscellaneous reporting requirements. Several of the more common ones are included in this section. In total they cover a wide range of potential report needs all the way from an Automobile Analysis to Stock Options and will benefit the user accordingly.

Exhibit 27-1

SUMMARY OF LEASED PREMISES

Location/Description	Sq. Feet	Lease Dates From	Lease Dates To	NNN Lease Y=YES N=No	Minimum Lease Payments 198	198	198	198	198	198	Options
Production Plant #3 2310 Willow St. Dallas, Texas	130,000	6/1/8	5/31/8	Y	$ 82,000	$ 82,000	$ 82,000	$ 82,000	$ 82,000	$41,000	No Options
Warehouse #1 5201 E. 15th S. Louisville, Kentucky	79,000	10/31/8	10/31/8	Y Except R.E. Taxes	60,000	60,000	60,000	60,000	60,000	35,000	Option to purchase at appraised value
Semi Truck & Trailer S.N. 8327585	-	6/15/8	6/15/8	Y	2,700	4,250	4,250	4,250	1,550	-	One 2 year option at same terms
Total minimum payments					$144,700	$146,250	$146,250	$143,550		$76,000	

Analysis of each company lease showing location, square footage, lease dates, options, and minimum lease payments.

MODEL REPORT #27-1

Key Use of Report:

Documents all facilities and equipment under long-term leases (more than one year) for management reference. If a company requires an outside audit, this schedule will be needed by the auditors.

Suggested Routing:

Administrative Manager, Property Manager.

Frequency of Preparation:

Updated each time a new lease is entered into.

Exhibit 27-2

SUMMARY STOCK OPTION LEDGER REPORT

Transaction Date	Type of Transaction (a)	Number of Shares	Balance Exercisable Now	Future
3/1/84	Grant	1,000		1,000
1/1/85	Grant	2,000		3,000
3/1/85	Portion Exercis.		200	2,800
1/1/86	Portion Exercis.		600	2,400
3/1/86	Portion Exercis.		800	2,200
3/10/86	100% Split	3,000	1,600	4,400
6/15/86	Exercised	(1,000)	600	4,400
8/19/86	Exercised	(600)	-	4,400
9/10/86	Grant	1,000	-	5,400
1/1/87	Portion Exercis.		200	5,200

(a) Option prices are detailed on individual employee ledger sheets.

Analysis of options showing transaction date, type of transaction, number of shares, and balance exercisable now and in the future.

MODEL REPORT #27-2

Key Use of Report:

Lists all stock option activity for analysis and control purposes.

Suggested Routing:

Administrative Manager.

Frequency of Preparation:

Updated each time stock option activity takes place.

Exhibit 27-3
EXPENSE REPORT

EXPENSE ACCOUNT
(SEE REVERSE FOR INSTRUCTIONS AND OTHER DETAILS)

NAME _____ TITLE _____

EXPENSES FOR PERIOD FROM _____ THROUGH _____ DATE PREPARED _____

PURPOSE OF TRIP AND/OR EXPENSE _____

_____

_____

DATE	TOWN	SUBSISTENCE		TRANSPORTATION			TOTAL	ACCOUNT CHARGED
		LODGING AND TIPS	MEALS AND TIPS	CODE OR MILES	WII CR. CARD CHARGE	ALL OTHER PAID BY TRAVELER		
SUBTOTAL								

CASH ADVANCE		LIMOUSINE OR TAXI		FROM REVERSE SIDE
TRANSPORTATION		TELEPHONE AND TELEGRAM TOLLS		FROM REVERSE SIDE
OTHER		TRAVELERS CHECK FEES		
TOTAL ADVANCES		TECHNICAL MEETING FEES		
LESS: TOTAL EXPENSE ACCOUNT		CUSTOMER CONFERENCE EXPENSES		ATTACH FORM EXP-1A
AMOUNT DUE TRAVELER		MISCELLANEOUS EXPENSES		EXPLAIN UNDER REMARKS
AMOUNT DUE WII (REMIT)		TOTAL EXPENSE ACCOUNT		

ANY BALANCE DUE WII MUST ACCOMPANY THIS REPORT	SIGNATURES	DATE
TRANSPORTATION CODES: A - RENTED AUTO	TRAVELER:	
AT - AIR TRAVEL G - GASOLINE	APPROVAL:	
GP - GARAGE, PARKING, AND TOLL FEES	AUDITOR:	

FORM EXP-1 (REV 10/83)

Exhibit 27-3 (continued)
EXPENSE REPORT

\<center\>TELEPHONE AND TELEGRAM TOLLS\</center\>			
DATE	PERSON CONTACTED AND AFFILIATION	ACCOUNT CHARGED	AMOUNT

\<center\>LIMOUSINE AND TAXI EXPENSE\</center\>			
DATE	FROM	TO	ACCOUNT CHARGED	AMOUNT

\<center\>REMARKS\</center\>			
DATE	EXPLAIN ANY UNUSUAL EXPENSES AND ANY APPARENT INCONSISTENCY IN ACCOUNT DISTRIBUTION WITH TIME REPORT	ACCOUNT CHARGED	AMOUNT

\<center\>WII CREDIT CARD CHARGES\</center\>			
DATE	EXPLAIN IN DETAIL ALL CREDIT CARD CHARGES	ACCOUNT CHARGED	AMOUNT

\<center\>EXPENSE DISTRIBUTION\</center\>			
DATE	JOB NUMBER	ACCOUNT CHARGED	AMOUNT

INSTRUCTIONS FOR PREPARATION OF EXPENSE ACCOUNT STATEMENTS

1. Expense accounts should be typewritten or prepared in ink and the original submitted to the Treasurer after approval by the department head, or his authorized representative.
2. Expense accounts must be submitted during the week after the traveler returns from his trip.
3. Employee must attach receipts for all hotels/motels, tolls, parking, etc.
4. In the event advances exceed expenses, a refund of the difference shall accompany this report.
5. When use of a personal auto is authorized, mileage is paid at the current rate specified by Winzen International, Inc.
6. Technical meeting fees -- report total registration fees paid for attendance at meetings.
7. Customer conference expenses are allowed only for Profiler or film sales and must be reported on Form EXP-1A.
8. All WII credit card charges must be listed and charge slips attached.

Exhibit 27-3 (continued)
EXPENSE REPORT

CUSTOMER CONFERENCE EXPENSE FORM

NAME _____ TITLE _____

EXPENSES FOR PERIOD FROM _____ THROUGH _____

DATE	AMOUNT	ACCOUNT CHARGED	NAME AND TITLE	AFFILIATION	OTHER WII EMPLOYEES	PLACE AND TYPE OF ENTERTAINMENT	PURPOSE

FORM EXP-1A (REV 10/83)

Detailed travel and entertainment expense report.

MODEL REPORT #27-3

Key Use of Report:

Used by employees to document their travel and entertainment expenses.

Suggested Routing:

For use by all employees making T & E expenditures.

Exhibit 27-4

PRODUCT PRICING REPORT

```
Product:  Model C-400-A

Suggested Retail Price:              $79.50
Dealer Price - 35%/10% Off List      46.51     41% Margin
Distributor Price                    37.20     20% Margin

                                  Amount Per
                                  Unit        Percent

Distributor Price                 $37.20      100%

Variable Production Costs          10.97       30
Variable Distribution Costs         7.84       21
        Variable Product Cost      18.81       51
Marginal Contribution             18.39       49

Fixed Costs:
        Promotion                   6.74       18
        General and Administration  8.45       23
Net Income                        $ 3.20        8%
```

Analysis of customer prices, variable and fixed costs, and net income
by product.

MODEL REPORT #27-4

Key Use of Report:

Allows management to evaluate the effects of various price and cost decisions on profits. This report is especially valuable when placed on a micro-computer where different variables can be quickly tested using "what if" analysis.

Suggested Routing:

Top Management, Marketing Manager, Sales Manager.

Frequency of Preparation:

Each time pricing and costs change.

Exhibit 27-5

MARKET/BUSINESS ANALYSIS—PRODUCT PERFORMANCE REPORT

	Product #1	Product #2	Product #3
Market:			
Market Size Overall	$145 MM	$1,000 MM	$400 MM
Estimated Annual Market Growth	7%	4%	8%
Business:			
Product Sales Volume	$3,500,000	$ 387,000	$1,100,000
Unit Sales Volume	2,750	210,000	242,000
Assets Employed	$ 875,000	$1,138,000	$ 589,000
Current Assets Employed	$ 530,000	$ 497,000	$ 351,000
Earnings After Tax	$ 110,000	$ 57,000	$ 152,000
Cash Flow	$ 159,000	$ 105,000	$ 203,000
Performance Measures:			
Market Share %	2.4%	-	.3%
Annual Product Sales Growth %	7%	13%	8%
Return on Sales	3.1%	14.7%	13.8%
Return on Assets	12.6%	5%	25.8%
Asset Turnover	4	.33	1.87
Cash Return on Assets %	18.2%	9.2%	34.5%

Analysis by product of market size and growth rate potential and current business performance levels.

MODEL REPORT #27-5

Key Use of Report:

Makes a business and market evaluation of how well existing products are doing for management analysis and planning. The more precise you can make the market data the more beneficial this report becomes because this information so often is a wild approximation.

Suggested Routing:

Top Management, Marketing Manager.

Frequency of Preparation:

Annually.

Exhibit 27-6

ADVERTISING AND SALES PROMOTION STATUS REPORT

Project	Project Budget	Actual Expen. Through Month End	Outstanding Purchase Orders	Total	Balance Left to Use or Reassign
Magazine Advertising:					
Plastic World	$12,500	$ 8,400	$ 1,410	$ 9,810	$ 2,690
Plastic Technology	8,000	6,920	2,150	9,070	(1,070)
Plastics Machinery	5,000	2,400	-	2,400	2,600
	25,500	17,720	3,560	21,280	4,220
Brochures:					
Corporate Update	14,300	-	12,350	12,350	1,950
	14,300	-	12,350	12,350	1,950
Trade Shows:					
Chicago	8,750	3,950	1,650	5,600	3,150
Denver	16,230	12,800	970	13,770	2,460
	24,980	16,750	2,620	19,370	5,610
Product Sheets:					
Model 10	2,150	1,940	-	1,940	210
Model 40A	1,360	1,620	100	1,720	(360)
	$68,290	$38,030	$18,630	$56,660	$11,630

Analysis by project of dollars budgeted, expended to date, outstanding purchase orders, and balance left to use or reassign.

MODEL REPORT #27-6

Key Use of Report:

Summarizes actual advertising and promotion activity compared to budget for all active projects. This is an important control report for management to use in evaluating current expenditures and the need for any modifications.

Suggested Routing:

Marketing Manager, Sales Manager.

Alternative Reports:

Model Report #5-9.

Exhibit 27-7

PROFIT CENTER "POINTS" ASSIGNMENT REPORT

	Points Assignment
Pretax Profit Performance:	
Pretax Profit:	
Exceeds prior year	2 points
Exceeds prior year by 20% or more	1
Exceeds prior year by 30% or more	1
Pretax profit as % of sales exceeds prior year	2
Pretax profit as % of profit center average assets exceeds prior year	2
Planning Performance:	
Pretax profit not less than 85% not more than 120% of budget	2
Pretax profit as % of sales not less than 90% of budget	2
Pretax profit as % of profit center average assets not less than 90% of budget	2
Asset Investment Performance:	
Cash accumulation over and above reinvestment needs exceeds budget	3
Cash accumulation over and above reinvestment needs exceeds budget by 20%	2
Accounts receivable turnover exceeds budget	2
Inventory turnover exceeds budget	2
Total Points	23 points

Note: Organizations weigh the various items according to what
they want to stress and base performance bonuses on
being able to achieve certain point levels. In the
above example, the firm was stressing cash accumulation
and weighed that point the heaviest. In this case, they
paid a 100% bonus to profit center managers if they
reached 20 points <u>and</u> had cash accumulation over and
above reinvestment needs that exceeded budget.

Listing of pretax profit, planning, and asset investment performance
criteria for bonus and incentive pay awards.

MODEL REPORT #27-7

Key Use of Report:

Used by Top Management to structure bonus plans for profit center managers.

Suggested Routing:

Top Management.

Frequency of Preparation:

Annually.

Exhibit 27-8

COMPANY AUTOMOBILE ANALYSIS REPORT

Vehicle #	Employee	Description	Initial Purchase Price	Quarterly Employee Payroll Deduction	Quarterly Odometer Reading Beginning	Ending	Usage	Average Total Cost Per Mile YTD	Miles/Gal YTD	Maintenance YTD
A-4	Bill Johnson	1980-300 CD Mercedes	$20,000	$150	63,249	65,505	2,256	$.29	10.9	$313.99
A-9	Phil Pauling	1981 Cutlass Wagon	6,268	62	106,984	111,489	4,505	.10	14.2	38.00
A-12	John Elden	1982 Ford Fairmont	7,445	75	52,847	59,701	6,854	.18	16.3	688.75
A-14	Pat McCormick	1981 Ford Granada	7,425	62	36,825	39,091	2,166	.10	15.1	35.00
A-16	Dick Zammira	1983 Chev. Celebrity	9,124	75	18,863	24,167	5,304	.06	21.0	14.70
A-23	Todd Kimbel	1983 Chev. Cavalier	7,513	75	20,715	27,282	6,567	.05	27.2	62.00

Analysis of company-owned automobiles detailing usage by quarter, average total cost per mile YTD, miles/gallon YTD, and maintenance YTD.

MODEL REPORT #27-8

Key Use of Report:

Measures the cost of maintaining a fleet of company vehicles.

Suggested Routing:

Top Management.

Frequency of Preparation:

Quarterly.

II

Graphics
and Charting Examples

TYPES OF GRAPHICS AND CHARTS

There are numerous kinds of graphics and charts available to managers, most of which are a variation of the nine basic types that follow in this Section. These examples epitomize the best in visuals. They are eye appealing, easy to comprehend, practice-tested, and allow the reader to quickly grasp the important points being made. Additionally, these examples have all stood the test of time. They have been in use for as long as visuals have been used in reporting.

Exhibit 28-1
LINE CHART—BASIC

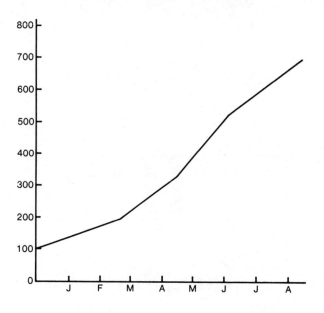

Exhibit 28-2
LINE CHART—CUMULATIVE

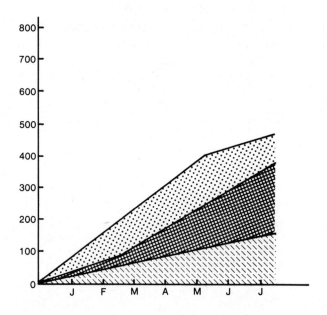

Exhibit 28-3
LINE CHART—SUPPLEMENTED WITH NUMERICS

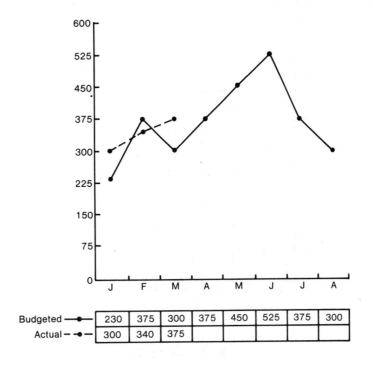

	J	F	M	A	M	J	J	A
Budgeted ——●—	230	375	300	375	450	525	375	300
Actual — ●—	300	340	375					

Exhibit 28-4
SURFACE CHART

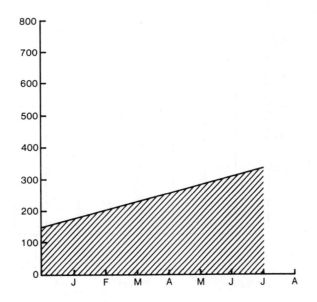

Exhibit 28-5
BAR CHART

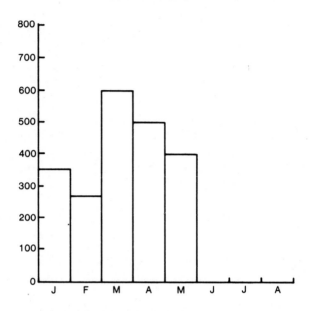

Exhibit 28-6
GROUPED BAR CHART

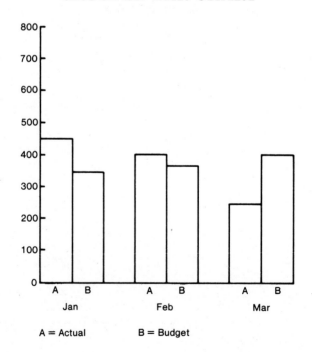

A = Actual   B = Budget

Exhibit 28-7
SYMBOL CHART

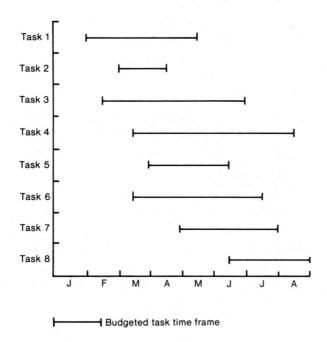

H——————H Budgeted task time frame

Exhibit 28-8
PIE CHART

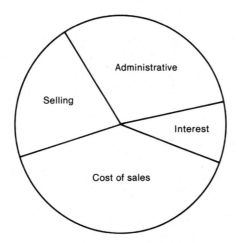

Exhibit 28-9
DEVIATION BAND SURFACE CHART

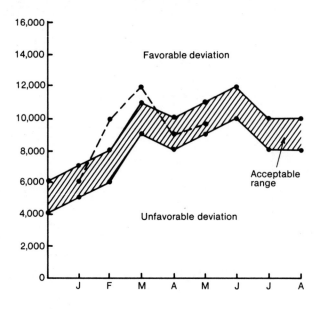

SPECIFIC GRAPHICS AND CHARTING EXAMPLES

The 29 examples that follow illustrate specific graphics and charts adaptable to your reporting system. They cover a wide range of possibilities to help you answer daily questions, in short- and long-range planning, and improving communications. They illustrate different combinations of the basic types of charts and graphs shown in Section 28.

Exhibit 29-1

BUDGET DETAIL

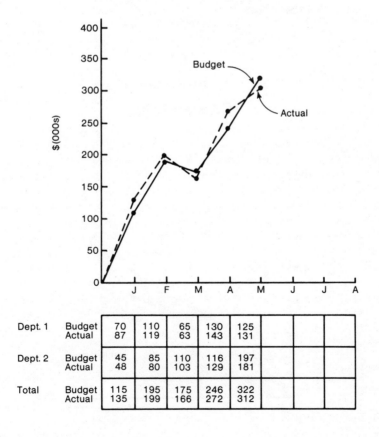

		J	F	M	A	M			
Dept. 1	Budget	70	110	65	130	125			
	Actual	87	119	63	143	131			
Dept. 2	Budget	45	85	110	116	197			
	Actual	48	80	103	129	181			
Total	Budget	115	195	175	246	322			
	Actual	135	199	166	272	312			

Exhibit 29-2
ACTIVITY SUMMARY YEAR TO DATE

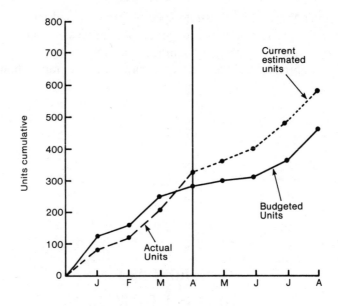

Exhibit 29-3
CASH FLOW

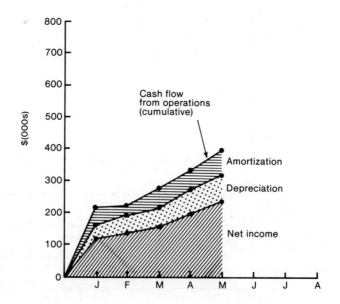

Exhibit 29-4
AVERAGE COLLECTION PERIOD OF RECEIVABLES

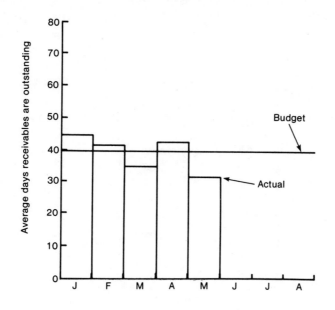

Exhibit 29-5
MAXIMUM/MINIMUM INVENTORY LEVELS

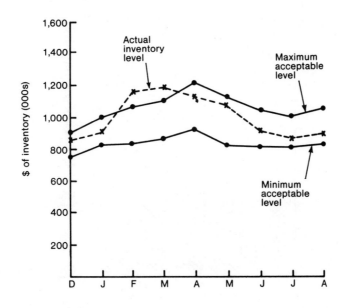

Exhibit 29-6

NUMBER OF DAYS SUPPLY IN INVENTORY

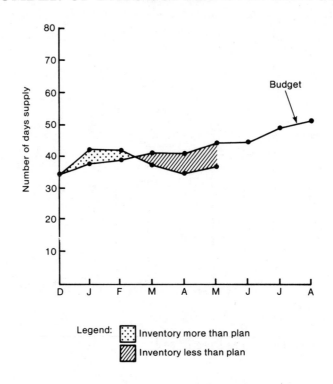

Legend: Inventory more than plan / Inventory less than plan

Exhibit 29-7

WORKING CAPITAL TURNOVER

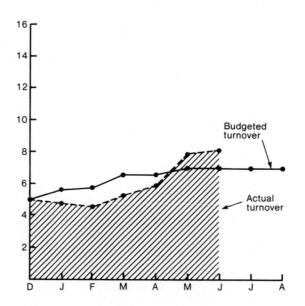

Exhibit 29-8
CURRENT RATIO

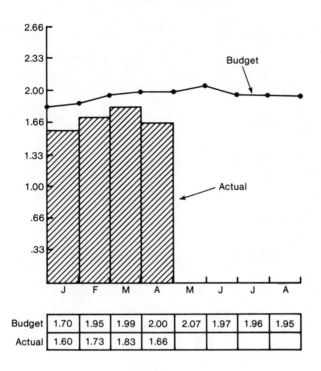

	J	F	M	A	M	J	J	A
Budget	1.70	1.95	1.99	2.00	2.07	1.97	1.96	1.95
Actual	1.60	1.73	1.83	1.66				

Exhibit 29-9
EQUIPMENT CAPACITY VS OUTPUT

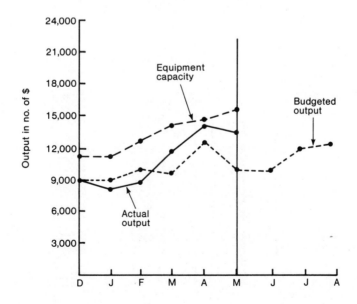

Exhibit 29-10

PLANT CAPACITY VS WORKLOAD

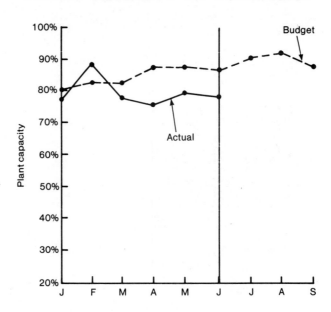

Exhibit 29-11

FIXED ASSETS TO NET WORTH

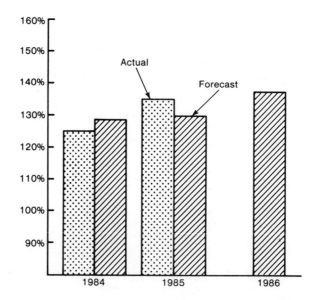

Exhibit 29-12
EQUIPMENT USAGE

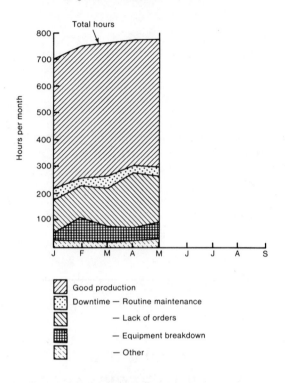

Good production
Downtime — Routine maintenance
— Lack of orders
— Equipment breakdown
— Other

Exhibit 29-13
TOTAL ASSETS

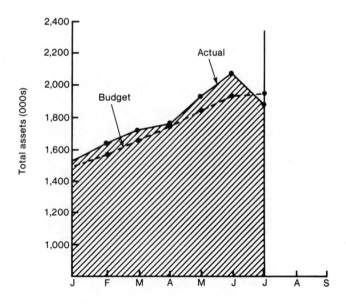

Exhibit 29-14
ASSETS PER EMPLOYEE

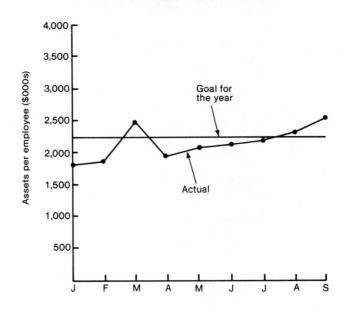

Exhibit 29-15
SALES TO RECEIVABLES

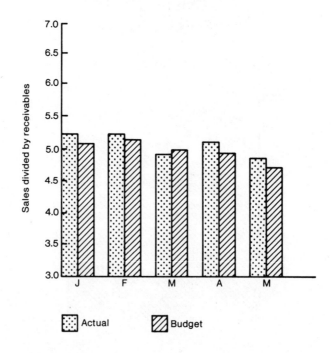

Exhibit 29-16
CUMULATIVE EXPENSES

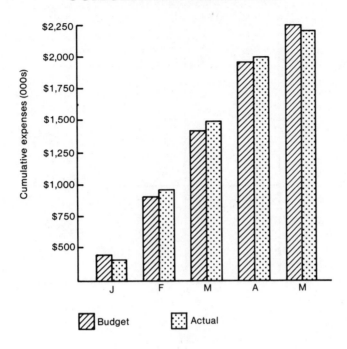

Exhibit 29-17
DETAILED COST COMPARISON

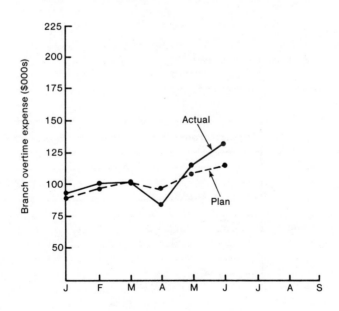

Exhibit 29-18
GROSS MARGIN

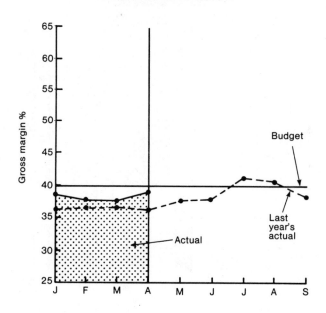

Exhibit 29-19

BALANCE SHEET RATIO PERFORMANCE

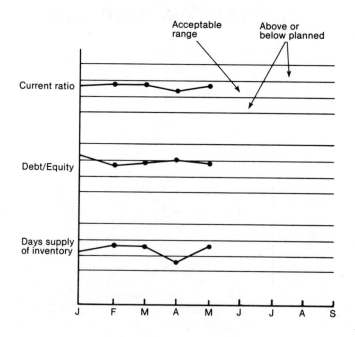

Exhibit 29-20

DISTRIBUTION OF INCOME

Exhibit 29-21

PROFIT AND LOSS

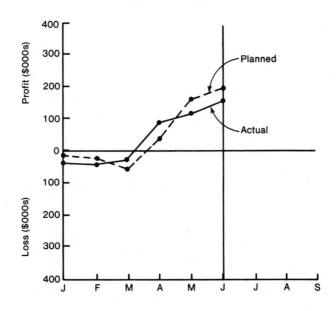

Exhibit 29-22
SALES AND PROFITS

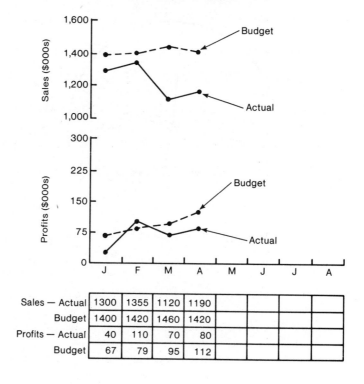

Sales — Actual	1300	1355	1120	1190				
Budget	1400	1420	1460	1420				
Profits — Actual	40	110	70	80				
Budget	67	79	95	112				

Exhibit 29-23
MANPOWER ANALYSIS

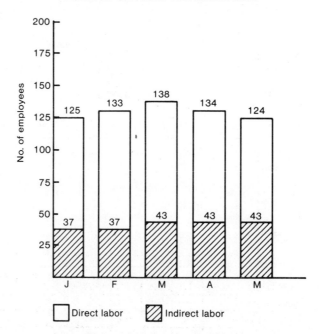

Exhibit 29-24
INVENTORY TURNOVER

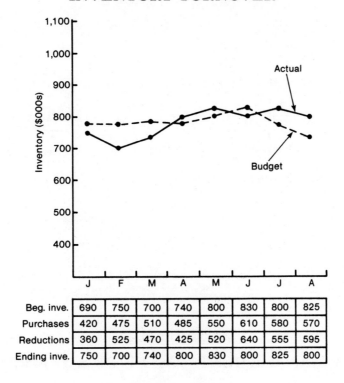

	J	F	M	A	M	J	J	A
Beg. inve.	690	750	700	740	800	830	800	825
Purchases	420	475	510	485	550	610	580	570
Reductions	360	525	470	425	520	640	555	595
Ending inve.	750	700	740	800	830	800	825	800

Exhibit 29-25
DEBT TO EQUITY RATIO

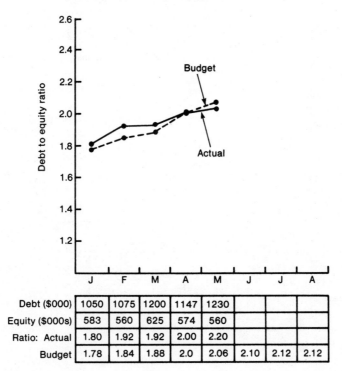

	J	F	M	A	M	J	J	A
Debt ($000)	1050	1075	1200	1147	1230			
Equity ($000s)	583	560	625	574	560			
Ratio: Actual	1.80	1.92	1.92	2.00	2.20			
Budget	1.78	1.84	1.88	2.0	2.06	2.10	2.12	2.12

Exhibit 29-26
QUALITY ASSURANCE

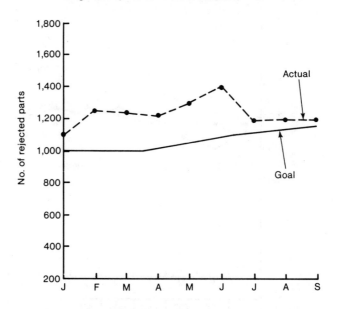

Exhibit 29-27
PROJECT MANAGEMENT—VALUE OF WORK PERFORMED

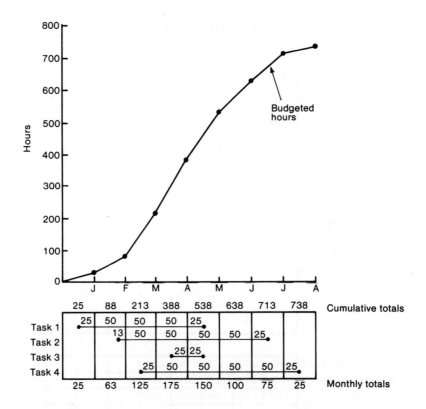

Exhibit 29-28
PROJECT MANAGEMENT—COST TO DATE VARIANCE

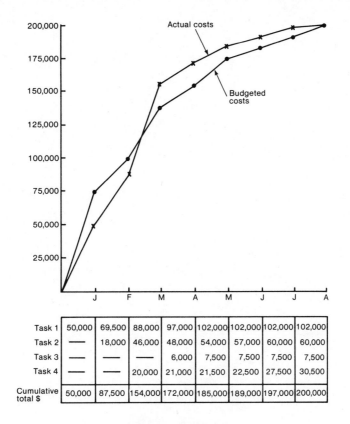

	J	F	M	A	M	J	J	A
Task 1	50,000	69,500	88,000	97,000	102,000	102,000	102,000	102,000
Task 2	—	18,000	46,000	48,000	54,000	57,000	60,000	60,000
Task 3	—	—	—	6,000	7,500	7,500	7,500	7,500
Task 4	—	—	20,000	21,000	21,500	22,500	27,500	30,500
Cumulative total $	50,000	87,500	154,000	172,000	185,000	189,000	197,000	200,000

Exhibit 29-29
PROJECT MANAGEMENT—TREND ANALYSIS

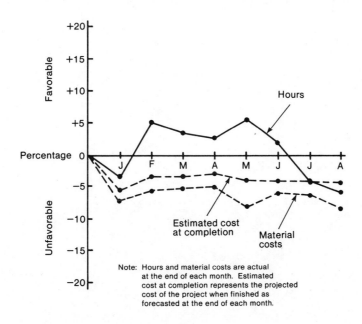

Note: Hours and material costs are actual at the end of each month. Estimated cost at completion represents the projected cost of the project when finished as forecasted at the end of each month.

III

How to Design Useful and Understandable Accounting Reports

Section 1

THE MECHANICS OF PRODUCING WINNING REPORTS THAT VIRTUALLY TALK TO MANAGEMENT

We live in an information age. Your firm has had to learn to manage large quantities of data that are often fragmented, constantly changing, and quickly obsolete. It has become as important a job as managing a firm's physical assets or people resources, yet more elusive. And computers, with their vast manipulative power and accessibility to hundreds of different data bases, have added to this "information overload."

The degree to which your firm succeeds in managing and reporting information, often is going to be the difference between profit or loss. Sloppy, ill-conceived reports have a negative impact on management. Recipients of such reports spend little time, if any, with them. Key data needed to make timely, informed decisions may be buried within such a report, but managers are not going to take the time to dig it out.

On the other hand, smartly designed reports that immediately capture the readers' attention, make a specific point, and do so quickly are the ones that will get used. They allow management to act on important matters *now* and not waste precious time trying to decipher what is important. There is no faster way to raise a manager's ire than to force him/her to untangle a web of data only to find that it falls within acceptable limits and does not require any action on his/her part.

We have all seen many examples of both types of reports. The obscure and wordy ones that challenge the reader to pick out key components, and the neatly assembled ones that quickly make a point as they virtually talk to management. There are 20 common characteristics of these winning reports, and having a thorough understanding of them is a decisive first step in improving companywide communications without a large investment of time or money. These 20 points should become second nature to all report preparers.

How to Construct Reports with an Impact

1. Do not hide key data in a report and expect readers to find it. They will not take the time to do it. Readers expect the preparer to do the work. How many times have you picked up a report and had to scan it high and low for its important point? It is frustrating and a waste of time.

2. Highlight key report data by boldly underlining them or somehow setting them off (indenting, italics). You may want to subdue secondary data to accomplish this.

3. Use 8½" X 11" paper.

4. Clearly label each report and make sure your caption is informative and tells exactly what the report contains.

5. Avoid small print in a report. It is difficult to read and hard on the eyes. For typewritten reports, pica type is more acceptable than the smaller elite type.

319

6. Use crisp, legible typeface. Script is out!

7. Leave plenty of white space at the top, bottom, and both edges. Margins should be at least 1⅛" to 1½".

8. Omit all cents. It is a rare report that needs accuracy down to the last penny.

9. Remove all unneeded numbers, subtotals, words, and other details. They blur a report's meaning and often lead to unnecessary questioning by readers as they analyze the content.

10. Initial and date (day, month, and year) all reports.

11. Show a report's distribution right on the face of the report.

12. Standardize a report's format. If it is prepared periodically, it should be structured the same way each time to facilitate comparisons and analysis.

13. Include a maximum of two minutes' worth of reading material in any uninterrupted portion of a report. If you have any more material than this, consider breaking it up into two or more sections. Tests have shown that two minutes is about the maximum concentration span of report readers before their minds wander.

14. Use columns rather than rows. Limit to three or a maximum of four, the number of columns in a particular grouping.

15. Refrain from including too much detail in the main body of your report, whether it is supporting numbers or narrative. It tends to slow the reader down and diffuse his/her focus from the key report elements. Detail is better left for exhibits and appendices.

16. Edit unnecessary duplication from reports. Detailed calculations or totals that are only for your benefit should be eliminated. Complete column headings should not be repeated if they are the same for each column. For example:

Incorrect	Sales Dollars 1984	Sales Dollars 1985	Sales Dollars 1986
Correct		Sales Dollars	
	1984	1985	1986

17. Avoid long, windy sentences, connectives, and a rambling narrative style often found in fiction. Keep descriptions, headings, titles, and sentences short and to the point. Use understandable wording, and be sure to put your report aside for a time after you have first prepared it. Picking it up again later, even if it is just a couple of hours, usually gives a fresh perspective and considerably eases your editing job.

18. Review all reports completely *before* they are distributed. This eliminates the embarrassment of having a report go out incomplete or with errors. Because many reports end up being prepared under tight deadlines, it is often difficult to review them thoroughly, but with careful planning this ongoing dilemma can at least be minimized.

19. If a report contains complicated material, it should not be distributed without letting the user know what is coming. This is often best accomplished by holding a short seminar or meeting to briefly overview the report's content.

20. Be imaginative. Do not get caught in the age-old rut: "We've always done it this way." Keep on the lookout for more effective ways to organize and present report material.

Example: I continually search current business literature and annual reports for better ways of doing things. Recently, I came across an understandable way to format a Statement of Changes in Financial Position. In the past I was continually having trouble constructing a funds flow statement that all managers could grasp. I immediately revised our company's funds flow reporting and quickly cleared up an age-old reporting problem.

How to Show Data the Same Way Managers Think About Their Operations

1. Limit a report's contents to a few key items.

Do not load up a report with numerous key points. Generally, a reader will successfully focus on one or two main ideas at most. If more are highlighted, they fail to catch the reader's attention.

2. Limit the numbers of reports a manager receives.

Just as too many items in a report will lose a reader, so will too many reports. It seems that many organizations, in an attempt to keep on top of the information "explosion," just keep grinding out report after report without ever stopping to think how inefficient and wasteful this practice is. Data becomes a blurred jumble, and readers quickly get worn down and lose track of which information is important and which is not. Limiting the number of reports to just the ones that are absolutely essential is an important step in keeping the reader focused on the key areas of his/her job.

3. Be careful when setting standards.

The most common method of evaluating actual results is to measure them against predetermined standards such as budgets, estimates, and so on. To have the intended impact, these standards not only must be thoughtfully developed, but they must be understood. The best way to accomplish this is to involve the employee directly responsible for the standard in the setting of the standard. For example, production managers, supervisors, and even foremen should be closely consulted when setting labor or piece rates. Their involvement will usually insure that they will take an ongoing interest in the standards because they "bought in" when they helped set them. They are more willing to be held accountable for performance because they actively participated in the process rather than sat idly by while top management dictated the planned numbers.

4. Sound a warning when management should take action.

In reviewing a report, managers do not have the time to think about and assimilate each piece of data. They should only be concerned with the most important information. When data falls outside acceptable parameters, a warning should be sounded alerting managers that there is a problem needing their attention. These warnings can take several forms such as asterisks or stars by the piece of information needing action or a written comment calling the manager's attention to the problem area. Whatever form this alert takes, it should be highlighted and easily identifiable. Also, managers must know that these particular messages call for their immediate action.

TIP: This last point is often overlooked. Reports are often circulated that flash various early warning alerts but are ignored by the reader because he/she is unaware that these problems require immediate action.

5. Use exception reporting whenever possible.

Reports that drone on with facts and figures are virtually useless as are reports that have so much crammed into them that you have to be a magician to sort out the pertinent information. Exception reporting reduces this problem. What exception reporting does is to highlight only good or bad results. This is the information a manager needs to be most concerned about. For instance, top management does not need to review actual results line item by line item. Most managers would be relieved if the reports they received highlighted only those items that were outside of acceptable limits. To institute this type of reporting means heavy initial involvement on both the report preparer's and user's part—the preparer to itemize what information is available and the user to decide what is important to see out of all the data that is available.

6. Highlight a report's results.

In addition to highlighting good or bad individual results, it is equally important to highlight the overall results of the report. In summary, what does the report show? Commonly, you will see a profit and loss statement that identifies major deviations from budget including the appropriate explanations for the individual deviations. But often these reports come to no overall conclusion. The reader is left hanging. Is the final result acceptable? In summary, what does the report say? Do the individual line item deviations add up to a favorable or unfavorable result?

TIP: Instead of highlighting the results at the end of a report, do it at the beginning. For example, in summarizing the important information from an updated balance sheet, consider starting with five or six important ratios (return on investment, return on assets, current ratio, inventory turn, etc.) before presenting the detailed balance sheet. This allows the user to obtain the "flavor" of the results before plowing through the entire balance sheet.

7. Conclude all reports with totals that are easily traceable to the next higher level of statements.

This goes without saying but is a common deficiency in many reporting systems. For instance, report totals of one department manager's operating statement did not readily agree with the P & L summary used by the General Manager without several reconciling entries. This was unnecessarily confusing and wasted precious time when they met monthly to go over their results.

8. Segregate controllable and uncontrollable expenses.

Costs that vary with production levels (variable costs), such as direct labor and materials, should be separated from costs that do not vary with production levels (fixed costs), such as rent, depreciation, and property taxes. Costs that are semi-variable should be divided into their fixed and variable components. Separating expenses is essential in determining a plant's or product's breakeven point. Additionally this cost breakdown is necessary to study the critical relationships between volume; fixed, variable, and total costs; and profits.

Section 2

HOW TO ENSURE TIMELY REPORT PREPARATION AND SPEEDY DISTRIBUTION

One of the most frequent criticisms of management information systems is that report preparation and distribution is generally not handled on a timely basis. Managers are constantly pressuring report preparers for faster information turnaround. Although there will always be a lag in any reporting system that partially relies on receiving outside paperwork such as vendor invoices, there will also be a lag in reporting when all information is internally generated. For instance, an inventory report will lag until the physical inventory can be reconciled with the book inventory.

The key to keeping the reporting process moving along is to minimize the delay caused by items over which you have control. Generally, if this is done, there will be enough time to reconcile discrepancies, track down missing paperwork, perform the needed analysis and still get reports issued on time before the information is stale.

Below is a 12-point program that should allow you to accelerate your reporting turnaround and at the same time enhance the value of the report in the user's hands.

1. Avoid setting arbitrary report completion deadlines. Involve the users in deciding on completion dates and make sure you come to an agreement. Be certain to get the agreement dates in writing and on to a master report schedule. This eliminates confusion about which report gets prepared first and when.

2. Do not necessarily wait until a full complement of reports is complete before dispersing them. Consider distributing reports as they are completed. For instance, instead of waiting until the full set of month-end financial statements is done, distribute the profit and loss statement first followed by the balance sheet and cash flow statement. You not only avoid bunching the distribution of data that leads to possible information overload, but by piecemealing it out, chances are the reports will be examined more closely because there is simply less to look at all at once.

3. Obviously, some reports are more important than others. It is critical that these be recognized and prepared first before time is spent working on incidental reports that may be needed but can wait until off-peak report preparation time. Again, it is a matter of proper coordination between preparer and user to determine what comes first and what waits.

4. Certain data, such as sales, cash balances, inventory, and order levels, may be so important in the operational scheme of things that managers cannot wait for 10-12 days after month's end to find out the information. In this case, companies will issue month-end hot item reports highlighting these items before the regular monthly financials are completed. Many firms highlight their most sensitive operating information in flash reports weekly.

5. To speed up the assembly of quick turnaround reports, especially flash reports, control totals should be used instead of supplying of all detailed information. Often, firms will present overall totals such as companywide accounts receivable aged 30, 60, and greater

than 90 days instead of breaking it down by profit center or account. The same goes for weekly cash receipts or inventory levels which should also be summarized for the company as a whole. The details can follow with the monthly financial statement package.

6. As a rule of thumb, daily reports should be published the following day, weekly reports within two or three days, and monthly reports within 10 to 12 days. Such turnaround times should be satisfactory in all except the most unusual circumstances.

7. Just as there is a need to schedule an anticipated report completion date, there is also a need to schedule due dates, for key data needed in the report. By injecting this bit of discipline into individual report preparation, a firm is able to meet tight reporting deadlines, and their entire reporting process is generally streamlined as a result.

8. As report preparers proceed with scheduling due dates for needed information, it is imperative they work closely with operations in setting up timetables. It must be a cooperative venture.

9. In the haste to publish timely financial reports, a firm must be careful not to cut off *too early* on items that affect the P & L. This not only distorts the current period's results, but a firm is constantly playing catchup the next period. The most common example of this is a "too early" cutoff of accounts payable whereby significant vendor invoices may not be accrued in the proper period resulting in an overstatement of profits.

REMINDER: It is often disruptive to have an early cutoff on items affecting just the balance sheet. Keep cutoffs open longer for items you know will affect the profit and loss; i.e., payables, expenses, accruals, and so on.

10. There are numerous steps one can take ahead of time in preparing a report before final information is available. These include entering all report headings, titles, column headings, and comparative data from prior periods. This allows report preparers to fully concentrate on entering and analyzing current data when it becomes available. It also streamlines the reporting process by spreading routine report preparation time to off-peak hours.

11. Often report preparers will load a report with all the information they have on a topic whether the user has requested it or not. Their thinking goes as follows: "When in doubt, put it in the report." Instead of deciding ahead of time what the user needs, a preparer wastes precious time taking for granted what might be needed. In addition to dragging out report preparation time, resulting reports in this situation are often ponderous and seldom allow the user to focus on the report's important points.

12. Periodically, every company should review their chart of accounts to purge outdated accounts and to consolidate others that serve no particular purpose in being split out. Unless this is done on a regular basis, charts of accounts will often bury an accounting department in a quagmire of extra detail. More time is spent coding invoices and costs. There are more accounts to analyze and more account numbers to remember. In many cases, the law of diminishing returns has long ago set in, and the extra effort of splitting costs so fine yields no beneficial operating help. Additionally, such a detailed effort can waste untold time in closing the books and preparing reports.

Section 3

SHORTCUTS TO UNDERSTANDABLE REPORTING: CLASSIC AND TIMELY TIPS

Five Basic Principles of Report Preparation

1. Performance should always be measured against benchmarks such as budgets, last period's results, or acceptable variances. This gives the reader a clear reference point from which to measure the current data and to decide whether any action is necessary.

2. Never count on keeping your audience's attention beyond a few moments and even when you have their attention, it is seldom that it is without interruption. Managers have a multitude of demands on their time, and interruptions are the rule rather than the exception. That's why keeping reports brief and to the point pays dividends.

3. The more points a report tries to make, the far greater the chance of the main point being overlooked altogether. Generally reports should conclude with *only* one or two major points, and these should be self-explanatory. A reader should not have to stop and think what the preparer meant by his conclusion or have to go to other sources to verify the conclusion. Users will rarely do this, and your report will lose its clout.

4. Higher level reports should contain summary information, while those below need more detail. An example of this is a financial package for the board of directors. It should rarely contain material other than balance sheet and P & L totals accompanied with selected operating and financial ratios; whereas, a controller needs a complete set of financial statements, detailing every individual balance sheet, cost, and revenue item.

5. The most effective means for an operating manager to monitor his/her progress is by using responsibility reporting. This type of reporting produces the results of items directly under his/her control. For instance, a plant manager would receive the consolidated plant P & L. His/her departmental supervisor would receive a detailed P & L for the portion of the plant under his/her responsibility; i.e., the machine shop supervisor would receive actual results of the machine shop measured against budget. This type of reporting should be instituted wherever possible, and is quite often the basis for incentive pay and bonus calculations.

How to Ensure That the Reader Quickly Grasps Your Message

1. Present data in terms the user understands and relates to. For instance, plant people are used to dealing in units of production, hours, pounds, and not as often in dollars. Whenever possible, confine plant reports to these items or at least include them in reports. On the other hand, corporate management is more used to seeing dollars in their reports rather than plant jargon. It is important to play to your audience—give them what they are comfortable with and can understand.

2. Do not expect readers to sort out the important points in a report. They will spend little, if any, time doing it. You must make sure to emphasize these points in your conclusion, summary, or a variance analysis.

3. Do not allow a report reader to lose his/her train of thought while reviewing a report. Keep to the point. For example, if your report covers new international marketing plans, don't start discussing domestic sales efforts.

4. Keep the flow of the report in a logical sequence. If you don't, you will lose the reader along the way, and you may never get him/her back. This is especially true of reports containing numerous charts and graphs. By requiring readers to hopscotch back and forth between narrative and exhibits, you are testing the limits of their concentration.

5. Many tightly constructed reports will meet all generally accepted reporting guidelines except one. They leave the reader baffled as to what assumptions the preparer used in writing the report. For instance, when preparing a five-year plan, tell the audience whether you are using inflation-adjusted data or not and tell them early in the report. This eliminates the need for a reader to jump around in the report looking for assumptions.

6. Eliminate any superfluous information in a report that does not help the user to understand the final result. Be tough on this one. A brief, to-the-point report will get attention. An overloaded report will "get" the file cabinet, or worse the circular file.

7. Schedule the release of reports throughout a period instead of all at once. This will help eliminate reports stacking up on managers' desks, none of which will receive adequate attention. Distributing one every few days is an ideal guideline and helps ensure that reports receive maximum management scrutiny.

8. The most meaningful reports are those that analyze a trend or change, not the ones that simply provide a pile of data for a period and then attempt to draw a conclusion. Instead of preparing a report summarizing plant labor hours and concluding that utilization is high, the report would be much more useful if labor hours and utilization were compared to some meaningful standard such as industry averages, a budget, or last period's results.

9. Intermittently, it is wise for report preparers to sit down with users and review each report's contents. These mini training sessions help to decide if the contents of a particular report are still meaningful or if changes should be made. These meetings are particularly important when a new manager starts receiving reports. These sessions should be informal, one-on-one meetings free from interruptions.

10. One of the quickest shortcuts to understandable reporting is to use visuals and charts. This topic will be covered in the following Section.

Section 4

HOW TO GET THE MOST FROM GRAPHICS

Graphics can dramatically simplify reporting and also the length of explanations that accompany a report. They are especially valuable when the user is not intimately familiar with accounting terminology or how to draw conclusions from columns and rows of numbers. To get the most from graphics so that accounting data come alive, the following 10 rules should be followed.

10 Simple Rules to Follow

1. As explained previously, the best reports should always present a trend or relationship between numbers instead of a pile of raw data. Many report users are not agile at discerning trends from accounting reports. No matter how the material is explained, the report remains a heap of numbers, totals, and statistics. A well-constructed graphic can overcome this hurdle. Complex data becomes instantly understood.

Pointer: Many accountants think their job is done once they have generated the numbers. They are not particularly happy to have to summarize data for charts and then actually construct the visual. They feel the numbers should speak for themselves. Do not accept this thinking. Use graphics wherever possible.

2. Graphics are an exceptional way to highlight important points in a report. Whereas in a written report, trying to present and support more than one or two key points often will lose a reader, using graphics is a convenient way to rapidly focus on several key points without losing a user.

3. If your audience is composed mostly of non-accountants, graphics is the safest communications tool. Highly complex financial data can become easily understood with the proper chart or visual.

4. Do not clutter a visual with more than one underlying theme. If you do, chances are high you will distract the reader. For instance, if you develop a chart analyzing how your firm's cash is flowing, only the major sources and uses should be included. You should not try to analyze accounts receivable and collection patterns on the same graphic. Simply show how much in total was collected for the period and leave the details for another analysis.

5. As much as possible, each visual should stand alone with one central theme, a straightforward heading and all pertinent data present. It is irritating and time-consuming to have to jump back and forth between visuals trying to keep track of relationships. It is too much of an effort, and most users won't do it.

6. Even if a graphic contains only one theme and stands on its own nicely, it still can be a disaster if you try to cram too much onto it. This crucial mistake normally takes two forms: (1) too much detailed data not sufficiently summarized, (2) too many headings or wordy explanations. Spend the time necessary to make your graphics visually appealing.

7. Be sure to print all letters horizontally. Do not make the reader turn a page sideways to read captions. I still see visuals in prestigious business journals that fail to follow this fundamental principle.

8. Earlier I mentioned that visuals are extremely useful when your audience has a non-financial background. Additionally, they are effective for audiences that do not possess much interest in a topic. For whatever reason, many firms overdistribute reports. It seems that every manager gets every report. Without passing on wisdom of the approach, if you feel there is a need for this type of reporting to keep managers informed, you will be much more successful if you liberally use visuals. A plant manager who receives manpower reports for every department of the company may spend some time examining the information if he gets a graphic. Otherwise he may glance at it in passing, if at all.

9. The more complex a business is and the more complex the data you are trying to present, the farther ahead you will be by putting it into graphic form. For instance, one firm with large, lengthy government contracts in process, shifted from a weekly written summary report that outlined due dates, task responsibilities, and all the various interdependencies to an End Item Completion Chart that visually laid out the same information, but it was understandable at a glance. As a result, project coordination was dramatically simplified.

10. Be sure it is perfectly clear which description goes with which graph line, chart column, pie slice, and so on. Use arrows and pointers to accomplish this. *Remember:* Do the work for the reader, and you will keep his or her attention.

Major Pointers for Different Graphics

Studies have shown that the easiest type of graphics to follow are either pie charts or bar charts. The least are line and surface charts. (Examples of different kinds of charts are shown on pages 295-315.) Specifically, there are certain points to keep in mind when working with each of the three major chart categories. They are outlined below.

Line and Surface Charts

1. Limit the number of lines to three or less whenever possible. If you have to use more, consider using two charts or use color codes to identify the lines.

2. Instead of setting up a legend similar to the ones you see on maps where each line is constructed a little differently and so identified in a chart on the map, place each line's description right near the line. As was mentioned above, use pointers or arrows if necessary to connect the two.

3. Do not crowd grid markings so close together that it becomes difficult to identify them. By spreading them apart not only does the chart become more visually appealing, but also chances of a user misreading the information is reduced.

4. Place each chart on the page so all information (headings, descriptions, labels, etc.) can be filled in horizontally. Vertical or diagonal labels are out on line charts!

5. Start both the vertical and horizontal axis at zero if possible. Readers are used to this from as far back as their grade school days.

6. When you have several line charts covering the same type of data, keep grid spacing and scales the same. For example, profit histories for several divisions should be displayed using similar graphs. The vertical axis should show the same profit increments (0, $100,000, $200,000, $300,000, etc.), while the horizontal axis should cover the same number of years (1980, 1981, 1982, 1983). Any deviation from the approach gives the reader the visual sense there is something different about each divisional chart other than just the numbers when, in fact, there are no other differences.

Bar and Pie Charts

1. Do not vary more than one dimension of each bar. For instance, make your point by varying the height or width but never both on the same graph. A person can better visualize differences when only one dimension is changed. If you change two, the eye has a much harder time picking these out.

2. Do not crowd numerous bars on a graph. It looks cluttered and can dilute the impact of your message.

3. Pie charts are notorious for vertical and diagonal labels. Remember the rule: Keep all labels horizontal.

4. Pie charts lend themselves nicely to lumping all minor breakdowns into an "other" category. This eliminates the chances of subdividing the pie so fine that you have no room for labels and more importantly it confines the focus to the larger segments where the emphasis should be.

Section 5

HOW TO DECIDE WHICH REPORTS MANAGERS REALLY NEED

A Practical Seven-Point Program That Identifies Reporting Needs

1. Each manager working in conjunction with his or her supervisor should list all important items under his or her control that need monitoring.

TIP: Often this can be conveniently done at the same time an employee's annual objectives are set or when his or her bonus goals are developed.

2. Next decide whether an appropriate report presently exists to provide all the needed facts and data. If one does not exist, now is the time it should be developed.

3. All reports a manager is receiving should be reviewed to see if they are still useful. Firms often forget the large cost of preparing a report, and if one is not helping a manager in his or her decision-making, it should be eliminated.

4. Strike a balance between the operating and financial data a manager receives. One complements the other and gives a supervisor a wide breadth of information to manage from both the numbers side and the plant side.

5. The report preparer needs to ask a series of questions before the format, timing, and content of a report is finalized:

- When is the data needed?

- How often is the data needed? Daily? Monthly? Quarterly?

- How accurate should the data be? If a report is needed quickly, estimates may have to be used.

- How will the data be used? This question gives the report preparer a chance to inject his or her thoughts on the approach being proposed as well as offer any suggestions on refining a report. Also, it is important to make sure the needed data are not already available in another report.

6. Next it must be decided what frame of reference the report should provide. Will it be most effective simply comparing current data with last period's or last year's? Should results be compared to standards, published statistics, averages, etc.?

7. A final step that is mandatory in solidifying a firm's reporting plans is to obtain top management support for the program. This is the needed catalyst to get a report program off the ground and moving.

How to Accurately Slot Your Reporting Tasks

Prioritizing reports within a reporting system is crucial to its efficiency. This approach not only establishes a flow as to which reports will be prepared first and when, but it also identifies which reports need a manager's scrutiny first and which are nice to have but can wait to be examined until time permits.

Generally, the best grouping is to slot your reports into these three categories:

1. Crucial—need immediate attention.

2. Secondary—familiarize top management.

3. Background—to review as needs permit.

It is also good to code each report with its priority so all users know exactly the importance of a particular report.

Important Point: When prioritizing reports, the ultimate determination must come from the users. Only they are in a position to know exactly what information they need to maintain operating effectiveness, and only they know exactly when they need it to best maintain control.

The way one general manager prioritized his needs was as follows:

Critical Reports:

Responsibility Operating Report
Product Contribution Report
Daily Direct Labor Report
Manufacturing Expense Variance Report
Plant Overhead Report
Daily Production Report
Plant Backlog Report
Inventory Analysis Report
Materials Utilization Report

Secondary Reports:

Flash Cost Change Report
Materials Requirement Plan
Master Capacity Report
Equipment Usage Report
Material Obsolescence Report
Gross Profit Analysis
Maintenance Performance Report

Background Reports:

Plant Automobile Report
Price Level Adjusted Profit and Loss
Fixed Asset Summary Report

How a Periodic Report Audit Will Keep Your Reporting System Streamlined

The Four Crucial Steps of a Report Audit

1. Assemble a list of *all* reports presently being produced by the firm. Don't stop with just the ones being generated by data processing. No doubt many manual ones are also being prepared.

2. Reports will normally take on a life of their own. Unless they are periodically reviewed to see who is using them, if anyone, they will continue on and on. Purge all that are trivial, not being used, or redundant.

3. Jot down any weaknesses that have been noted in any operational area. Reach a consensus as to whether any of the weaknesses are a result of having no information or the wrong information. If so, a new or different report is needed.

4. All reports should be cross-referenced and reconciled to all others. This step is often not done or done haphazardly. Nothing can dim the credibility of a reporting system faster than reports that show up with the same information differing from report to report.

Case Study of an Actual Report Audit

The divisional Marketing Vice President of a midwest distributor finally called for a report audit after several instances of conflicting data kept reoccurring between the Contribution-by-Product Report, Marketing Variance Report, and Marketing Performance Report.

The first step for the Controller was to review the last four months of each report. The discrepancies showed up each month's end. Instead of examining older reports to see when the differences first started appearing, he instead started examining the differences themselves which centered on inventory usage. The Product Report was calculating a monthly running average of inventory usage, the Marketing Variance Report was using average beginning and ending inventories, and the Marketing Performance Report was using actual monthly usage.

After conferring with the Marketing Department, it was determined that the actual monthly usage was the figure all the reports should contain, although it was discovered that at the time the other usage numbers were employed in the reports, there was a valid reason for so doing. These reasons, however, were no longer applicable, and in the future actual usage was now to be used in all three reports.

Section 6

INEXPENSIVE WAYS THE COMPUTER CAN SLASH YOUR REPORTING TIME WITH VERY LITTLE WORK

Signals That Tell You a Company Could Use Data Processing Reporting Help

The telltale signals that a business needs data processing help are numerous. The list below is by no means complete but does cover most of the major signs.

- Managers are unfamiliar with current costs.
- Invoices are not being done on a timely basis.
- Billings are inaccurate.
- Information is taking longer and longer to collect.
- Information is spread among various divisions and departments.
- Order entry accuracy is suspect.
- Customer inquiries are not handled fast enough.
- Problems are reacted to very slowly.
- Records are slow to be updated.
- Month-end closes are slow.
- Data is overhandled.
- Information is unavailable.
- Data entry and storage costs are rising.
- "What if" analysis is unavailable. Instead all information must be entered to judge impact.
- Posting errors are numerous.
- Order status is uncertain.
- Information is redundant. The same information is being reported on and stored in several departments.

How to Isolate an Underlying Reporting Problem

Isolating a reporting problem requires managers to wear their detective hats. The signs are often subtle and tough to pick out. In most cases it requires a keen amount of observation and thought.

Below are five telltale signs to help managers identify reporting problems. One should be on guard for these at all times.

1. Users do not trust a report's data. They sidestep it and instead rely on intuition to make decisions.

2. Users spend inordinate amounts of time analyzing the ramifications of a decision. This simply may be the user's nature, but often means the right data are unavailable or are difficult to manipulate so various assumptions can be tested.

3. Users continue to make current decisions relying on old data. Either new data is delayed in reaching the manager or never reaches him or her at all.

4. Managers are not using report data once they receive it. This may result from distrust as pointed out in Item 1, or it may result from information overload. Too much data is reaching a manager's desk all at once.

5. Users cannot find available information. This is causing managers to "wing it" in their decision-making and sets a dangerous precedent.

How Data Processing and Other Office Automation Apparatus Can Streamline Your Operations

Automating a firm's operation has many benefits. If you have any employees who devote much of their time to collecting, verifying, organizing, or distributing information, there could be substantial help available, such as:

- Decision-making can be speeded up. Anyone who has had to construct a complicated spreadsheet before making a decision knows what a relief computerization has been in accelerating the entire process.

- Data can be examined more quickly through the availability of small mini- and microcomputers. Users become more productive because their efforts can now be directed towards analyzing data rather than assembling it and making calculations. Additionally, one's attention span for analyzing data is heightened because the mind-numbing crunching of numbers has been eliminated.

- Information overload can be minimized by computerization. A busy executive can quickly sort through an abundance of data segregating what is relevant. Companies intent on computerization will generally focus on one or more of the 11 needs listed below. The solutions data processing offers a company in the area of information control and reporting are numerous and are almost a necessity in this ultracompetitive age we live in. Additionally, computerization is now within financial reach of almost all companies. Prices of desktop computers continue to fall and have become a way of life for progressive companies. As one small company executive recently told me, "Micros have enhanced my capabilities for growth beyond my wildest expectations." This comes from an owner who three years ago had a completely manual system. Parts of it are still manual, but the most important parts—inventory control, budgeting, order entry, and financial modeling—have now all been effectively automated to the delight of management.

Computer Needs and Capabilities Analysis

Need: Accounts Receivable Control

Computer Capabilities:

- Prompt organization of customer billings.
- Current preparation of customer history files—name, billing address, shipping address, last purchase date, last payment date, credit limits.
- On-time preparation of month-end customer statements.
- Immediate aging of customer balances by invoice.
- Quick preparation of past-due notices.
- Accurate calculation of finance charges.
- Speedy preparation of mailing labels for customer lists.
- Immediate organization of various sales reports by customer, salesperson, or geographic area.
- Easy processing of cash receipts, especially partial or unidentifiable payments.
- Quick development of reports on anticipated cash by due date.
- Accurate preparation of reports on credit memos, no-charge items, and adjustments.

Need: Accounts Payable Control

Computer Capabilities:

- Invoice processing.
- Invoice aging by due date.
- Cash requirements by future due date.
- Check registers providing control over checks issued, voided, returned, or lost and to assist in bank reconciliation.
- Year-to-date purchases by supplier.
- Vendor historical information files—alphabetic listing, yearly volumes, payment amounts, peak volume, telephone numbers, addresses, last payment dates.
- General ledger account number assignment.
- Payment duplication eliminated.
- Partial payment features.
- Purchase order number control.
- Check writing with a manual override to allow for handwritten checks.

Need: Fixed Asset Control

Computer Capabilities:

- Depreciation calculations, both book and tax.
- Fixed assets located by tag or control number.
- Life, class (building, equipment, improvements, etc.).
- Additions, sales, transfers, write-offs, gains/losses on disposition analysis.
- Capital budgeting control.
- Capital requisition control.
- Insurance coverage control.
- Repair and maintenance costs summarized.

Need: Financial Modeling

Computer Capabilities:

- "What-if" analysis (change one or more variables of a problem and examine alternative impacts). This technique is particularly useful for budgeting, cash planning, sales forecasting, material, and labor planning.
- Make-or-buy and make-or-lease decisions.
- Capital investment analysis.
- Marketing planning and performance analysis.

Need: General Ledger Reporting

Computer Capabilities:

- Production of profit and loss statements, balance sheets, changes in financial position, and other related reports.
- Completion of trial balance.
- Summarization of end-of-period closings and processing.
- Maintenance of charts of accounts.
- Analysis of a single account for a period in the year.
- Processing of general journal entries.
- Analysis of finances—ratios, variances, trends.

Need: Inventory Control

Computer Capabilities:

- Inventory balance by location.
- Inventory balance by type—raw, in process, finished.
- Inventory analysis by obsolete item.
- Inventory item data—part number, name, description, unit of measurement, unit price, cumulative usage, turnover, reorder point, lead time, minimum reorder point, last day ordered and received, last day physically counted.
- Out-of-stock reports.
- Price lists.
- Shipping reports.
- Picking tickets.

Need: Order Entry

Computer Capabilities:

- Shows customer order files with order entries, backlog, and status for each customer.
- Provides current credit status and receivable data so orders can be immediately reviewed as they are received.
- Advises customers of backorder delivery times; can suggest substitutions for out-of-stock items.
- Provides customer order acknowledgements.
- Reports on all open orders by date.

Need: Payroll Processing

Computer Capabilities:

- Writes payroll checks and computes withholding.
- Provides outstanding check register.
- Allocates employee earnings to proper general ledger account.
- Provides Federal and state tax reports and year-end W-2 earnings records for each employee.
- Provides vacation, sick pay, and overtime reports.

Need: Personnel Reporting

Computer Capabilities:

- Employee master file—name, address, social security number, hire date, exemptions, earnings rate, workmen's compensation classification, termination/retirement date, medical coverage status, pension/profit-sharing entry dates.

- Employee head counts by department and other labor statistics required by government agencies.
- Employee turnover rates.
- Employee record of sick days, vacation days, and other time off.

Need: Production Planning, Scheduling, and Reporting

Computer Capabilities:

- Records of labor expended, material used, and overhead incurred.
- Records of job status.
- Records of location of orders.
- Records of scrap.
- Records of projected item availability.
- Records of bills of material.
- Records of component parts inventory.
- Records of deviation from standard or budget.
- Records of quality control performance.
- Records of capacity and equipment usage.

Need: Word Processing

Computer Capabilities:

- Provides text composition and editing—deletes, inserts, and moves text; instantly corrects errors.
- Provides "spelling checkers"—spelling errors are automatically corrected by a control feature within the system comprised of a "dictionary" of commonly misspelled words.
- Organizes reports automatically in predetermined formats.
- Does math computations.
- Stores all information on disks.
- Prints pages in 25 seconds.
- Provides foreign language capabilities.
- Accesses computer data for inclusion in a letter or report.

How to Organize Your Office

Increasing white-collar productivity, many feel, will be the key to future gains by American business. Currently, there are a number of automated devices and operating systems available for offices. They are versatile and cost-effective, and allow a company to start small and expand as needs arise, simply by adding new software or work stations. Details of the most popular tools available to organize and automate the office are outlined below:

Work Stations

- Provide stand-alone computers and terminals.
- Allow user to do a multitude of tasks without ever leaving a work area, such as word processing, order entry, electronic mailing and filing, spreadsheet analysis, accounting, and time management.
- Share data with other work stations, computers, and common files.

Time Management Programs (Often called "electronic calendars")

- Contain an appointment book for scheduling multiple daily meetings.
- Contain a phone book allowing thousands of individual listings and instant dialing capabilities.
- Contain a notepad that can be called up on a screen to jot down information.
- Contain an index card file that resembles a mini-database. One current file being marketed contains 36 lists with 500 cards per list.
- Provide a calculation capability for doing math.
- Contain current date and time, always visible on a screen.

Electronic Mail

This concept is more easily visualized when it is called a computer telephone. Messages can be sent to and from a computer over phone lines without the use of a phone.

- Allows you to create, display, and list messages in addition to sending and receiving.
- Confirms that message has been seen by receiver.
- Provides "urgent" warnings that flags important transmissions.

Desktop File

- Replaces a secretary's card file.
- Contains a large indexed file cross-referenced in numerous ways—zip code, name, dates, area, rating, alpha, etc.

Document File

- Provides large document storage system.
- Stores and recalls documents as needed, instantly.
- Distributes documents electronically wherever they are needed within an organization, whether it is across the hall or across the country.

Graphics

- Create charts, graphs, or any combination.
- Plot graphics on paper or transparencies and store them.
- Create what you want—make axes thick, border lines thin, solid or broken lines, pies, bars.
- Write comments on graphics using various typesets.

Project Management

- Report on various project milestones, cost estimates, staffing levels, slack time, late finishes, durations, and deadlines.
- Analyze alternative scenarios—material, people, costs.

Section 7

HOW TO QUICKLY DESIGN A REPORT FOR ANY SITUATION

Obviously, it is beyond the scope of any book to present every report that could be used in every situation. Needs will arise where you will be confronted with preparing a report that is not covered in this book. To simplify this task and to allow you to respond quickly to this type of request, it is important that the fundamentals of preparing any report be at your fingertips. There are 14 steps to follow that will allow you to focus quickly on what exactly is needed, by whom, and in what form. Furthermore, when you follow these steps, you will be able to format the report so it is simple to follow, crystal-clear to the reader, and eye-appealing. In short, these steps, which are discussed below, help you establish the impact you desire.

14 Steps to Designing Any Report

1. Determine what type of report is needed: an exception report that designates key results as acceptable or unacceptable or action required or none required; a summary report where results are abbreviated without detail; or a detailed report where all the information surrounding the topic at hand is included.

2. Determine who the audience is. Is it for the department manager only? Is it for a department meeting? Will the CEO be getting a copy? Knowing who gets the report will often dictate how detailed a report should be; i.e., the higher in the organization it goes, the more its contents should be summarized.

3. Select the best construction for the report under the circumstances. There are four basic types:

   a. Tabular
   b. Narrative
   c. Graphic
   d. A combination of a, b, and c.

Once these first three steps are complete, the following steps will ensure your report is easy to read and invites immediate interest.

4. Use a tight, to-the-point report heading. For instance, Aged Accounts Receivable Report is more descriptive than Accounts Receivable Analysis.

5. Use columns not rows for numbers. They are much easier to follow.

6. Double underline, asterisk, or highlight important data in bold type.

7. Summarize detailed data so the reader does not get lost in a myriad of numbers.

8. Stick to one or two key ideas. For example, if you are going to develop an exception report highlighting only deviations from plan greater than $10,000, do not start commenting on other information in the report.

9. Always compare report data to budget, previous month's actual, last year's results, or whatever is appropriate. This establishes a basis of spotting exceptions or trends.

10. Leave ample room in the report for notes and comments.

11. Show any key assumptions early. Readers want to know this information. For instance, the projected inflation rate is 8%, GNP growth will average 4%, expenses are based on a sales volume of 10,000 units.

12. Keep column headings and descriptive labels to the point. Be sure to label every line.

13. Round off cents to dollars.

14. Make sure you include enough data so the reader can make decisions. This point sounds simple enough but very often reports reach a user's desk with insufficient information to make an informed decision. Conversely, many reports contain too much data. The reader is lost. He or she cannot determine what is critical or not. *Important:* Report preparers must continually put themselves in a user's shoes and concentrate on exactly what the reader will need to make a decision.

Report Preparation—Case Study

ABC Company's Operational Vice President made an urgent request to the Controller for a report on branch expense activity. Not having any guidelines to go by other than the 14-step process just outlined, the Controller was able to focus quickly on exactly what was needed and designed an effective, to-the-point report for the V.P.

In a meeting he determined the V.P. wanted an exception report highlighting a select group of 15 branch expense accounts compared year-to-date to both plan and last year's actual. The audience was the Operational Vice President and Branch Manager. The Controller decided a tabular report entitled *Select Branch Expense Analysis* would be appropriate. A standard layout was used that had columns headed as follows:

	Current Year to Date		Last Year Actual	
Expense Account	Actual	Plan	Year-to-Date	Comments

The requested 15 expense accounts were listed down the left side of the report in account number order and appropriately labeled. Because all the data was important, it was equally emphasized in the report. Ample room was left in the comments section for notes and explanation. No key assumptions were needed because the column headings and title gave all the explanation necessary. All numbers were in whole dollars, and the report presented only the information the V.P. requested. No additional analysis or information was included to distract the users.

Section 8

HOW TO DESIGN REPORTS USING THE COMPUTER

Until the late 1970s, financial spreadsheets had to be done by hand. Then in 1979, the VisiCalc electronic spreadsheet became available for desktop computers and a whole new era of financial modeling, analysis, and report writing dawned. In 1982 Lotus Development Corporation introduced its version of the electronic spreadsheet called 1-2-3, and it along with VisiCalc quickly became the premier worksheet programs. Coupled with the affordability of smaller computers, these popular programs have changed the way firms control their business.

There are several substantial gains available for firms who employ spreadsheet programs.

1. They are affordable. For only a few hundred dollars plus the cost of a microcomputer and related hardware you are in business. There are no backbreaking capital investments nor need for special programmers, analysts, and the like. You handle all of this activity yourself and with relative ease. Many managers can become fairly proficient with an electronic spreadsheet in just a few hours.

2. They save time and maximize productivity. The big benefit of using electronic spreadsheets is that it frees managers from tiresome calculations to spend more time analyzing and understanding information; whereas, in the past so much time was spent entering data, analysis often went unfinished, budgets were often not completed on a timely basis, and alternative outcomes to questions could not be sufficiently examined because there was never enough time to make all the necessary calculations. These concerns are a thing of the past. You now can get all arithmetic done instantly. You don't need to type reports; just print them out. Changing a number involves one or two keystrokes and all totals and calculations are immediately updated.

3. They permit "what if" analysis that dramatically improves decision-making ability. For example, you want to know how changes in inventory levels affect your cash flow budget. By simply plugging in different inventory levels you can instantly explore as many options as needed until a sensible answer is obtained. Without the computer, financial managers dreaded this type of analysis because it was 99% arithmetic and erasers and only 1% good, sound learning. One financial wag likens reviewing a detailed manual spreadsheet to doing a post-mortem!

The list of possible "what ifs" you can explore with an electronic spreadsheet is endless. Some of the typical questions that firms are answering are:

● What effect will a speed-up or slowdown in accounts receivable collections have on overall cash flow?

● How is working capital affected by financing capital expenditures out of operations instead of borrowing?

- What if inventory turnover decreases? What effect does this have on profits?
- What is the effect of net profit if sales do not reach planned levels?
- Should I purchase or lease this piece of equipment?
- How will our balance sheet be affected by this acquisition we are looking at?

How Electronic Spreadsheets Work

If, for example, you wanted to conduct an analysis of various sales patterns, it would be extremely useful to devise a spreadsheet similar to the one below. This example happens to use VisiCalc, but the identical worksheet could just as easily be constructed on 1-2-3 or any number of other available financial spreadsheets.

	A	B	C	D	E	F	G	H
1								
2				ABCO, INC.				
3				SALES ANALYSIS				
4								
5								
6		ITEM		UNITS	SALES		GP%	GP
7								
8		MODEL A		500	9,000		.4333	3,899
9		MODEL B		750	42,000		.4214	17,698
10		MODEL C		450	27,900		.3822	10,663
11		MODEL D		800	53,200		.4000	21,280
12		MODEL E		1,250	90,375		.3845	34,749
13								
14		TOTAL		3,750	222,475		.3968	88,289
15								
16				PROD INFO				
17			MODEL	PRICE	COST			
18			A	18.00	10.20			
19			B	56.00	32.40			
20			C	62.00	38.30			
21			D	66.50	39.90			
22			E	72.30	44.50			

A VisiCalc worksheet contains 254 rows and 63 columns for information, depending on what size your computer memory is. Rows are numbered 1 through 254 while columns A through BK (A-Z, AA-AZ, and BA-BK). Our example above contains 22 rows and 6 columns (A through F). *Coordinates* on the worksheet represent the intersection of rows and columns. They can hold three types of information:

1. Labels
2. Values
3. Variables

Labels in our example are the report heading, column headings, and row descriptions. *Values* represent the numbers typed in by the user such as units, price, and cost in our example. *Variables* represent a number that is calculated from a formula you place in the computer. Again going back to our example, the numbers included in the sales, GP% and GP columns are variables. Also the numbers along the total row are variables. Sales are calculated by multiplying units × price. The GP% is calculated by subtracting cost from price and then dividing by the price. GP is calculated by multiplying sales × GP%. Totals are calculated by adding rows 8 through 12 for units, sales, and GP. The GP% total is calculated by dividing total GP by total sales.

How the formulas are actually constructed is beyond this book, but there are numerous instructional manuals available for any spreadsheet from its supplier, a nearby library, or a bookstore.

Upon reviewing the spreadsheet you now decide to test a few alternatives, checking for impact on total company gross profit. You type in 300 sales units for Model A and 650 sales units of Model C. Instead of extending the rows, retotaling the columns and recalculating the total GP%, you merely push a key and all the work is automatically done. If you do not like this answer, you can change the mix of sales again, or you can change the product information in any way you want. Formulas entered into the computer memory instantly recalculate the outcome throughout the example. Also, if you do not like the statement layout, you can rapidly reformat any portion of it.

How to Use This Book in Conjunction with Electronic Worksheets

Every report example in this book lends itself nicely to an electronic spreadsheet. Although you will have to invest up-front time programming a report, you will quickly make up the time when you update information or perform what-if analysis.

TIPS: What many companies do is first, permanently enter original spreadsheet information. Going back to our example, they would enter this original data on pricing, cost, and units and leave it. Separate columns are then set up next to this original data for what-if analysis. Any changes made in the what-if columns leave the original columns unaffected. This initial information provides a convenient base of data against which to measure the new information you have just entered in the what-if columns.

Other companies enter the original information, but instead of constructing a second set of what-if columns, they print out this original data which is then used to compare against any what-if changes made in the original information columns.

Either way works, and either way gives you a powerful tool for eliminating the number-crunching usually associated with manual financial analysis and decision-making.

Many electronic spreadsheets also now feature graphics. After designing a tabular report, you can construct a visual, whether it be a pie chart, bar chart, or line graph, from the same information. As can be done with tabular information, you can test various graphics before choosing the best one suited for your needs. Because graphics have such a high degree of positive impact when part of a presentation, using the computer to help in this vital area gives you another potent tool for financial reporting.

Reportamatic Locater Index